Library of
Davidson College

DESIGNATION

DESIGNATION

MICHAEL DEVITT

1981
Columbia University Press/New York

Library of Congress Cataloging in Publication Data

Devitt, Michael, 1938–
Designation.

Bibliography: p.
Includes index.
1. Reference (Philosophy) 2. Semantics (Philosophy)
I. Title.
B105.R25D48   149'.946   80-26471
ISBN 0-231-05126-3

COLUMBIA UNIVERSITY PRESS
NEW YORK   GUILDFORD, SURREY

COPYRIGHT © 1981 COLUMBIA UNIVERSITY PRESS
ALL RIGHTS RESERVED
PRINTED IN THE UNITED STATES OF AMERICA

CONTENTS

PREFACE ix

PART I

CHAPTER 1: DESCRIPTION THEORIES OF PROPER NAMES 3
1.1 Mill's View 3
1.2 Reasons for Rejecting Mill's View 4
1.3 The Main Problem 6
1.4 Ambiguity: Types and Tokens 9
1.5 The Refutation of Description Theories 13
1.6 Circularity 21

CHAPTER 2: A CAUSAL THEORY OF DESIGNATION (1) 25
2.1 The Problem 25
2.2 First Uses of a Proper Name 26
2.3 Later Uses of a Proper Name 29
2.4 Ambiguous Names 32
2.5 Donnellan's Distinction 36
2.6 Demonstratives 42
2.7 The Semantic Significance of Donnellan's Distinction 46
2.8 Multiple Groundings 56
2.9 Other Ways of Naming 57
2.10 Criterion of Identity 60

PART II

CHAPTER 3: A SEMANTIC PROGRAM 67
3.1 Main Outline of the Program 68
3.2 The Language of Thought 75
3.3 Speaker Meaning and Conventional Meaning 80

v

CHAPTER 4: DEFENSE OF THE PROGRAM — 87

- 4.1 Semantics and Conceptual Analysis — 87
- 4.2 Semantics and Particular Languages — 90
- 4.3 Semantics and Linguistic Competence — 92
- 4.4 Linguistic Competence and Knowledge-That — 95
- 4.5 Linguistic Competence — 101
- 4.6 Testability — 110
- 4.7 Convention T — 113
- 4.8 Principles of Charity and Rationality — 115
- 4.9 The Need for Theories of Reference — 118

PART III

CHAPTER 5: A CAUSAL THEORY OF DESIGNATION (2) — 129

- 5.1 Abilities to Designate — 129
- 5.2 Groundings — 133
- 5.3 Reference Borrowings — 137
- 5.4 Partial Designation and Designation Change — 138
- 5.5 Identity Statements — 152
- 5.6 The Distinction between Designational and Attributive Terms — 157
- 5.7 The Fundamental Notions — 160
- 5.8 Truth Value Conditions — 161

CHAPTER 6: EMPTY TERMS — 167

- 6.1 The "Tough" and the "Tender" — 167
- 6.2 Fictitious Names within Fiction — 170
- 6.3 Fictitious Names outside Fiction — 171
- 6.4 Empty Names and the Causal Theory — 174
- 6.5 The Distinction between Designational and Attributive Empty Terms — 177
- 6.6 Truth Value Conditions — 179
- 6.7 Pseudonyms — 185
- 6.8 Singular Existence Statements — 186

CHAPTER 7: OTHER TERMS — 189

- 7.1 "Observational" Natural-Kind Terms — 189
- 7.2 Mistakes and Reference Change — 191

7.3	Knowledge of "Meaning"	195
7.4	"Theoretical" Natural-Kind Terms	199
7.5	Other Terms	202

PART IV

CHAPTER 8: MODAL CONTEXTS — 207

8.1	Substitutivity and Essentialism	207
8.2	Distinctions of Scope	209
8.3	Rigid Designation	211
8.4	Truth Conditions	214

CHAPTER 9: CONTEXTS OF PROPOSITIONAL ATTITUDES (1) — 219

9.1	Background	219
9.2	Vividness and Knowing-Who	221
9.3	Having-in-Mind	224
9.4	Paradigm Cases	226
9.5	Other Cases	229
9.6	Logic	233
9.7	Truth Conditions: First Approximations	235
9.8	Truth Conditions: Refinements and Additions	243

CHAPTER 10: CONTEXTS OF PROPOSITIONAL ATTITUDES (2) — 251

10.1	Negative Attitude Statements	251
10.2	Multiple Attitude Contexts	257
10.3	Attributions of Self-Knowledge to Others	260
10.4	Opacity in Certain Verbs	263
10.5	Intentional Identity	267
10.6	Difficult Cases	270
10.7	Conclusion	274

GLOSSARY OF SPECIAL SEMANTIC TERMINOLOGY	277
NOTES	281
BIBLIOGRAPHY	295
INDEX	305

PREFACE

This book is an essay in the semantics of natural language. My aim is to give a theory of a particular semantic relationship, which I call *designation,* and to bring out the bearing of this relationship on the meanings of various simple and complex expressions. Designation usually holds between proper names and the objects they refer to; it often holds between demonstratives, pronouns, and definite descriptions, and the objects they refer to. I offer "a causal theory" of designation.

This book contains, therefore, "a causal theory of proper names." Such theories have enjoyed plenty of attention but not a great deal of popularity. There are two main sources of resistance: first, causal theories have not been worked out in sufficient detail for it to seem plausible to many that they can handle the difficult cases; second, several popular programs in semantics seem to leave no place for causal theories of reference. A major concern of this book is to overcome this resistance.

Parts I and III are focused on the details of a causal theory of names and so are directed at the first source of resistance. Some key ideas in handling difficulties are as follows: the identification of a name's "meaning" with its underlying causal network; the claim that a name is usually *multiply* "grounded" in its object; a Gricean distinction between speaker meaning and conventional meaning; a distinction, like Keith Donnellan's for descriptions, between designational and attributive names; the application of notions of *partial reference* to names.

Part II takes up very general questions about the nature of semantics and the place of causal theories of reference in semantics, and so is directed at the second source of resistance. The semantic programs of such influential writers as Donald Davidson, Paul Grice, and Michael Dummett seem to have no place for causal theories of reference. Drawing on the ideas of Hartry Field in "Tarski's Theory of Truth" (1972), I describe a program that gives a central role to causal theories of reference. I relate this program to the well-known ones. I reject the popular view that it is the main task of semantics to describe or explain what the speaker knows, and also the view that what he does know are semantic propositions (for example, "T-sentences"). I reject the "Principle of Charity" and give "Convention T" no significant role.

It will help the prospective reader if I bring out now the relationship between my views and those of the two best-known causal theorists of names, Saul Kripke and Keith Donnellan.

There are two steps in my causal theory of proper names: a causal theory of *reference borrowing* and a causal theory of *grounding*. The theory of reference borrowing explains how those of us who have never grounded a name in its bearer can get the benefit of the groundings of others. The theory of grounding explains how, ultimately, names are linked to their objects. In 1967 I attended a series of lectures by Kripke at Harvard, parts of which later became the paper "Naming and Necessity" (1972). From those lectures I took the idea of a causal theory of reference borrowing. Donnellan has a similar idea (1972, 1974). Further, in "Reference and Definite Descriptions" (1966), Donnellan describes a distinction between two uses of definite descriptions—"referential" ones and "attributive" ones. This distinction and Kripke's idea suggested to me a twofold development. First, draw a distinction at token level, based on Donnellan's at type level, and then apply this new distinction across the board, covering names, demonstratives, and pronouns, as well as definite descriptions. Second, give a causal theory of the "referential" ones. A corollary of that theory is my causal theory of grounding for names.

Kripke is opposed to Donnellan's distinction (1977) and so would presumably be even more opposed to my across-the-board distinction based on it. He has never said much about grounding. However, his discussion of "fixing the referent" in his 1972 paper suggests a "description theory" of grounding. His criticism of Donnellan's distinction confirms that he would reject a causal theory of grounding of the sort offered here.

Donnellan's main argument for his distinction comes from a consideration of cases of confusion and error. My main argument for it comes from a consideration of "imperfect" descriptions (like 'the man') which in their normal use are more like demonstratives than Russellian descriptions. Donnellan does not consider the implications of his distinction for other singular terms, nor does he offer a *theory* of referential descriptions. He does not directly address the question of the grounding of names. However, he might be sympathetic to the twofold development suggested here.

In Part IV I consider the bearing of my theory of designation on the problems of referential opacity, including Quine's problem of "exportation." I use the theory in urging a solution to the semantic problems of singular terms in propositional attitude contexts.

My interest in this subject has led to several earlier works. My doctoral dissertation at Harvard, "The Semantics of Proper Names: A Causal Theory" (1972), was an early version of some of the main ideas for this book. "Singular Terms" (1974), "Suspension of Judgment: A Response to Heidelberger on Kaplan" (1976a), "Semantics and the Ambiguity of Proper Names" (1976b), and "Brian Loar on Singular Terms" (1979b) were all on this subject; modified versions of parts of those articles constitute a small part of this book. "Donnellan's Distinction" (1980), a response to Kripke (1977), is in progress. It draws on ideas in this book. An earlier version of chapter 9 was delivered at La Trobe University in August 1972. An earlier version of chapter 6 was delivered at the University of Adelaide in April 1974. Earlier versions of parts of chapters 3 and 4 were delivered at various places in Australia in August 1978.

While I have been working, others in the field have not been idle. Where I am aware that they have arrived independently at similar conclusions, I have not made a point here of saying so; where I am aware that they have arrived at different ones, I have said so.

Causal theories of reference, particularly of grounding, promise an answer to age-old questions about how language "hooks onto" the world. Such an answer is important if we are to resist the current trend away from "full-blooded" realism, a trend influenced by such writers as Michael Dummett and Donald Davidson in semantics, and Thomas Kuhn and Paul Feyerabend in the philosophy of science. Dummett leans explicitly toward antirealism as a result of his identification of the metaphysical issue of realism about the external world with an issue about truth. This identification seems to me quite mistaken. However I do think, as many do, that the issues of truth and realism are related. So I think that the rejection of truth by Kuhn and Feyerabend makes their realism an "anemic" kind. These important matters could not be argued in a book of this nature. [I have used causal theories of reference against the "incommensurability thesis" of Kuhn and Feyerabend in Devitt (1979a).] Davidson's views are discussed here in some detail. In my view, his rejection of realist reference, and hence of causal theories of reference, makes his realism "anemic" also. If we do not view reference as an objective relationship between words and the world, we cannot view truth as a property a sentence has in virtue of an objective correspondence to that world. A proper defense of "full-blooded" realism must be left to another time.

Preface xiii

My debts to Kripke and Donnellan are obvious by now. In that respect I should also mention Charlie Martin. I was first drawn to a distinction like Donnellan's when Martin urged it in lectures and discussions in Sydney in 1966. Not obvious from the above is my debt to Hartry Field. His influence began when we both attended Kripke's lectures in 1967. The discussions that preceded his paper of 1972 were important in forming my general views about semantics. Over the years since then I have benefited greatly from discussions and correspondence with him. I am also indebted to David Armstrong, John Bigelow, Bill Lycan, Graham Nerlich, Hilary Putnam, J. J. C. Smart, Kim Sterelny, and Barry Taylor for written comments on parts of earlier drafts. Other earlier debts are too numerous to list. Suffice it to say that I am grateful to the many people with whom I have discussed this subject. Finally, my thanks go to Anthea Bankoff for her cooperation and efficiency in typing the final drafts.

Although my main ideas on designation have not changed over several years of thinking about it, my views of the details change constantly. I have good reason to suppose, therefore, that I shall soon come to recognize errors in the present work.

Michael Devitt

Sydney, Australia
1980

I

Chapter One
DESCRIPTION THEORIES OF PROPER NAMES

> "Don't stand chattering to yourself like that," Humpty Dumpty said, looking at her for the first time, "but tell me your name and your business."
> "My name is Alice, but ___"
> "It's a stupid name enough!" Humpty Dumpty interrupted impatiently. "What does it mean?"
> "Must a name mean something?" Alice asked doubtfully.
> "Of course it must," Humpty Dumpty said with a short laugh: "my name means the shape I am—and a good handsome shape it is too. With a name like yours, you might be any shape, almost."
> Lewis Carroll: Through the Looking Glass

1.1 Mill's View

It was Mill's view that "proper names are not connotative: they denote the individuals who are called by them; but they do not indicate or imply any attributes as belonging to those individuals" (1867:20). We can vary the language a little: a proper name designates an object but has no other meaning; it does not describe that object; it says nothing about the object.

This view does not take us far but it is a promising start:[1] it accords with our first intuitions about names.[2] It is striking, then, that the view has been rejected by nearly all subsequent theorists. For one reason or another, it was thought necessary to conclude that names have "senses" or are otherwise logically associated with descriptions.

The first aim of this book is to reject these "description theories," replacing them with a theory that is Millian in spirit.

1.2 Reasons for Rejecting Mill's View

Plausible though Mill's view is, various reasons have been adduced for rejecting it in favor of description theories.

(i) We need to explain the fact that 'Socrates is wise' differs in meaning from 'Aristotle is wise'. This seems easy enough for a Millian. The meaning of a name is simply its role of designating a certain object; or more extremely, its meaning *is* that object (Russell 1956:186). 'Socrates' and 'Aristotle' designate different objects and so differ in meaning.

A consideration of identity statements suggests that this explanation is inadequate. Frege indicated the difficulty:

Now if we were to regard equality as a relation between that which the names 'a' and 'b' designate, it would seem that '$a = b$' could not differ from '$a = a$' (i.e., provided that '$a = b$' is true). A relation would thereby be expressed of a thing to itself, and indeed one in which each thing stands to itself but to no other thing. [1952:56 (cf. Hume 1739:200)]

How can a Millian explain the differing "cognitive values" of '$a = b$' and '$a = a$'? Each name here concerns the one object.

The problem posed by identity statements faces all theories of names. Awareness of the problem has pushed some philosophers away from the view that identity is what it seems to be— a relation between the objects designated by the names—toward the view that it is a relation between the names themselves. This had been Frege's view.[3] Objections to that view led Frege to his theory of names. (They have led others to more desperate expedients.)[4]

Frege saw that the solution to the problem of identity statements is to be found by focusing neither exclusively on the signs nor exclusively on the objects designated; we must focus on what mediates between sign and object. Frege called this the "mode of presentation." Frege's theory, the classical description theory of names, is that each name has a "sense" wherein the mode of presentation is contained (1952:57). The sense is something "grasped by everybody who is sufficiently familiar with the language" to which the name belongs (though there may be different opinions about it among those who use the language). It is the same as the sense of some definite description. It supplies a criterion of identification; the object the name designates is the one and only one that fits the description. The differing "cognitive values" of '$a = a$' and '$a = b$' are to be explained by the differing senses of 'a' and 'b' (Frege 1952:57–58; see also Frege 1918).[5]

(ii) The next reason for rejecting Mill's view is the long-notorious problem of singular existence statements. If the role of a name 'a' is merely to designate, then it seems "tautologous" to say 'a exists'. If the name is meaningful at all, then there must exist something it designates; it is "strictly nonsense" to talk of the existence of actual things in the world (Russell 1956:233, 241). More seriously, it seems impossible to make any sense of 'a does not exist'; it seems "contradictory."

Russell distinguished ordinary proper names from "logically proper names." Ordinary ones are abbreviated descriptions amenable to treatment by the theory of descriptions. Logically proper names are the only genuine ones. They stand in a relationship of the utmost intimacy to their bearers. The relationship is epistemologically fundamental; a name immediately and directly focuses attention on an object, and that's *all* it does. Only 'this', it seems, qualifies as a logically proper name. It cannot meaningfully appear in a singular existence statement. On the other hand, an ordinary proper name can; the statement affirms that there exists or does not exist exactly one object fitting the associated description.[6]

(iii) A closely related difficulty for Mill's view arises from the fact that some names like 'Pegasus' and 'Santa Claus' are "empty." Mill says that "all names are names of something, real or imaginary" (1867:16). So there exists something which 'Pegasus' names. But no such entity exists. So 'Pegasus' does not name anything. So its meaning cannot be simply its role of naming something. It is tempting to say that it must have a sense which can be expressed by a definite description (Russell 1956:54). And if we allow this for empty names, why not allow it also for the others?

(iv) Finally, there is the problem of opaque contexts. The peculiar feature of such a context is that the rule of substitutivity of identity does not hold for it: if we replace a name by a codesignational name, there is no guarantee that we will preserve truth. The role of a name in such a context cannot, it would seem, be merely to designate. However, suppose that a name has a sense. A way out of the difficulty then suggests itself. In these peculiar contexts a name shifts its referent to what is normally its sense; the name still designates, but it designates something different. Such a solution was Frege's ("On Sense and Reference," 1952).

Any theory of proper names must take account of these four problems. I consider identity statements in section 5.5. Singular existence statements and empty names are the whole concern of chapter 6. Opaque contexts are the concern of chapters 8 to 10.

1.3 The Main Problem

The main semantical problem for proper names is that of explaining the nature of the link between name and object in virtue of which the former designates the latter. Description theories seem to supply the first step in a solution: the name designates the object in virtue of the object being the one and only one to which the associated description applies. This leaves the problem of explaining the nature of the link between *description* and object in virtue of which the former applies to the latter. However, we have that problem anyway: two problems seem to have been reduced to one.

A very obvious concern with this main problem has led many recent theorists to emphasize that the user of a name must, in some way, be able to *identify* an object.[7] Usually the form of identification required has been the production of an identifying description of an object. To this point, such recent theories remain close to those of Frege and Russell. However, the identification requirement has usually been part of more complex description theories than the classical ones. A name is not tied tightly to one description but loosely to many: a name has logically associated with it a cluster, or "presupposition-set," of descriptions.[8] These complications have been prompted by the implausibility of the classical theories.

In describing the main problem, I have used the term 'designate' to refer to a certain relationship between name and object. We might ordinarily use that term for this purpose; or we might say that the name "refers" to the object; or that it "denotes" the object; or that the object is "its bearer." 'Designate' seems the most apt ordinary semantic term for the relationship, but nothing hinges on its choice. More must be said about this, for it leaves the precise nature of the problem unclear. And so long as the problem remains unclear, the methodological question of *how we should test a proffered solution to it* remains unclear.

Our problem is to investigate the semantically important relationship that holds between a name and a certain object, whatever that relationship is called. The relationship in question is picked out by its crucial bearing on the *truth conditions* of sentences containing the name. Consider any simple predication containing a name. For the predication to be true, a certain object must have a certain property. Which object? In my usage it is the object the name "designates." And we could give examples of name-object pairings to teach this usage.[9] That is all I can and could say initally to explain my usage. Beyond this, the term is explained as we develop a theory. I shall have occasion to modify my usage. On the one hand I shall widen the extension of 'designate' because a relationship exists between certain other singular terms and their objects that is similar to that between a name and its object. On the other hand I shall narrow the extension because a relationship exists between *some* names and their objects that is different from the paradigm. I shall not attempt an analysis or definition of 'designate' in the sense of offering a *synonym*. To do so would be pointless, for our task is to explain and describe the nature of the relationship that *any* such term refers to. The overall aim in semantics is to explain semantic relationships like designation in nonsemantic terms. Perhaps we can expect a *physicalist reduction* in the end; I am not sure.[10] In any case my explanation falls far short of it.

These remarks raise a number of questions about the nature and scope of semantics which are discussed in more detail in Part II. We must wait until then to say much on the methodological question (see section 4.1 particularly). Meanwhile I shall say only that we cannot rely uncritically on "what we would say" in this or that circumstance to test a theory of designation; for "what we would say" is laden with undeveloped folk semantic theory. Clearly enough, nevertheless, we must look to our ordinary intuitions for tests because there is nowhere else to look.

It is important to distinguish our main problem from another. Our problem is to explain the nature of the link that certain kinds of words have to the world. The other problem is to explain how words come to be so linked to the world: what is the historical or causal explanation? Causal theories of reference are sometimes seen simply as solutions to this other problem. As such they may seem true enough but trivial. However, they are offered primarily as solutions to the main problem: they claim that the nature of the link is to be found by looking to the historical explanation.

Two further points on usage. I follow Quine in using 'refer' as a generic term: proper names, predicates, variables, and so on, may all refer. I use 'apply' to express the special relationship between predicates and the world; so 'raven' applies to each and every raven and to nothing else.

1.4 Ambiguity: Types and Tokens

Proper names typically have more than one bearer. I shall stretch ordinary usage a little and say they are typically "ambiguous." It is convenient to bring out the contrast between description theories of names and the theory to be offered here by considering the way they handle the problem this ambiguity gives rise to. The problem is that of determining which one of the many objects bearing a certain name is designated by a particular token of that name. What is it about a particular token of 'John' that makes it designate *this* John and not any other of the millions of Johns?

It is common to distinguish *types* and *tokens*. When we say, "'John' is among the words used in a certain book," what we are talking about is a type. 'John' is used 107 times in the book. The result of each use is a token. The idea of a word token is clear enough: tokens are inscriptions on the page or sounds in the air; they are datable, placeable, parts of the physical world; they have causal histories. But more needs to be said about word types.

What is it that is ambiguous? What, for example, are we referring to by the expression 'proper names' in the opening sentence of this section? We are referring to *sorts of sounds or inscriptions*, each sort being identified by the overt physical characteristics of the sounds or inscriptions that make it up. When we say that 'John' is a proper name in this sense, we are saying that a certain sort of sound or inscription is used (implicitly, in English) with the semantic properties of a proper name. And it is ambiguous because it is so used in more than one way. So, what is a proper name in this sense, and what is ambiguous is a *sound type* or an *inscription type* defined only by overt physical characteristics.

This fact is a little obscured in languages like English where ambiguities in sound types and inscription types tend to go together. Thus the statement, "'John' is ambiguous," can be taken to be referring either to a sound type or an inscription type. In Japanese, however, things are quite different. The spoken language is full of ambiguous sound types for which there are no corresponding ambiguous inscription types; and there are also ambiguous inscription types for which there are no corresponding ambiguous sound types.

Call sound types and inscription types "physical types." Words like 'word' and 'proper name' are often used to refer to physical types. They are sometimes used to refer to tokens. They are also used to refer to types of a different sort which I shall call "semantic types."

Suppose that in the above book the physical name type 'John' is used to designate three different people. So the 107 tokens exemplify three meanings of the physical type. We may wish to talk about one of those three uses or meanings: "'John' names a well-known figure in the Sydney underworld"; "that name makes a true sentence if joined to 'is rich'." The reference here is not to any particular token and it cannot be to the physical type; it is to a semantic type. Or, consider a common semantic remark like the following: "'Pegasus' is an empty name." This is not a remark about the sound or inscription type 'Pegasus', for such types are used to refer successfully to many things; it is about a semantic type. (When we use the expression 'the English Language', we are mostly referring to something to be defined *semantically*.)

Two tokens that are in different media—for example, in speech and in writing—cannot be of the same physical type but they can be of the same semantic type. Semantic types are defined only by semantic characteristics.

The problem of ambiguity that concerns us here can now be put as follows. What settles which semantic name type a given token of an ambiguous physical name type belongs to?

Description Theories of Proper Names 11

Does our main problem, outlined in the previous section, concern physical types, semantic types, or tokens? Utterances are the primary vehicles of truth (Quine 1950:xi). Utterances are tokens. Similarly it is name tokens that are the primary vehicles of designation. (Because of this I shall feel free to talk of the person responsible for a token, as well as the token, designating something.) Indeed, my talk of types seems nothing but a convenient *façon de parler*. To say that a token is of a certain physical type is just to say that it is F, where 'F' is a certain physical predicate. To say that it is of a certain semantic type is just to say that it is G, where 'G' is a certain semantic predicate.

Having made these distinctions, I shall not be pedantic about them. I shall use words like 'word' and 'proper name', without more ado, to refer to tokens and to types of both sorts unless there is danger of confusion. A word token surrounded by single quotation marks may refer to a certain physical type, or to a certain semantic type, or to a certain token; it will never refer to itself.

Which object did a particular name token designate? It is natural to say that it designated the object the speaker *had in mind* or *meant*. This was an insight of some description theorists (particularly, Strawson 1959:182). The ordinary notion of *having-in-mind* is a very suggestive one in the semantics of singular terms, as we shall see (sections 2.4–2.7, 9.3–9.6). However, it is too unclear to be helpful without some sort of explanation. If we had one, a solution to our problem of ambiguity would be in sight; a speaker designated one object and not another by 'John' *because he had it in mind*.

What sort of explanation might description theorists offer of this notion? The first step is clear enough. The speaker associates with the name an "identifying description." He has in mind the object picked out by that description. So he has one and not another object in mind by 'John'.

In what does this association of identifying description with name consist? It consists, it seems, in the speaker's readiness to produce that description if asked what he has in mind; it consists in something he could or would do.[11]

How are we to understand this claim? One way that is sometimes suggested by the writings of description theorists is what we might call a "behaviorist interpretation." It is as follows: A person has uttered a sentence including the use of a name. If he were asked soon afterward what he had in mind by the name, he would offer a certain identifying description. The object picked out by this description was the object he had in mind.

This view is unsatisfactory, for it makes a certain sort of error impossible. It prevents a speaker from being *wrong* about what he had in mind. Suppose he uses the name 'John'. When asked whom he had in mind, he produces a description which identifies an object with that name. Could the object picked out be the wrong John? With this view, it seems not. The description *determines* what he had in mind. Yet clearly he could be mistaken about his mental states so that he would offer the wrong description; he does not have "incorrigible knowledge." He might, for example, have become confused about, or forgotten, what he meant. Perhaps he didn't notice what he was doing.

A more plausible way of understanding the claim is given by a "centralist interpretation."[12] The association of identifying description with name consists in *the holding of a belief* which the user would express using the name and the description. Whenever a speaker uses the name, such a belief has a *causal role*. Which object the speaker had in mind, and hence designated, depends on which such belief had the causal role: the object is the one picked out by the description "involved in" the belief. Knowledge of his own mental states would, in normal circumstances, lead the speaker to offer that description on request to explain his use of the name. However, circumstances may be abnormal. What matters is not the description he offers, but the description that was *in fact* involved in the above way in the production of the name.

Description Theories of Proper Names 13

This centralist interpretation contains more than a grain of truth. I shall return to it in developing my own theory (sections 2.4 and 5.1–5.3). However, description theories under this interpretation, as under all others, are open to Kripke's objections. In my view these objections are decisive.

1.5 The Refutation of Description Theories

Kripke's long article, "Naming and Necessity" (Kripke 1972),[13] weaves together many strands of thought including several on proper names. My purpose in this section is to outline what I see as the strongest Kripkean argument against description theories. Description theories are mostly offered as theories of the *meaning* of a name. As such they have certain modal statements as consequences: for example, the consequence that *necessarily*, if Aristotle existed, he was such and such.[14] Much of Kripke's article is taken up with discussing the nature and truth value of such modal consequences. He argues that names are "rigid designators" and hence that these consequences are false. Therefore, description theories of this type are false. His discussion of necessity has been the focus of much subsequent comment. It is important to notice that the article contains another argument against description theories.[15] This argument is independent of the modal argument, has a more powerful conclusion, and is in my view a better argument.

Kripke points out that description theories may be offered not as theories of meaning but as theories of reference. As such they claim simply that the reference of a name is determined by the descriptions associated with it. According to Kripke, description theories of this sort do not have the above modal consequences. Because of this he makes no call on claims about modality in his argument against them. It is in that respect that this argument is independent of the earlier one.

The conclusion of the argument is more powerful in that it entails the earlier conclusion: if descriptions do not determine the reference of a name, they do not express the meaning which determines the reference.

It is well known that modal statements containing definite descriptions suffer from ambiguities of scope. At bottom, Kripke's modal argument against description theories rests on the intuition that names are different from descriptions in this respect. I think he is largely right, but intuitions here seem laden with the theories in question: Dummett's vigorous response to Kripke, arguing that names are in this respect just like descriptions, has considerable plausibility (Dummett 1973:111–35).[16] The argument below seems to me to be better in that it does not suffer from this defect.[17]

I shall take all description theories to require at least this:

> For any name token x and object y, x designates y if and only if y is an object correctly described by most of the descriptions, or a weighted most of the descriptions, associated with x by the speaker, and no other object is so described.

This is general enough to include the classical theories of Frege and Russell and the more modern Wittgensteinian ones.

According to description theories, therefore, if a name designates an object, the descriptions associated with the name will be ones *correctly believed true* of that object. There seems no reason to withhold the term 'knowledge' here. So, for a person to designate an object by name he must *know something* about the object sufficient to identify it. This claim is implicit (at least) in all the standard description theories. It is implicit also in my earlier "centralist interpretation" of these theories. It is false.

There are three sorts of examples which cast doubt on description theories: (i) examples where we do not associate an appropriate definite description with a name; (ii) examples where we associate a definite description but it identifies "the wrong object"; (iii) examples where we associate a definite description which identifies no object, but the name is not empty.

(i) Consider the name 'Cicero'. Most of us who use this name

Description Theories of Proper Names 15

associate with it ' = Tully' and 'the denouncer of Catiline'. These are identifying descriptions, but they are not *appropriate* ones to satisfy the demands of description theories. Their defect is that they themselves contain names which also must be supplied with identifying descriptions. I can do no better for 'Catiline' than 'the person denounced by Cicero'. I have now indicated near enough the full extent of my knowledge of Cicero (Tully) and Catiline. My efforts to produce an identifying description for each of these names will simply run around the same circle of descriptions involving the names. Many people could do no better.[18] Even those who are much wiser might find it difficult to satisfy the demands of description theories here: it might take a good deal of classical knowledge to produce identifying descriptions containing no names.

The situation is no better with a well-known name like 'Einstein'. It is not sufficient to offer 'the discoverer of the Theory of Relativity' without being able to identify that theory independently of reference to Einstein. Very few of the many who use the name 'Einstein' could manage that.

Despite our failure with 'Cicero' and 'Einstein', it seems that our uses of each of these names designate a certain object: the predications containing those uses are true or false according as that object does or does not have the property specified.

A way out of the difficulty suggests itself: we manage to designate because we "borrow our reference" from others.[19] We have allowed that there are some experts who could satisfactorily identify Cicero and Einstein. Perhaps they can carry the rest of us? This is a sound suggestion, but it does not save description theories from implausibility.

What form does reference borrowing take in description theories? A person may designate an object in using a name '*a*' in virtue of associating a description: 'the person *b* referred to by '*a*' in such and such circumstances'. The problem for description theories is, once again, that they require knowledge where none may exist. First, the user of a name must remember at least one other user. In doing this it is not sufficient for him simply to produce the name of another user: an identifying description is required. This may, of course, set the user off on further reference borrowing, which in turn will require of him further knowledge. Second, the reference *lender* must be able to supply an identifying description or, alternatively, identify someone else from whom *he* borrowed his reference. And so on. There is a danger of circularity here (1.6). Aside from that it is implausible to claim that the knowledge required here is in fact present with most names; we naturally *forget* most of this information. We forget where we got a name from. Or we remember but can't identify the person satisfactorily. Or we identify him but he is no better off than we are: he is no expert. The resort to reference borrowing may help us in a few cases, but in the main it merely staves off disaster for a while.

It may be objected that the claim of implausibility here is too hasty. "Perhaps it would be appropriate if only "descriptions proper" could appear in identifying descriptions. But it is common to allow the descriptions to contain demonstrative elements. This widens our ability to identify objects considerably."[20] Construed in this way, description theories include theories that require the speaker to associate a *criterion of identification* with a name:[21] either he must be able to offer a "description proper" of the object, or he must be able to point it out "when the occasion arises" (Ayer 1963:145).

Description theories of this sort are more plausible, but they still seem to require too much knowledge. There are severe limitations on the number of objects most of us could successfully point out. We could manage it for our friends, many of our acquaintances, and some of our famous contemporaries. However, we can but dimly call to mind many people whose names we seem quite competent to use. We certainly cannot manage this sort of identification for the likes of Cicero, for they are no longer around to be pointed at. Nevertheless the objector is clearly right in thinking that this further method greatly increases the range of objects we can identify; in particular, it makes reference borrowing more useful, for the potential lenders will often be people we could indicate though not describe. I suggest, however, that we would still fail to produce an identifying description for many names.

(ii) We could sum up the discussion so far by saying that description theories require us to have beliefs that we do not in fact have. A more striking defect is that these theories seriously underestimate the number of *false* beliefs we have. Public opinion surveys show that many people are quite mistaken about famous and historical figures. Many will say, for example, that Columbus was the first person to think that the earth was round and that Einstein invented the atomic bomb. Often the *only* (nontrivial) belief held by someone about an object is a false one. Yet it is clear that the truth or falsity of remarks by such a person using 'Columbus' do not depend on the properties of some ancient Greek but on the properties of *Columbus*.[22]

Suppose that a person intent on misleading his audience launches on a narrative without making it clear that he is storytelling. Or, to avoid deliberate deception, suppose the person tells something that is in fact a vivid dream but which he, deluded as he is, thinks is true. The audience believes the narrative and later passes it on to others. Now it turns out that there are some people, none of whom the narrator could have known, who fit the descriptions of his characters (or mostly fit them). *Must* we say that he (and hence his audience) was talking about those people? Of course, if the parallels were striking enough, we *might* say this; some of us might see it as a case of extrasensory perception. There is another alternative, however: we might say that the parallelism was *purely a matter of chance*—that, despite the fact that the descriptions used pick out those people, the narrator did not designate them.

Even identification by means of demonstratives can be mistaken. It is *possible*, indeed it is likely, that our memories of many people would be so dim that we would point out the wrong person in a crowd for many names we use. The object we identify for a name may thus be quite irrelevant to the truth conditions of statements containing the name.

This discussion reveals further hazards to reference borrowing as a way for the ignorant to get by. The reference lender may be misidentified. Or *he* may be mistaken: someone who rightly thinks that Einstein discovered the Theory of Relativity may, when pressed to identify the designatum of 'Einstein', place his trust in a close (easily identifiable) friend who wrongly thinks Einstein invented the atomic bomb.

To sum up, we have earlier seen that we may fail to associate any appropriate definite description with a name. We see now that we may associate one that identifies the wrong object.

(iii) Consider Wittgenstein's example of Moses (1953:§79). Suppose we were to discover that there was no one man who satisfied all (or most, or even any) of the descriptions normally associated with 'Moses'; for example, 'the man who led the Israelites out of Egypt', 'the man who as a child was taken out of the Nile by Pharaoh's daughter'. In the face of this we would say, and probably say rightly, that Moses did not exist and that 'Moses' was an empty name designating nothing. But there is an alternative, an alternative which may be overlooked. This can be brought out by considering the case of Jonah.

It is unlikely that the biblical story of Jonah *as a whole* is true of any actual man or even that *substantial parts* of it (particularly the parts about the big fish) are true of anyone. Does it then follow that 'Jonah' is an empty name? It does not, *because Jonah may have been a real person about whom a legend has grown.* Imagine we discover that the facts were as follows: There was an ordinary man called 'Jonah' who lived out his life in an ordinary way. The only unusual thing about him was that he was regarded in a superstitious way by his associates; they tended to tell peculiar stories about him. After his death these stories blossomed into what we now know as the story of Jonah; *all* the truths about this man, except the trivial ones like 'being a man', were quickly forgotten. This is the alternative that may be overlooked.[23]

In the situation imagined, our uses of 'Jonah' designate the man described: earlier predications using the name, such as those in the Bible, are mostly false because that man lacks the required properties; on the other hand, present predications, reflecting this discovery, are true because the man has the required properties. Description theories cannot accommodate these claims.[24] Reference borrowing is no help here, for we *all* were wrong about Jonah. A description theory must conclude that the imagined discovery shows that 'Jonah', in its earlier uses at least, is an empty name: none of th earlier predications, even the trival ones we still think true, can be true. We have not replaced a false theory about a certain man, Jonah, with a true theory about him; until the "discovery" we had no theory *about him* at all. Note that it is *not possible*, according to description theory, for an earlier scholar to speculate, or to find evidence, that Jonah was a certain ordinary man that he, the scholar, has tracked down; that Jonah was the subject of superstitious stories; and so forth. Such speculations and evidence cannot be *about Jonah* because they deny the descriptions on which our use of the name depends. This is not a plausible claim.

The examples in (i) to (iii) strongly suggest that description theories are wrong not merely in details but in fundamentals; the whole "research program" seems mistaken. The examples do not, of course, *entail* that it is mistaken. Moves can still be made to continue it. The evidence of the examples can simply be denied ("The ignorant do *not* designate Einstein," and so forth). More plausibly, attempts can be made to accommodate the evidence (Kripke considers some), but these have the look of "degenerating problem shifts."[25] I shall consider a surprisingly popular attempt in the next section. However, what we most need to complete the rejection of this program is a new program for theorizing about designation. *How* can we succeed in designating an object with a name when we are unable to identify the object? *We designate the object in virtue of a causal network stretching back from our uses of the name to the first uses of it to designate the object. The important thing to consider in deciding whether and what a name designates is the historical explanation of its use.* This is the central idea of "causal theories" of proper names. With Kripke's discovery of this new program, his objections to description theories become, in my view, decisive.

Description theorists have been impressed by a certain fact: a person's ability to use a name is accompanied by various beliefs about its bearer. Their error has been to think that some of these beliefs, a sufficient number to *identify* the bearer, must be *true* in order for the name to designate the object. The discovery that most of our beliefs about the bearer of a name are false is, of course, a large one. However, we have no need to see this discovery as changing the "meaning," or any other semantic property, of the name. It simply changes our beliefs about the bearer, as I said.

Description theories are not without any truth, nevertheless. They are half true for some names (2.5, 5.6). And they contain a number of insights which can be included in a causal theory.

It is natural (and correct) to think that, for the most part, we "know what we mean" by the words we use. However, this expression should not mislead us into exaggerating, as description theories do, the degree to which we are experts on the semantics of our language, and in particular, the degree to which we are experts on what our terms refer to: *there is a sense in which we do not, for the most part, know what we mean.* Questions of meaning and reference are *theoretical* questions requiring empirical investigation. We can talk without knowing the answer to these questions just as we can eat without being able to explain digestion and ride a bicycle without knowing any physics. I shall return to these matters in later sections (4.4–4.5).

1.6 Circularity

Kripke placed the following condition on a description theory of names:

(C) For any successful theory, the account must not be circular. The properties which are used in the vote [to determine the name's referent] must not themselves involve the notion of reference in a way that it is ultimately impossible to eliminate. (1972:283)

An obvious violation of condition (C) would be provided by a theory that offered as the identifying description associated with a name '*a*' by a speaker, 'the object I am designating by '*a*''. A more interesting violation could occur with the description theory of reference borrowing explained briefly earlier (1.5). The speaker offers the description 'the person *b* referred to by '*a*' in such and such circumstances'. Now suppose that *b* borrows from *c* in a similar way and *c* borrows from the original speaker. We have come full circle: we have not explained what determines the referent of *any* of these uses of '*a*'. A satisfactory description theory that allows reference borrowing of this sort *must require that some lender can manage reference on his own.*

This might seem too obvious to be worth more than a passing mention were it not for the fact that philosophers who are presumably aware of condition (C) and of Kripke's detailed discussion of it (Kripke 1972:283-86, 297, 766-68) are still urging theories that take very little account of it.[26]

What these theories do is include in the descriptions a person associates with the name '*a*', 'is called '*a*'', or 'was named '*a*'', or 'is commonly referred to by '*a*'', etc. The appeal of this move is that it is plausible to claim that these are descriptions that users of the name do correctly believe true of the object x. It is easier then to build an identifying description around one of these which it seems plausible to say is associated with the name in difficult cases. Kripkean arguments from ignorance and error like those in 1.5 still apply but they do not seem so persuasive.

Our task is to explain the nature of the relationship between a name and its bearer. I have called this relationship "designation"; others may prefer "naming," "reference," or whatever. The term is not important (1.3). What all these description theories do, in effect, is explain the fact that a person designated x by 'a' partly in terms of *a community's present practice of designating x by 'a'*, a practice that may be dependent on a past one.

Consider first a present practice that is not dependent on a past one. Suppose that the description the speaker adds to 'is designated by 'a' in community K' to get an identifying description is 'F'. What these theories tell us is that the speaker of 'a' designated x because it is an F that the members of K, a community he can identify, are in the practice of designating by 'a'. In virtue of what is it x that they are in the practice of thus designating? We are told the same story for each one of them. Each one designates x only because everyone does. We have no *independent* route to x. This sort of community reference borrowing is no better than the individual borrowing we considered earlier. It violates (C) and is circular.

The situation is not significantly better if the speaker's borrowing takes us back to a past practice of designating x by 'a'. (In one respect it is worse: the speaker or one of his fellows will have to be able to identify the relevant past community, a task that is likely to prove harder than that of identifying the present one.) We do not have immediate circularity in this case because the present community is dependent on the past one but not vice versa. For this reason Kripke seems to regard it as not a violation of condition (C) (1972:766). Nevertheless it is just as objectionable unless we are given some way of eliminating the notion of *the past community's reference*.[27] We need to be told in virtue of what it was x that the *past* community referred to by 'a'. These theories tell us only that each member of it referred to x because all the others did. The circularity has reappeared but in this case it is in the past. This is what we should expect, of course, because there was a time when the past community was a present one like the community above, entirely dependent on its own resources. Reference borrowing from the past simply transfers the problem.

A satisfactory description theory of reference cannot simply rest with identifying descriptions like 'the F called 'a' by K': it must say more. However, as soon as more is said the theory is open to the usual arguments from ignorance and error.

The first move to avoid circularity seems clear enough: *some* members of the community on which we all ultimately depend must be able to designate x by 'a' *without* relying on the community. How is that requirement to be filled?

An easy way would be to say that the community rests on *all* those who do not rely on reference borrowing; on *all* those who have an identifying concept which does not include *being called* 'a'. But this easy way leads to disaster. Among those courageous enough, or foolhardy enough, to "go it alone" will be many who are simply *wrong* about x; no single answer will emerge, let alone a correct one.

The theory must somehow specify *the experts*. How is that to be done? The theory can't, on pain of circularity, say that they are *the people who are expert about what 'a' designates*. It seems that the theory must require that the members of the community identify the experts. But then we can forget about the community altogether. We are back to reference borrowing from individuals (the experts). The theory must, of course, avoid violating condition (C) (a thinks b is the expert, b thinks c is, and c thinks a is). Still there is the problem that a member of the community may not know the experts; or he may know one but not have an identifying individual concept of him except one that involves *is called* and so raises the same problems; or he may *mis*identify the expert; or he may identify the expert but the expert may be *wrong* about the referent. Problems of ignorance and error loom again.

I conclude that description theories are not to be saved by making use of reference borrowing from the community. We must seek an alternative theory.

Chapter Two
A CAUSAL THEORY OF DESIGNATION (1)

This chapter outlines a causal theory of nonempty proper names and certain other singular terms which resemble them semantically. The filling out of the theory must wait until chapter 5, after we have placed the theory (in Part II) within a general program for semantics.

I start with names (2.1-2.4). I then consider definite descriptions, arguing that a distinction drawn by Donnellan is to be partly explained in terms of causal links to objects similar to those for names (2.5). I draw a similar distinction for demonstratives and pronouns (2.6) and consider the significance of these distinctions for semantics (2.7). Making use of these distinctions, I return to the discussion of names (2.8-2.10).

2.1 The Problem[1]

The central idea of a causal theory of names is that our present uses of a name, say 'Aristotle', designate the famous Greek philosopher Aristotle, *not* in virtue of the various things we (rightly) believe true of him, but in virtue of a causal network stretching back from our uses to the first uses of the name to designate Aristotle. It is in this way that our present uses of a name "borrow their reference" from earlier uses. It is this social mechanism that enables us all to designate the same thing by a name.

This central idea makes our present uses of a name causally dependent on earlier uses of it. These causal links do not, however, take us *to the object*. In virtue of what do the *first* uses of a name designate a certain object? We can see, perhaps, how we are dependent on our ancestors, but how did *they* manage? Other questions occur to us. What is the nature of this causal network? How did it begin and how did it grow? What has my causal connection to Aristotle got to do with my present act of designating him?[2] Could a use of a name be causally linked in the appropriate way to more than one object?

Our main problem was to explain in nonsemantic terms the nature of the link between name and object in virtue of which the former designates the latter (1.3). I have claimed so far that part of that link is a causal network. So, if we explain the nature of that network by answering the questions in the last paragraph, we have partly explained designation. What would remain to be explained would be the initial link to the object, the subject of the previous paragraph. It would be unrealistic, of course, to expect that we could come near to completing either explanation at this time and in this place.

2.2. First Uses of a Proper Name

A paradigm situation for naming is one in which a name is given to a previously unnamed object by a "naming sentence" in a face-to-face confrontation at a "naming ceremony." The sort of ceremony that leaps to mind here is a christening ceremony or the launching of a ship. Mostly, however, such formal and elaborate procedures merely give religious and public expression to what has already been established informally and privately.

The object in the paradigm is likely to be a humble one, and so we shall take such an object to illustrate a naming ceremony. (Thinking about names has not been helped by limiting attention to the famous and the grand.) Consider the case of our late cat. We acquired her as a kitten. My wife said, "Let's call her 'Nana' after Zola's courtesan." I agreed. Thus Nana was named.

This is the typical way for a name to be bestowed, but there are others. I shall discuss these in section 2.9.

What happened to those present at the naming of Nana? They *perceived* the ceremony, using at least their eyes and ears. To perceive something is to be causally affected by it. As a result of the effect it had on them, they were in a position to use the name 'Nana' later to designate the cat. What they gained at the ceremony, we might say, was "an ability to designate Nana by 'Nana'."

Let us expand this story a little, considering my situation at the naming. I gained that ability to designate from perceiving the complex event that constituted the naming ceremony. I saw Nana. I saw my wife. I heard the naming sentence. I was aware of agreeing. I knew which object my wife was suggesting a name for. As a result of the causal interaction at that ceremony among my wife, Nana, and myself, an interaction in which Nana occupied a unique place (that of the object being named), I gained my ability which is thus "grounded in" Nana.

In order to gain this ability I must already have several abilities. To gain the ability to use *this* name, I must already have the ability to use names *in general*. And I must realize that a name can be bestowed on an object by a ceremony of the sort witnessed. This requires, inter alia, that I understand my wife's use of 'her'. Indeed, it was because that use designated Nana that the name was bestowed on *her* at this ceremony. I discuss the role of personal pronouns in 2.6. Foreshadowing that discussion, we can say now that 'her' designated the cat because of the place *she* had in the causal explanation of my wife's use of the term. And had my wife used 'our cat' instead because Nana was absent, we can say, foreshadowing a discussion in 2.5, that the term would have designated the cat because of her role in the causal explanation of the use. The same would be true if there had been another name for Nana available, and if my wife had used that.

A few minutes later I exercised my new ability: I said "Nana is hungry." That *first* use of the name designated Nana. How? It designated her because it was *in fact* produced by an ability that arose our of the above ceremony in which *she* had a certain place; the ability is grounded in Nana. In other words, it was because Nana had that special place in the causal explanation of my utterance that the name designated her.

The central idea of a causal theory was that present uses of a name are causally linked to first uses. I claim now that first uses are causally linked to the object (but see 2.5 and 5.6).[3]

Designation is causal network plus initial causal link. There is good ground already for our earlier pessimism about the extent of explanation possible here. My description of the initial link, the grounding, rests on a notion of *perception* and it presupposes various *linguistic* skills in those present at the ceremony. Furthermore, I talk of "abilities to designate objects by name." These abilities constitute an important part of the designational link, but what are they? Such an ability is a mental state which is brought about in a language user by perception of a naming ceremony (and in other ways to be described) and which is apt to produce (in part) certain sorts of utterances—utterances using the name in question. In 5.1 I say more about these abilities and in 5.2 more about groundings. However, even in the final analysis we have to talk of mental states which remain largely unexplained.

How concerned should we be about these explanatory failures? Given our present lack of knowledge of the mind, of language, and of the relation of the one to the other, it seems to me that the answer is, "Not very."

I take it that our attribution of a language to an organism—our assumption that the sounds, etc., that it emits have meaning and reference—is part of our attribution to it of a human mind. We attribute to it complicated beliefs, hopes, desires, etc., which we think its words express, as part of our theory to explain the complicated way it behaves (cf. 3.1). Notions like designation are part of this explanation: to see a person's expression as designating *x* is to apply this theory. To fully explain designation, therefore, we would need to fit it into a psychological and linguistic theory that related linguistic behavior to other behavior and offered an explanation of it all. We are clearly a long way from having such a theory.[4]

Nevertheless, what we are attempting here should be a contribution to such a theory. We are attempting to explain designation in nonsemantic terms by relating it to psychological and nonpsychological reality.

Can we look forward to having, someday, an overall psychological and linguistic theory in nonpsychological and nonsemantic language? Can we look forward to a reduction to physics? I share the physicalist dream but I am uncertain what we can expect here, as I have already indicated (1.3). Certainly I think that every token object, event, and state is physical. What seems to me much less clear is the status of laws in, for example, psychology, for reasons given by Jerry Fodor and Hilary Putnam. I do not think that a semantic relation like designation *is* a (first order) physical relation. It is, like psychological relations, a functional relation which can be realized by various physical relations.[5]

I shall say that "underlying" a name token is a "causal chain" "accessible to" the person who produced the token. That chain, like the ability that partly constitutes it, is "grounded in" the object the name designates. The chain underlying my first use of 'Nana' begins with Nana at her naming ceremony; it runs through my perception of that ceremony; from then on it is my ability thus gained to use 'Nana' to designate her. I shall call such a causal chain a "d-chain," short for "designating-chain."

2.3 Later Uses of a Proper Name

Two of us gained our abilities to designate Nana by her name at the naming ceremony. All others, directly or indirectly, "borrow" their reference from these two (but see 2.8).

Many gain the ability directly from one of the two. I might introduce them to the cat: (i) "She is called 'Nana'," or (ii) "This is Nana." This ceremony plays the role for them that the earlier naming ceremony played for me. Their perception of Nana in that introduction will mean that underlying their later uses of 'Nana' will be d-chains grounded in her.

I might pass on the ability in Nana's absence: (iii) "Our cat is called 'Nana'," or (iv) "Nana is our cat." An ability thus gained would also be causally grounded in Nana, although this is not so apparent because Nana is absent. In using or mentioning the name 'Nana', I have exercised *my* ability which is causally grounded in Nana. The person addressed *hears* my remark. This causally links him through my ability to Nana. The question arises whether he is also linked to Nana through the role of 'our cat'. So far we have barely mentioned the role of the other singular terms used to designate Nana at the time when abilities are gained. There was, for example, my wife's use of 'her' in the naming ceremony, my use of 'she' in (i), 'this' in (ii), and now 'our cat' in (iii) and (iv). We must set aside consideration of the role of such terms in grounding abilities with names until we have discussed the terms (2.5–2.7).

There is one important way I might pass on the ability: I might use the name in an ordinary predication. For example, I might say, (v) "Nana is hiding." Someone who hears this and correctly classifies 'Nana' as a sound with the role of a name can borrow his reference from me. If he does, he gains an ability that is causally grounded in Nana via the ability I exercised in making the remark. Underlying his future use of 'Nana' will be a d-chain grounded in the cat.

Contrast this view with that of description theories. They require extensive *knowledge* of an object for a person to succeed in designating it. I have already rejected this requirement. I am now going further: it is not necessary that a person have any substantial set of *beliefs* involving the name (whether true or false).

This may seem to go too far. "We would not say that someone who comes to use 'Nana' merely as a result of overhearing (v) *understands* the name; he has not *fully grasped its use.*" Perhaps not, but what we would say depends on more than what is the case. I have already raised this methodological question in 1.3 and will return to it in 4.1 and 4.5. *I claim that the person who overhears (v) is in a position to gain the ability to designate Nana with the name.* He is able to ask questions about her ("Who is Nana?"), give orders concerning her ("Show Nana to me!"), and make true or false statements about her ("Nana is hiding because she is frightened"). I can see no reason, aside from devotion to the description theory, for denying this.

We have seen how those present at a naming ceremony can pass on the ability to designate an object by its name. There are many users of a name who were not at the naming ceremony and have not come by their use from anyone who was at it. We are all in this position with 'Cicero'.

Consider again the case of 'Nana'. Those who gained the name from the two of us present at the naming ceremony were then in as good a position to pass it on as we were. And they pass it on in similar ways. People are told, "The Devitts' cat is called 'Nana'," or "Nana is an unusually patterned cat," and thereby gain the appropriate ability. Their later uses of the name designate Nana because the d-chains underlying their tokens, chains that run through several people's abilities, are in fact grounded in her. And so the chains continue: people acquired and used the name long after Nana was with us

Under each token of a semantic name type (1.4) lies a d-chain. These chains are linked together to form the *causal network* for the name type.

The nature of reference borrowing will be discussed in more detail in 5.3.

So far we have considered only those uses of a name which pass it on. In fact, most uses of a name are to an audience that already has it. Each of these uses reinforces in a member of the audience the ability he has with the name. It establishes *further* causal linkages between him and the object. Therefore, there may be *many* d-chains grounded in the object underlying a person's use of a name: there may be a causal network underlying *his* token. The overall network for the name is the union of all such individual networks.

It is a commonplace that a person in a position to pick up a name may fail to do so: he may fail to pay attention at an introduction; the required ability to designate the object is not acquired. Further, a person who has the ability may lose it; it fades through lack of exercise.[6] This loss of ability is a failure of memory. For a description theorist, what are forgotten are the descriptions required to identify the object. My explanation is somewhat different (see 5.1).

2.4 Ambiguous Names

So far I have ignored, as writers on proper names are prone to, the fact that most proper names are ambiguous. The ambiguity of the physical type 'Nana' was clear from the start, for it was Zola's use of it that led to its being bestowed on our cat. And there are many names much more ambiguous than 'Nana'.

In 1.4 I mentioned an insight of description theorists which seems helpful here: a name token designates this object and not that because the speaker had it in mind. The problem was then to give a satisfactory explanation of this unclear notion. My best effort to do so following description theories, the "centralist interpretation," fell victim to Kripke's refutation.

This insight of description theorists is an important one. The ordinary notion of *having in mind* points the way to the solution of several problems in semantics involving singular terms. It underlies Donnellan's distinction (2.5). Most important of all, and related to this, is its bearing on the role of singular terms in the contexts of propositional attitudes (9.3–9.6). Our present interest in it is that, when embodied in the above insight, it supplies another route to a causal theory of names.

What is it to have an object in mind? As a first step in answering this, I suggest that *there is an object which a person has in mind if and only if there is a certain sort of causal connection between his state of mind and the object* (so what you have in mind is not determined by what is in your head!). We are interested in a more specific notion, *having an object in mind in using a name (or meaning an object by a name)*.[7] This requires a special sort of causal connection. I suggest the following rough explanation:

> For any x, y, and z, x had y in mind in uttering name token z (x meant y in uttering name token z) if an only if there was a d-chain accessible to x underlying z which was grounded in y.

Apply this to the above insight and we have a causal theory of names: a name token designates the object in which the d-chain underlying it is grounded.

What bearing does this have on the problem of the ambiguity of names? Take a physical type 'John'. It is probably the case that most of us can designate about 30 different people with this name. Most of us, therefore, have about 30 distinct abilities involving the name, each one causally based on a distinct person. When we utter the name having a certain person in mind, there is (normally) one and only one of these abilities exercised in the production of the token. Which object a person designates depends on which ability he in fact exercises. Or, putting this another way, which object a person designates depends on which d-chain in fact underlies his utterance and on which object that d-chain is in fact grounded in.

My concern here has not been to produce a precisely accurate explanation of *having an object in mind in using a name*. In fact, what I have said is not strictly correct, as the cases considered in 5.4 show. My aim has been to give a rough account of the notion and to show that those who have seen it as an important clue to the explanation of designation were correct. However, it is only a clue, for it stands as much in need of explanation as does designation. My explanation must rest on a description of d-chains and their role.[8]

A feature of our problem is that of distinguishing which among the many causal links between a token and objects is the appropriate one. It is striking, for example, that more than one ability to use a name, hence more than one object, may be involved in the causal explanation of an utterance even though only one object is designated. Consider my earlier-mentioned utterance, "Nana is hungry," which contains a token of an ambiguous name. If we reify Zola's courtesan for a moment, we can say that I have an ability to designate her with the name as well as one to designate our cat. Furthermore both abilities appear in the explanation of my token: it was partly because I and others had abilities to designate the courtesan with the name that the cat got the name. Nevertheless I designated our cat by the token because it was the ability that concerned her that was exercised. Each of my abilities with an ambiguous name is distinct. The ability concerning the cat was exercised because it was the one that played the direct causal role in producing the token. The ability concerns only the cat because at its creation only she played the appropriate role (2.2; see also 2.3); only she played the grounding role. *The explanation of what caused that particular grounding to take place, involving as it does other abilities and objects, is irrelevant to designation.* The underlying d-chain begins at the cat.[9]

Each time we *hear* a name used, we must, in understanding it, associate it with an ability (unless we form a new ability on the strength of it). It is possible to do this *wrongly* and hence to *misunderstand* the remark. Misunderstandings are common with ambiguous names like 'John'. I shall consider the consequences of them later (5.4). As a result of many remarks using the name type 'John', we acquire many beliefs concerning various people of that name. The beliefs concerning different people are, in some sense, "stored" separately with their respective abilities.

How is it that we do not more often misunderstand the use of an ambiguous name? According to the causal theory, the designatum of the name is settled by something to which the audience has no access. Clearly we rely primarily on the (external) context for clues. It is usually a reliable guide to what the speaker has in mind. Some have thought that the context has more than merely epistemic significance here: it *determines* which object the name designates. I have criticized this view elsewhere.[10]

It is important to note that what clues we get from the context depends very much on *what we already believe*, particularly about the speaker; understanding a person's words is part of the task of understanding *him*. We know that people who utter sentences are usually aiming to communicate something and so they will try not to mislead. Taking account of this, we consider what in this context is *likely* to be the designatum. We are guided by what we think the speaker *can* designate with that name, and also by what we believe he thinks we can designate by it and he thinks we know about his designating abilities. By and large, a speaker utters names he can use, names he thinks his audience can use and understand, and names he thinks his audience expects him to use. Sometimes, however, he will use a name that is new to his audience; he introduces the audience to a semantic type.

A further important clue to the interpretation of a name token is the predicate used with it: "Whom is he likely to be saying *that* about?" Our answer to that will be guided by what we think the speaker might know about various objects, by what we think he would be likely to think worth saying to us, and so on.

Where the context leaves us in doubt, we can usually ask the speaker about his intentions. The descriptions he will offer supply further clues.

Mostly the context, together with a well-chosen question or two, enables us to settle on an interpretation. And mostly we will be right. However, we may be wrong. Misunderstandings are possible: the context may mislead; our relevant beliefs about the speaker may be erroneous. Further, his answers to our questions may be incorrect: he may be wrong in one way or another about what he referred to (1.5).

We shall return to the discussion of proper names in 2.8.

2.5 Donnellan's Distinction

I have claimed that names refer to their objects because they are causally linked to them. Can we say anything similar about definite descriptions? At first sight it seems not: a definite description refers to the one and only object that its description applies to. However, investigation of a distinction made by Keith Donnellan suggests that this is too hasty (1966, 1968).

Donnellan distinguishes two uses of definite descriptions—an "attributive" use and a "referential" use:

A speaker who uses a definite description attributively in an assertion states something about whoever or whatever is the so-and-so. A speaker who uses a definite description referentially in an assertion, on the other hand, uses the description to enable his audience to pick out whom or what he is talking about and states something about that person or thing. (1966:285)

Donnellan brings out his distinction by giving a number of examples, particularly of situations where he claims a person is speaking "about" (1966:285), "referring to" (1966:295), or saying something "*of*" (1966:301) someone in using a description, *even though the description does not correctly describe that person*. These are referential uses of the description. Attributive uses differ in this respect. We would naturally mark the distinction by saying that in a referential use the speaker *has a certain object in mind* in using the description, whereas in an attributive use he does not.[11]

Causal Theory of Designation (1)   37

Consider two of Donnellan's examples. Suppose

> someone said ... in 1960 before he had any idea that Mr. Goldwater would be the Republican nominee in 1964, "The Republican candidate for president in 1964 will be a conservative." (1966-293)

Suppose the judgment was based on an assessment of overall trends within the party. The description in that utterance is used attributively: the speaker does not have any particular object in mind; he is speaking about whoever happens to become the candidate in 1964. In contrast,

> suppose that Jones has been charged with Smith's murder and has been placed on trial. Imagine that there is a discussion of Jones's odd behavior at his trial. We might sum up our impressions of his behavior by saying, "Smith's murderer is insane." (1966:286)

The description here is used referentially. The speaker has a certain object in mind, namely, Jones.

Now I take it that what is being suggested in this talk of "two uses" of descriptions is that there are two different *conventional* uses of descriptions. If that is so, it is a fact of considerable semantic significance. In my view Donnellan has not *established* that there are these two conventions, but he has made it seem intuitively plausible that there are. I shall argue later that there are the two conventions (2.7). Meanwhile I shall simply assume that Donnellan is right.

On this assumption, there is a convention to use a description "referentially." How *could* there be? Suppose, in the case just described, that Jones did not murder Smith. According to Donnellan there is nevertheless "a *right* thing to be picked out by the audience" (1966:304), namely, Jones, and the speaker "referred" to that thing with 'Smith's murderer'. How *could* a person manage to refer to an object using a description that does not even apply to it, let alone apply uniquely? How *could* he have that object in mind?

Causal Theory of Designation (1)

I have earlier given a causal explanation of having an object in mind in using a name (2.4). This points to what we need to say here. It was *because* of our experiences of Jones during his trial and our beliefs about him that we used 'Smith's murderer' in that utterance. Similarly, it was *because* of my experiences of Nana and my beliefs about her that I used 'our cat' in those earlier remarks aimed at passing on her name, (iii) and (iv). In a sense, *the object itself* leads us to use the definite description in such cases. I shall mark these similarities between descriptions used in this way and names by extending my terminology to them. I shall say that such a token description *designates* the object to which it is causally linked in the appropriate way, and that *underlying* it is a *d-chain grounded in* the object.

There can be a causal link of the required kind even though a speaker has had no direct experience of the object: it will be a d-chain running *through others* back to speakers who did experience the object. Thus, someone who has heard about our cat from me, but has never met her, can have here in mind and designate her by 'the Devitts' cat'. And we can all designate Aristotle by 'the philosopher who taught Alexander the Great'. One can borrow the ability to designate in using a description just as one can in using a name.

So far I have said next to nothing about the nature of the d-chain which makes the referential use of a description possible. Rather, I have relied on the very obvious *difference* between the causal explanations of referential and attributive uses; in particular, on the very obvious difference in the causal role of the object described. Jones clearly had a role in bringing about the use of 'Smith's murderer' which Goldwater did not have in bringing about the use of 'The Republican candidate for president in 1964'. In the latter case there was no causal link between the speaker and Goldwater in virtue of which the speaker uttered what he did. Refinements in this account will soon be called for.

Donnellan emphasizes that the description in a sentence can on one occasion be used attributively and on another referentially. I have illustrated a referential use in 'Smith's murderer is insane'. Now consider the following situation:

we come upon poor Smith foully murdered. From the brutal manner of the killing and the fact that Smith was the most lovable person in the world, we might exclaim, "Smith's murderer is insane." . . . assume . . . that . . . we do not know who murdered Smith. (Donnellan 1966:285).

The use of the description is attributive. We do not have, nor in the circumstances could we have, anyone particular in mind. Yet clearly there is a causal link between the murderer and us (via the corpse) in virtue of which we used the description 'Smith's murderer'.

What distinguishes the causal link in this case from the earlier links is that it does not involve *experience of the object*. Before, we had actually *seen* Jones at his trial; and it was *my acquaintance with* Nana that led to my use of 'our cat'. Now, however, we may never have seen the murderer. Or, if we have, seeing him could not lead us to use that description: we do not associate the person we saw with the murder. It is for these reason that the causal link to the murderer in this case is not a d-chain.

The d-chain that enables a speaker to have an object in mind in using a description starts with the perception of the object. (The speaker need not have perceived the object *himself*, of course. Those who have perceived it can pass on the ability to others.) It is indeed appropriate enough that having an object *in mind* should be based on perception of it.

There are elements of vagueness about *perceiving an object*. The clear-cut cases are those of "face-to-face" perception of the object. These are also the cases which yield paradigms of *having the object in mind*. Consider a case at the other extreme. Suppose that, at the time we come upon Smith foully murdered, we barely notice movement in the distance which we rightly take to be the murderer fleeing. Do we perceive the murderer? I shall not attempt to answer this question. However, I shall say that we could not, on the strength of this perception, have the murderer in mind in using 'Smith's murderer'; something close to "face-to-face" perception is required for a grounding. (See also 2.10 and 5.7 on grounding perceptions.)

I shall say more about d-chains for descriptions, relating them to d-chains for names (and other terms soon to be discussed), in later sections, particularly in 5.1 to 5.3.

Donnellan seems to have detected, at the level of intuitive semantics, a difference in meaning or function. We mark the referential use with an ordinary expression like 'having an object in mind' and the attributive with an ordinary expression like 'whatever it is'. Assuming (for the moment) that the distinction is a good one, I am claiming that the referential use of descriptions is made possible by d-chains. It is in virtue of a d-chain linking a person to an object that he can use it having that object in mind. Thus, the causal theory goes a long way toward explaining Donnellan's distinction.

For me, unlike Donnellan, 'refer' is a generic term (1.3). Donnellan's distinction is best captured in my terminology by replacing his term 'referential' by 'designational'.

I have pointed out earlier that a definite description may be used at a naming ceremony to pick out the object to be named (2.2). So the connection between a name token and its object may be mediated by a description. Clearly if that connection is to be a d-chain, that description must be a designational one; only such a description can be *grounded in* the object. And what we find in a normal naming ceremony is that any mediating description is designational.

Abnormal naming ceremonies are possible, however. An example would be the introduction of the name 'Jack the Ripper' for whoever committed that famous series of London murders.

We can invent a more extreme example. "Let us call the heaviest fish in the sea 'Oscar'." In these cases names are introduced by means of attributive descriptions. I shall call such names "attributive" to distinguish them from the more normal "designational" ones. (Since most names are designational, I will call them simply "names" unless it is confusing to do so.) Attributive names are not causally grounded in their objects and so do not have d-chains underlying them nor do they designate their objects.[12]

Description theories have a good deal of truth in them if they are restricted to attributive names: such names *are* associated with identifying descriptions which determine their reference. However, the description theory's account of reference borrowing is as wrong for them as for any name. In 2.1 I pointed out that the link between name and object has two parts—causal network and initial link to object. We have seen now that the initial link is not always a causal one. But even when it isn't, the causal network grows in the usual way: the name is passed from person to person; later references depend on earlier ones. Though an attributive name was associated with an identifying description at its introduction, many of those who now use it may not know this description. Indeed, it is possible, though not likely, that nobody now using the name should know it. I return to the subject of attributive names in 5.6.

I have been led by Donnellan's distinction to a distinction between two sorts of names. However, this distinction is of such a different kind than Donnellan's that is doubtful if it is appropriate to regard it as an *extension* of Donnellan's distinction. Note particularly that whereas a description seems to have just two uses, one designational, the other attributive, a name seems to have many, some designational and some attributive.

Donnellan's distinction is between ways of using descriptions; it is a distinction between semantic types (1.3). I have already indicated a preference for talk of tokens to talk of types (1.3).

Following that preference here will enable me to draw a distinction based on Donnellan's that can be applied across the board to singular terms. It is *a distinction between designational and attributive tokens*. A designational use of a description yields a designational token that depends for its reference on designation, as we have seen. An attributive use of a description yields an attributive token that depends for its reference on what I shall call "denotation": an attributive token of 'the F' denotes an object if and only if the object is the one and only one 'F' applies to. (Note that either a designational or attributive token may fail to refer: the problems this gives rise to are taken up in chapter 6.) I shall say that designational and attributive tokens of 'the F' *apply to* all objects 'F' applies to. Suppose 'F' in a *designational* token of 'the F' applies to one and only one object. Does the token denote that object? Let us say that it does for the moment, though I shall find reason later for preferring to say that no question of denotation arises for it (2.7). Finally, a token of a designational name is designational; one of an attributive name is attributive. And each attributive name token *applies to* and *denotes* whatever the attributive description token that introduced it applied to and denoted.

So far I have simply assumed what is in fact controversial: that there really are two conventional uses of descriptions as Donnellan suggests, and hence that his distinction is semantically significant. I shall argue for this assumption in 2.7. The next section will clarify the nature of the distinction.

2.6 Demonstratives

We next consider simple singular demonstratives and pronouns (often briefly, "demonstratives"): for example, in English, 'this', 'that', 'I', 'you', 'he', 'she', 'it'.

When such a demonstrative is used "out of the blue" to refer to an object, when a use is "deictic," it is clear that there is some causal link between the speaker and the object in virtue of which he uses the demonstrative. He is *perceiving* the object (introspecting it in the case of 'I') or has recently perceived it. It is the causal action of the object on him that led him (in part) to do what he did. Because of this we can truly say that he had that object in mind in using the demonstrative. Thus, at our earlier naming ceremony (2.2), my wife had Nana in mind in using 'her' in that it was the causal action of Nana on my wife that (partly) led her to use the pronoun. Once again I extend my terminology to mark similarities. I shall say that such a demonstrative token *designates* its object because it is causally linked to the object by a *d-chain grounded in* it. It is a *designational* demonstrative token.

Commonly the deictic demonstrative will be accompanied by a pointing gesture of hand or eye toward the object. On its own this gesture would often be insufficient to identify the referent. What determines that one aspect and not another of the vaguely indicated environment is referred to is that the speaker had that aspect in mind. We look to what played a certain causal role in the behavior in order to remove ambiguities. Sometimes no gesture is called for—it is not with 'I'—and other times, none is given. Again we look to the cause of the utterance to determine the reference.

When a demonstrative is not used "out of the blue," the speaker may not have a particular object in mind. And a demonstrative is often not used deictically: it "may depend for its reference upon determinants in antecedent verbiage" (Quine 1960:113); it is a way to *cross*-refer; it may be "anaphoric." In such a case the demonstrative borrows characteristics from the singular term on which it depends. If that singular term is linked to an object by a d-chain so that the speaker had that object in mind and designated it, then so also is the demonstrative. If not, then the demonstrative is not. If the term is dependent on an earlier designational demonstrative, or a designational name, or a designational description, then it will be so linked (unless they are empty). It will be a *designational* demonstrative. If, on the other hand, it is dependent on an attributive name or description, then it will not be linked. It will be an *attributive* demonstrative. For example, both the definite description and the pronoun designate an object in the first of the following sentences and denote one in the second:

> Our cat is hungry because she hasn't eaten for several hours.
>
> The heaviest fish in the sea is not a shark nor is it a whale.

Note that the designational/attributive distinction does not cover pronouns that depend for their reference on indefinite singular terms; these are like variables but will not be discussed here except briefly in 10.4 and 10.5.

I have extended my distinction at token level, based on Donnellan's at type level, to simple demonstratives. However, Donnellan's distinction *itself* cannot be so extended. Note that the anaphoric or cross-referential uses of a demonstrative may yield *either* designational or attributive tokens (ignoring those like variables). Further, the deictic ones yield *only* designational tokens. Our move to the level of tokens has paid off in greater generality for Donnellan's insight. This becomes more striking when we see that his distinction at type level does not even apply to all uses of descriptions.

It will help to bring this out if we first extend our treatment to *complex* demonstratives. Consider 'that book'. It can be used to designate a book in front of the speaker. It can be used cross-referentially, borrowing its referential properties from an earlier designational or attributive term. The designational/attributive distinction applies to the resulting tokens.

Definite descriptions, like demonstratives, can be used to cross-refer. Thus 'the book', like 'that book', might be used to refer to a book described in more detail by an attributive or designational description in the antecedent verbiage. What I said above for cross-referential demonstratives applies as well to cross-referential descriptions. *Donnellan's distinction covers only the deictic uses of descriptions.*

Cross-reference is a familiar enough example of the way in which one token can depend for its reference on another. What I am urging in my theory of reference borrowing is that an analogous type of dependency is the lot of most singular term tokens. Indeed, the only difference between reference borrowing and the familiar cross-reference is a relatively trivial one: terms typically cross-refer to ones of a different type that "convey more information"; terms typically borrow their reference from ones of the same type "conveying just the same information." Where there is cross-reference there is a causal network, though usually a short one.

In sum, my stand on Donnellan's distinction and related distinctions is as follows (still ignoring all terms like variables). Donnellan's distinction is between two deictic uses of descriptions, one yielding designational tokens and the other attributive ones. There is also an anaphoric use of descriptions. Demonstratives have an anaphoric use but only one deictic use, yielding designational tokens; so Donnellan's distinction cannot be extended to demonstratives. Anaphoric uses of descriptions and demonstratives may yield either designational or attributive tokens. Names are basically anaphoric: reference borrowing is of the essence of their role. We distinguish name types according to whether they are linked ultimately to their objects by designational or attributive means. The two sorts of name types yield two sorts of tokens, designational and attributive. *So my distinction at token level, based on Donnellan's at type level, applies across the board to all (definite) singular term tokens (except variables).*

My aim in this book is to describe the relationship between a token and an object in virtue of which the token designates that object, and to argue for the semantic significance of that relationship. I shall set aside matters that are irrelevant to that aim.

Thus, whereas the distinction between attributive and designational tokens is important for me, the nature of the link between attributive tokens and the world is not.

Finally, as preparation for the argument about semantic significance in the next section, consider the following question. How would we *give the meaning*, the conventional meaning, of the semantic type 'that book'? It will simplify our discussion without cost if we ignore anaphoric uses. Making use of our semantic terminology, I suggest an answer along the lines of "a designated book."

We could treat simple demonstratives in a similar way. The core of their conventional meaning is "a designated object." This misses the nuances of meaning that distinguish the simple demonstratives from each other. For my purposes we can mostly ignore these. However, it will help to notice the difference between the group 'this', 'that', and 'it', and the group 'he' and 'she'. "A designated object" near enough exhausts the meaning of the members of the first group but we capture the members of the second group better with "a designated male" and "a designated female," respectively. So the latter have "a descriptive content" just as 'that book' has, albeit a more general one. And it would be in accord with our usage to say for example, that 'he' *applies to* all males.

In this section and the preceding one I have adopted Donnellan's distinction and developed it in two ways. First, I have derived from it a distinction for tokens and then applied that distinction across the board to all singular terms. Second, I have offered a causal theory to explain the designational side of these distinctions.[13] I shall now argue for the distinctions and their significance.

2.7 The Semantic Significance of Donnellan's Distinction

We have already found some semantic significance in the distinction I have derived from Donnellan's. We need to explain how demonstrative tokens are linked to their objects. In some cases they are linked via definite descriptions to objects denoted (the object is denoted by the demonstrative because the description on which the demonstrative depends applies to that object only). In some other cases, the deictic ones, they are not so linked. I have explained the different link in the latter cases in terms of d-chains. The distinction between attributive and designational tokens is significant for at least these two groups of demonstratives: it distinguishes demonstratives according to the way in which their referents are determined. This significance must carry over to some name tokens, for names can be linked to their objects in virtue of deictic demonstratives designating those objects or in virtue of descriptions denoting them.

What has not been established is the significance of Donnellan's distinction for descriptions at type level and hence mine for descriptions (and dependent demonstratives and names) at token level.[14] The issue is whether or not there are two conventional uses of descriptions. A reason for doubting that there are two uses is that one seems to be enough. It seems that a description typically applies to one and only one object, thereby denoting it. We can rely on denotation to identify the object we wish to say something about. Why suppose that there is another use relying on designation?

So far, we have two reasons for supposing that there is this other conventional use. First, Donnellan's discussion of various cases of confusion and mistake makes it plausible to think that there is. However, perhaps the phenomena he points to can be otherwise explained.[15] Perhaps he has discovered some sort of distinction but it is not one between two conventional uses of descriptions. Second, I have shown how another use of a description is possible. It is possible because it can depend on designation, a relationship that links descriptions to objects by d-chains. This is far from conclusive as a reason, of course, because it does not show that there is an actual convention relying on this relationship of designation in using descriptions. It doesn't show that this relationship has any bearing on the truth conditions of sentences containing descriptions.

(1) Donnellan often seems[16] to make claims which, if true, would go a long way toward establishing that he has discovered another use of descriptions and hence a distinction of semantic significance. These claims concern the role of designational descriptions and, related to this (and more importantly), the truth conditions of sentences containing one.

According to Donnellan, a designational description "refers" to the object the speaker had in mind *even when it does not denote that object*. Further, the sentence containing the description is true or false according to whether the predicate in it does or does not apply to *that object which the speaker had in mind* (e.g., Donnellan 1966:295).[17] In all Donnellan's examples the designational description does not denote anything; so the choice is between reference to what the speaker had in mind and reference failure. Donnellan plumps for the former. He does not discuss any example where the speaker has one object in mind but the description he uses denotes *another*. However, the implication of his discussion is clear: in such a case the description refers to the *first* object and the truth value of the sentence depends on *its* characteristics (1966:301, particularly the sentence, "It does not matter here whether or not the woman has a husband *or whether, if she does, Jones is her husband*" [my emphasis]).

Donnellan's claims are too strong. First, many of his remarks using the term 'refer' *seem* to presuppose that there exists, pretheoretically, a clear-cut notion picked out by this term which it is our task in semantics to investigate (e.g., 1966:293).[18] This is not so (cf. 1.3 and 4.1). This term in philosphy is largely *a term of art*, gaining its meanings from its use in semantic theories. This is true of Donnellan's use, as it is also of mine. The pretheoretical ("ordinary") use of the term is so loose that it is easily adaptable to a variety of such meanings. Donnellan's claims about "reference" become substantial, rather than merely verbal, only when we see their bearing on his claims about truth.

Suppose that I was under the misapprehension that Nana was our neighbor's cat which we were looking after for a while; my wife had told me this story in order to get Nana into the house. The day after her arrival, she disappears. Talking about this later in the day, I say, "Our neighbor's cat has disappeared." Now, in fact, our neighbor has a cat, Jemima, whom I have never seen nor heard of and who is safely at home. Did 'our neighbor's cat' refer to Nana or Jemima? My claim is that, taken on its own, this is a purely verbal question. Clearly, my description is linked to *both* cats, though the links are of a different kind. I have marked this difference by saying that I "designated" Nana but "denoted" Jemima. Others might choose different terms. What we say here is of no interest until we see what follows within the semantic theory from saying it.

This brings us to the second point. Donnellan would say (it seems) that I referred to Nana and, hence, that what I said was *true*. We are here faced with a substantial question to which Donnellan gives a simple answer. I think that the correct answer is far from simple. When we attend to the link to Nana we are indeed inclined to say that the sentence is true, but when we attend to the different link to Jemima we are inclined to say it is false. Considering the whole picture, we don't know what to say. So much for our pretheoretical intuitions about 'true'. To advance further we need a semantic *theory*; we need to bring out the place of designation and denotation in explaining descriptions in particular and language in general.

If Donnellan's discussion established his claims about truth values, then it would be fairly decisive evidence that he had discovered a distinction of semantic significance. But the discussion does not. This is not to say that the discussion does not give *some* support for the hypothesis that there are two conventional uses of descriptions. We need to explain our intuition that *Nana* has something to do with the truth value of "Our neighbor's cat has disappeared," with the result that the sentence does not seem *simply false* (though we have found no basis for Donnellan's view that it is *simply true*). This is odd because 'our neighbor's cat' does not denote Nana. The hypothesis that there are two uses, together with my causal explanation of the designational use, give a very plausible explanation of Nana's involvement: the description was a designational one picking out Nana. I shall say more in explanation of these cases of mistake and confusion later.

(2) We can do better for the distinction than this. It has often been noted that many definite descriptions, used deictically, fail to denote because they apply to many objects; Russell's uniqueness condition is not satisfied. Yet usually such a description seems to refer to just one object. Consider the sentence, "Put the book on the table"; the world is full of books and tables, yet the reference may be clear. Call these definite descriptions, in their deictic use, "imperfect."[19]

What normally determines the reference of an imperfect description? The striking thing about such a description is that *denotation normally seems irrelevant to determining its referent.* Not only does 'the book' not apply uniquely to any object, but it would not normally be uttered with the intention of applying uniquely, nor would it normally be taken by its audience to be uttered with that intention. It would normally be *common knowledge* that 'the book' was not purporting to denote. *There is a conventional use of some descriptions at least which seems not to depend on denotation.* What then does that use depend on?

Just as the solution to the problem of determining the reference of ambiguous names has been sought in the external context, so also has the solution to our present problem with imperfect descriptions. One is inclined, as Donnellan points out, to save Russell's view by relying on the context "to supply further qualifications on the description to make it unique" (1968:204n.). Donnellan himself seems to suggest that the context settles which object an imperfect description refers to.[20] Note, however, our intuition that the description refers to the object *the speaker has in mind*. The intuition is parallel to the earlier one for names (1.4).

I explained that earlier intuition in terms of causal links to objects (2.4). The proposed explanation of designational descriptions enables me to do the same here: *an imperfect description normally refers to the object it designates.* The earlier speaker referred to this book and that table (in the sense that the truth value of his remark depends on the relationship between that pair of objects) because of their special place in the causal explanation of his utterance: he exercised abilities grounded in those objects.[21] The external context is merely a guide to this reality.[22]

So if we take the normal uses of imperfect descriptions to be designational, we have a plausible explanation of the way in which their reference is determined. The plausibility of this explanation is increased by the earlier discussion of deictic demonstratives (2.6). I argued that those demonstratives depend for their reference on designation. What I am now claiming, in effect, is that *there is a deictic use of at least some descriptions that makes them just like demonstratives.*

We have already considered the conventional meanings of various demonstratives (2.6). Making use of my semantic terminology I gave some of them as follows:

this:	"a designated object";
he:	"a designated male";
that book:	"a designated book."

On the basis of the present discussion we can now add:

the book:	"a designated book."

Doubtless this ignores some differences in nuance between 'that book' and 'the book'. My point is simply that there is a conventional way of using 'the book' that makes it nearly synonymous with 'that book'. Furthermore, both terms are related in meaning to 'this' and 'he'. *A token of any of these terms used deictically would normally refer to the object the token designated.* How else could the reference be determined, for no question of denotation arises?

I have been careful always to write of the "normal" use of imperfect descriptions. I do not want to suggest that a description like 'the book' *cannot* be used just like 'the Republican nominee for president in 1964' in Donnellan's example. To use 'the F' attributively, depending on denotation, one has to believe (roughly) that one and only one object is F. Clearly, if one has crazy enough beliefs, one could use even 'the book' attributively.

I have established that some descriptions, at least, have two conventional uses, a designational one and an attributive one. I have called these descriptions "imperfect." But what really *is* an "imperfect" description? It is simply one whose "normal" use is designational. But is there any reason for not supposing that *any* description can be used designationally, just as any one can be used attributively? How could we possibly draw the line between ones that can and ones that cannot be used designationally?

I have just given the designational meaning of four terms listed in order of increasing "descriptive content" (the last two being equal). We can continue increasing the content until we may have a denoting description:

that red book:	"a designated red book";
the red book about reptiles:	"a designated red book about reptiles";
the red book on the table:	"a designated red book on a designated table";
the red book of Fred's:	"a designated red book of Fred's."

Now if I am right in thinking that the previous four terms can be used so that they have those meanings depending on designation, it is hard to see a good reason for denying that the present four terms can be used so that they have these meanings depending on designation. *At what point on the spectrum do we draw a line beyond which designation cannot be relevant to determining reference?*

One reason for supposing we draw no line here is that *any* description, however rich in descriptive content, can be linked to an object in the causal way that makes a designational use of it possible. If we have a convention that takes advantage of this with descriptions like 'the book', then it is plausible to suppose our convention takes advantage of it with other descriptions too. Another reason for supposing we draw no line is given by our earlier explanation of intuitions about cases of mistake and confusion: descriptions like 'our neighbor's cat' and 'Smith's murderer' are rich in descriptive content and yet seem to be used designationally in these cases.

In sum, 'the F' is ambiguous. It has two conventional uses which we might capture as follows:

whatever is alone in being F;
a designated F.

The first of these is the attributive use; the second the designational. Donnellan is right. *The object that bears on the truth value of a statement containing a designational token is the object it designates. On the other hand, the object that bears on the truth value of a statement containing an attributive token is the object it denotes.*

Since denotation is irrelevant to the designational use of 'the F', an adjustment in my terminology seems called for. *I shall no longer say that a designational token of 'the F' denotes an object even if 'F' should happen to apply to that object uniquely* (cf. 2.5); no question of denotation arises for it.

A person might be in a position to use a description designationally and yet use it attributively. He might, for example, suspect Jones of Smith's murder and yet want to express the belief, suspicions aside, that *whoever* murdered Smith is insane. He could do this by saying, "Smith's murderer is insane." Whether a token description is designational or attributive is determined by which convention the speaker *in fact* employs (cf. 3.3; see 5.6 for a qualification).

I have said that no question of denotation arises for a designational use of 'the *F*'. Does any question of *application* arise? Consider the sentence, "The book is on the table," where 'the book' is designational but where the d-chain underlying it is grounded not in a book but in a box (which looks like a book perhaps). Does this failure of application matter semantically? I don't think we have any strong intuitions here but I suspect that our theory, particularly our theory of convention (3.3), will require that it does matter. So, although 'the book' designates the box, it does not *identifyingly refer* to it because it does not apply to it; and the sentence is not true even though the box is on the table. I am not convinced that this is the correct line but I shall take it because it seems preferable to others. So far as I can see, nothing very significant for the theory depends on this line. I summarize its bearing on truth conditions in 5.8.

We now have the further semantic theory needed to complete the explanation of cases of confusion and mistake of the sort that first suggested his distinction to Donnellan. The description in my utterance, "Our neighbor's cat has disappeared," is designational. It designated Nana. It is because of this that it seemed, intuitively, that I had Nana in mind and that she had something to do with the truth value of the sentence. It is because the description does not apply to Nana (she is not a cat of our neighbor) that the sentence is not, despite Nana's disappearance, true. Although Jemima is our neighbor's one and only cat, she is irrelevant to the truth value of the sentence; for no question of the denotation of 'our neighbor's cat' arises when it is used designationally.

Donnellan's distinction at type level applies only to deictic uses of descriptions, and so I have thus far ignored cross-referential uses in this discussion of semantic significance. However, my distinction at token level is significant across the board. A cross-referential description or demonstrative token will depend for its reference on an earlier token. If that token exemplifies the designational use of a description, the token that depends on it will be designational; if it exemplifies the attributive use it will be attributive. If the cross-referential token depends on a deictic demonstrative, it will be designational. The token will also be designational if it depends on a name linked to an object by such a demonstrative or by a designational description. On the other hand, it will be attributive if it depends on an attributive name. The designational mode of identifying reference for deictic demonstratives and for one use of descriptions, and the denotational mode for the other use of descriptions, spread to cover all (definite) singular term tokens. The designational/attributive distinction is crucial to the explanation of reference for all such tokens.

(3) An important aspect of the significance of the distinction between attributive and designational terms cannot be discussed now: it has a bearing on the semantics of statements attributing propositional attitudes. Quine has distinguished two sorts of contexts here, "opaque" and "transparent," and has suggested that the "exportation" of a singular term involved in the inference from opaque to transparent is in general implicative. However, this leads to difficulties. The solution, I shall argue in chapter 9, is that only designational terms may be exported.

Throughout our discussion of definite descriptions we have ignored the fact that some descriptions are *superlatives*: they have the form not of 'the F' but of 'the most FG'. The reasons adduced in (2) above for seeing Donnellan's distinction as semantically significant do not mostly apply to these, for they are not in the spectrum we described. However, the intuitive grounds for the distinction discussed in (1) seem to apply to them as well. And the distinction has as much bearing on their role in the contexts of propositional attitudes as on any other singular term.

It is not my concern here to offer a theory of attributive terms. However, my discussion has committed me to certain views on the matter. First, I agree with the familiar view that attributive terms refer to whatever they denote. Second, they may, like designational terms, have a network underlying them generated by cross-reference or reference borrowing. However, that network will not be grounded in an object.

We return now to the discussion of (designational) names that we left in 2.4. Discussion of other terms will resume in 5.1.

2.8 Multiple Groundings

Nana is involved in the causal network for her name at more points than its beginning at her naming ceremony; the network is *multiply* grounded in her.

This arises in the first place because of the role of other singular terms in passing on and reinforcing abilities with names. Suppose I pass on 'Nana' by means of (ii), "This is Nana," together with a pointing gesture. Nana will be both mediately and immediately causally involved in this passing on. She will be mediately involved via the ability I exercise in using her name, an ability grounded in her at the naming ceremony. She will be immediately involved because 'this' is a designational demonstrative: she is present at the utterance, and her presence leads to my use of the demonstrative. Thus, someone who gains an ability from this utterance will gain one that is grounded in Nana by means of two entirely distinct d-chains.

Nana is always mediately involved when her name is used to designate her. However, in the second place, she may be *immediately* involved in that use (even though no other singular term features). Suppose Nana is present and her presence leads someone to designate her by name, thus exercising his ability to do this. He is in the position where he has her in mind *quite independently* of his ability to use her name. She is again causally involved both mediately and immediately in that utterance.

In the situations we have just considered, the person involved is in the presence of Nana, and so he could designate her by a demonstrative. Suppose, however, that Nana is absent and a designational description or another name is used. Suppose, for example, that I pass on Nana's name to someone by means of (iv), "Nana is our cat." I have already allowed that a name can be initially grounded in an object at a naming ceremony (or equivalent) by means of a description or other name (2.2, 2.5), for if that term is designational, the name is then causally linked to the object in the appropriate way. It may seem therefore that the person to whom I say (iii) acquires or reinforces an ability which is then *doubly* grounded in Nana, once through my use of 'Nana' and once though my use of 'our cat'. However, I shall adduce reasons for thinking this is not so when I consider certain confusions (5.4).

If an object is picked out by an attributive description at its naming, then the resulting name will be attributive (2.5); the object is not involved in the causal network for that term at the network's beginning. It may become involved later, however, in ways just indicated. If it does, then the network becomes grounded in the object; an attributive name becomes designational.

Multiple grounding is very important: it enables a causal theory to explain reference *change* and various mistakes and misunderstandings (5.4). Causal theories of reference for names, or indeed for any terms (7.2), leave themselves open to easily produced counterexamples if they make the initial grounding at a naming ceremony (or equivalent) bear the entire burden of linking a network to an object.[23]

I say more about groundings in 5.2.

2.9 Other Ways of Naming

It is common for people who become wives, kings, popes, and so on, to adopt new names at the time of so becoming. And babies in our culture have a surname waiting for them at birth. In many of these cases there is an entirely automatic procedure by which a certain name is bestowed on the object: for example, the next person called 'Charles' to become king of England will be called 'Charles III'. Any ceremony in such cases is not *primarily* a naming ceremony but counts as one nonetheless. In all these cases the name is likely to be grounded in the object, usually by face-to-face confrontation with it, sometimes by the use of a designational description.

An important consequence of the existence of an automatic procedure for name bestowal is that anyone who knows the procedure, and correctly makes a few assumptions, can use a name to refer to an object without that use being grounded in the object or even dependent on a causal network. The resultant use will, or course, be an attributive name. To take an extreme example, if Evans is right about the Wagera Indians, then a person who correctly assumes that someone has three children could, simply on the strength of this, use the name of the children's maternal grandfather to refer to the third child (1973:195).

Many names are acquired not at a naming ceremony but *through use*. Nicknames, in particular, are commonly not bestowed ceremonially, but rather are used, seem apt, and hence catch on. Other names may be similarly acquired. A previously unnamed animal or place may be called by a certain name on some occasion and the name may catch on. In criminal and underground political circles, people often *adopt* new names. Authors often adopt pseudonyms.

A naming ceremony or an automatic procedure for name bestowal *immediately* creates the convention that the name in question is a name of the object in question. A nickname, on the other hand, may have to be used several times for an object before the convention is established. But this is not important. Each of these uses, even the first, designates the object. (Convention is discussed in 3.3.)

How can this be? In virtue of what does such a first use designate the object? The answer is along familiar lines. The speaker had the object in mind. He had it in mind in virtue of a causal connection. This connection *might have* led him to use a certain description *had he been searching for a description to designate it*, or a certain demonstrative *had he been searching for a demonstrative*, but the connection *did* lead him to use a certain name *when he was searching for an apt name for it*. Part of what he intended was to bestow the name (provisionally, perhaps) on the object.

It is possible, though perhaps not likely, that a naming ceremony might be similar to this. Instead of "Let's call her 'Nana' after Zola's courtesan," my wife says simply "Nana." We have no need to insist that the naming ceremony be explicit and include other singular terms, even if they are mostly explicit and do include other terms.

A name can be grounded in its object *indirectly* by being grounded in certain sorts of *representations* of the object. Thus, perceiving a film or painting of an object can serve as well to ground a name in the object as perceiving the object. I shall not attempt to specify the necessary and sufficient conditions for such a grounding perception. However, my talk of "perceiving the object" should not be taken to rule these out.

Many have claimed that we cannot refer to "future objects" by name.[24] My theory accords well with such claims: causes must precede effects, so the naming ceremony involving the object must precede the causal network that it gives rise to. However, these claims seem unduly rigid: there seem to be occasions where we do use the name of a future object.

Consider, for example, the situation where there exists a plan or blueprint for a ship or building. We could introduce a name for that future object and it would seem to function like an ordinary designational name. This requires a small modification in our theory: the network for a name may be grounded initially not in the object itself but in some plan to produce the object according to certain specifications. Later, of course, the network becomes grounded in the object so produced.

Those who make these claims about naming future objects are

struck by the oddity of now naming, say, the first child born in the twenty-first century. The oddity arises, I suggest, because we could not have any particular object in mind in using the names so introduced. This is striking because we mostly do have an object in mind in using a name. However, sometimes we don't; attributive names are possible (2.5). There seems to be no good reason for disallowing attributive names for future objects.

In sum, we can allow designational names for some future objects with a small modification of theory. Attributive names for future objects pose no problem.

2.10 Criterion of Identity

Some philosophers have claimed that the user of a name must associate with it a *criterion of identity*. Sometimes they claim what I have already denied (1.5): that the user must be able to pick out the object ostensively, if not by description proper. Sometimes, however, they claim that the user must associate some "sortal" term 'F' with the name which supplies the criterion of identification for the object, 'the same F' (e.g., Geach 1962:ch. 2). (This is a different claim, for I might be able to specify that any object that is a must be F without being able to recognize or describe *which F* it is.) This latter claim arises out of a valuable insight. It is, however, hard to give precise theoretical content to the insight. My discussion of it will be brief.

First, it seems extremely dubious that we ordinarily require users of a name to associate a criterion of identity with it: we would not think that a statement by a person using a name for which he could not supply a correct "sortal" predicate is, on that ground alone, not true. Nor, in the light of the present theory, does there seem to be any reason why we *should* think it: there is a d-chain underlying the use which is grounded in an object; the truth conditions of the statement are quite determinate. Thus, someone who comes by the name 'Nana' under the misapprehension that it names my grandmother could still use that name to make some true statements (and some false ones) about Nana. Even more radical error does not seem to interfere with the semantics of a name: a person might think that the name for a university designated a person or a river without preventing the name from functioning normally. Such errors might well make us *doubt* that the person had the use of the name, but that is not in question (cf. 2.3, 4.1, 4.5).

To say that each user of a name need not associate a "sortal" predicate with it that applies to the object designated is not to say that a name is not *in some way* linked to a criterion of identification expressible by a predicate. Think once more of the naming of Nana. I have said that *she* was the object named because of her special role in the ceremony. (a) But in virtue of what was it Nana, and not a time-slice of Nana having apparently the same role in the ceremony, that we named? (b) Would it have made any difference if what we had taken to be a cat was in fact something else? Just how wrong could we be?

These are difficult questions to which I shall attempt only incomplete answers. The settling of each involves decisions on the reference conditions for my wife's 'her'; it played an important role in determining what we named.

Consider (a). It is clear that the only difference between naming a cat and a time-slice of a cat is in the intentions;[25] see a cat and you have seen a time-slice of a cat. These intentions could be made explicit: "I name this time-slice of a cat 'Nana'." In the case in question, however, they were not; my wife *had a cat in mind* in using 'her' as did I in agreeing to the naming. What can we make of this? The external object, whether cat or time-slice of a cat, causes its audience to have certain experiences which are "conceptualized in a certain way" in the act of naming. Perhaps it helps to say further that to conceptualize experience as that of a cat in some process of thinking is to apply an ability to use the predicate 'cat' (or some synonym) to that experience in that process: the ability has a certain causal role in the process. It was because that ability was in fact causally active, rather than the complex of abilities involved in the use of 'time-slice of a cat', that we named a cat. This does not take us far, but it is as far as we can go without tackling many new problems.

The same question we have just considered for the naming ceremony arises at each of the multiple groundings of a causal network in an object (2.8). What object the network is grounded in depends, in part, on the mental processes of the person involved in the grounding.

Consider (b). Suppose what we believed to be a cat at the naming or later grounding was in fact a mongoose, a robot, a bush, a shadow, or an illusion (like Macbeth's dagger); neither cat nor time-slice of cat was present to cause anything. One thing is obvious about such cases: *we have to draw the line somewhere, saying that some sort of error invalidates reference. Reference failure is possible* and, in the case of illusion at least, it is actual. My explanation for having in mind and designation focuses on the cause of the speaker's state of mind. Clearly we must add something, for in all cases, we may presume, there will be *some cause* of the experiences that lead to our error.

At one extreme we could require that for a person to designate an object or have an object in mind in one of these face-to-face demonstrative situations, the cause must be an object *of the sort* he has in mind. So, in our example, if what we took for a cat was a mongoose, my wife did not designate anything by 'her' and nothing was named 'Nana'. At the other extreme we could require only that there be *something external to the mind* immediately responsible for the experiences in question. So Macbeth did not designate anything, but a person who attempts to designate a mirage under the impression that it is an oasis does. The first extreme is too severe; the second too lenient. I suggest that we would allow that a person intending to designate a cat (in these demonstrative situations) designated a mongoose if what he took to be a cat were a mongoose. And if it were a catlike robot he would designate that. But if it were a shadow he would designate nothing. If it were a bush, or some such object, the decision would become difficult. (As evidence that we are as liberal here as I claim, think of the role of 'it' in, "Is it a bird? Is it a plane? No! It's Superman!!")

What lies behind these ordinary views? Our interest in truth (1.3, 4.1) gives us an interest in distinguishing designation from designation failure, but it gives us no very clear guideline here as to where to make the distinction. There seems to be no sound theoretical reason for not being as liberal about reference as we ordinarily are: we insist only that the object be in the same *very general* category as it is taken to be. There is an element of arbitrariness in our determination of these categories.

If a naming ceremony is unsuccessful because, unbeknown to all present, there is no object of the appropriate category there to be named, the name will be "empty." It may be used nevertheless, passing from person to person in the usual way. Underlying later uses will be a network of causal chains just like that for a nonempty name except that none of the chains will be grounded in an object. I shall discuss this in detail in chapter 6.

Our discussion allows, in effect, that a name is associated in some way with a general categorial predicate. This differs from what I have earlier disallowed in not requiring the users of the name to have *knowledge*. Most notably it does not require that those who borrow their reference from people present at groundings should know what general category the object designated fits. It does not even require that those responsible for the groundings should know this. A successful grounding will be in an object that fits a category determined by the mental states of some person. It would be odd indeed if the person did not have knowledge of this mental state, but the semantic role of the name does not depend on his having it. Finally, such (noncategorial) "sortal" predicates as users of a name associate with it may be *false* of the object: Nana is not a cat but a catlike robot.

Our main problem was that of explaining the nature of the link between name and object in virtue of which the former designates the latter. In considering this problem, many have seen that the user of a name must, in some way, *identify* an object—the object he "has in mind." What does this identification amount to? The received answer has been that it is the speaker's ability to produce an identifying description of the object. This is mistaken.[26] The speaker is indeed important, but the identification depends not on anything he *could* or *would do* but on what he *did*, for underlying what he did was a causal network grounded in an object. Only in this way does a speaker identify an object. Causal networks link names to the world.

Overlooking the difficulties discussed in 5.4 and 5.6, we can say that a name token designates an object if and only if underlying the name is a d-chain grounded in the object. D-chains consist of three different kinds of link: groundings which link the chain to an object, abilities to designate, and communication situations in which abilities are passed on or reinforced (reference borrowings). I say more about abilities to designate in 5.1, groundings in 5.2, and reference borrowings in 5.3. But first we must consider some very general questions about semantics.

II

Chapter Three
A SEMANTIC PROGRAM

The matters discussed in this part deserve at least a book on their own, although we must treat them more briefly. The plausibility of the theory of designation offered here depends to a degree on the way it fits into an overall program for semantics. The need to set out such a program is made especially pressing by the following two considerations. First, there is amazingly little agreement in semantics; it is a field in which many flowers bloom. Second, relative to the flowers that bloom most vigorously, my views are, in certain respects, radical.

Given the scope of the views that I state here, there is a greater than usual chance of their containing errors. What is the consequence of such errors for the theory of designation offered? It is impossible to say in advance. It seems to me likely that that theory requires a program *something like* the one proposed here, but it could probably survive many errors in the actual proposal. Correspondingly, the program as it stands requires theories of reference *of some sort*, probably even causal theories, for in the final analysis there seem to be no others, but it does not require the particular theory of designation proposed here.

I am more concerned to describe the program and to relate it to other well-known programs, particularly those inspired by Donald Davidson, Paul Grice, and Michael Dummett, than I am to argue for it and against the others. However, some arguments are to be found here and some are suggested. Sometimes I can rest on the arguments of others.

The program is described in this chapter and defended in the next. I begin with the main outline of the program (3.1). I fill this out by adopting the view that there is *a language of thought* (3.2). I claim that this explains *speaker meaning* but is also partly explained by *conventional meaning* (3.3).

3.1 Main Outline of the Program[1]

Our problem in semantics is posed by a part of human behavior, the verbal part. People produce sounds and inscriptions which play a strikingly important role in their lives. Early in our theorizing about people, at about the time we attribute minds to them, we see their sounds and inscriptions as items of language: we see the items as having such semantic properties as *being meaningful*, of *referring* to parts of the world, of *being true or false*. We attribute to people complicated beliefs, hopes, desires, and so on about the world, which we think their words express, as part of our theory to explain the complicated way they behave in the world. I take the main problem of semantics to be to explain the semantic notions that appear in the theory. In virtue of what does this sound refer to that object? What is it for an inscription to be meaningful? Why is that sound true?

What semantic notions *should* appear in our theory of people? In my view the central notion is *truth*. I can see no plausible account of language, of the sounds and inscriptions we produce and react to, that does not see many of them as having a truth value. Part of our theory of people runs as follows: they have an interest in controlling and manipulating the world to satisfy various needs. It is clear that language plays a significant role in furthering that interest. It seems best to see its role in a typical case as follows. The speaker has a belief, which he uses language to express to a listener; he thinks the sentence he utters is true.

A Semantic Program   69

The listener treats the utterance as a guide to reality: if he thinks the speaker reliable in this matter, he will treat the sentence as true; this may well amount to a *change* in his beliefs, a change that will be reflected in his nonverbal behavior. In one sort of case it is the nonhuman reality that concerns speaker and listener. Both have an interest in cooperation to achieve their practical ends with rabbits, wheat, wine, or whatever. The point of talking is that it helps: the speaker has information about that reality that the listener lacks; they will both benefit from the listener gaining it. In another sort of case they are concerned with human reality. The point here is once again to convey information, but this time it is information about people, their feelings, desires, and so on, to serve the interests of social intercourse. We as theorists explain what speaker and listener are doing by assigning truth values to their utterances, beliefs about those truth values to them, and also to them, the aim in most cases of speaking the truth. (For more on the importance of truth, see 4.1 and 4.5.)

To explain truth we need notions of reference, which must then also be explained. Do we need any other semantic notions? We detect differences among coreferential words that we might well call differences in *meaning*. These differences can be accounted for, I claim, by differences in the "mechanisms of reference" which we posit to explain reference. Everything that the philosopher of language finds interesting and important about meaning seems well enough captured by truth and reference and what goes into explaining them. The phenomena we seek to explain do not, in my view, require any notion of meaning beyond this.[2]

An important qualification is needed to these remarks. They are written as if all utterances were assertions. Clearly they are not. Many sentences are not in the indicative mood. I set aside the problem of mood for a moment.

Given that semantic notions like designation appear in a theory of language which is part of a general theory of people, we cannot expect full explanations at this time. Full explanations would require psychological and linguistic theories explaining all behavior (2.2).

The problem of truth is to explain the truth conditions of sentences (*complex* expressions) in terms of the referential properties of the words (*simple* expressions) that make them up. This can conveniently be divided into two tasks. It leaves the further task of explaining the referential properties of words. Setting aside the problem of mood, we have then the following three tasks in the program.

(i) The first task is to explain the truth conditions of each kind of indicative natural language sentence in terms of the truth conditions of a certain kind of canonical "underlying" base-sentence, a sentence in the deep structure. A paradigm of this type of explanation is that of the passive in terms of the active. The aim is for base-sentences in a relatively simple language analogous to the predicate calculus. The talk here is of *grammatical categories* and *transformations*. The structure of each sentence token that counts as being in a natural language is revealed in a way that pairs it with a base-sentence which is synonymous with it. The tokens can be regarded as "generated" by transformations from the base-sentence.

We look mostly to the modern generative grammarians to fulfill this part of the program. This is not to say, of course, that they conceive of their task in this way. Typically they see themselves as explaining "linguistic competence." However, there are many signs that these linguists hope for the fulfillment of something like our first task from their researches (e.g., Chomsky 1965:v, 99; Lakoff 1972:545; Seuren 1972:237). And I think that their claims that they are describing or explaining parts of psychological reality are mostly mistaken. I shall return to that question later (4.4–4.5).

(ii) The next task is to show how the truth conditions of each kind of canonical base-sentence depend on the referential properties of its parts. The guide here is Tarski as interpreted and developed by Field (1972; a discussion of "The Concept of Truth in Formalized Languages" in Tarski 1956).

Suppose that we restrict our study for a moment to base-languages of the following simple form. Formulas are made up in the usual way from (definite) singular terms, one-place predicates, variables, a universal quantifier, a negation symbol, a conjunction symbol. Sentences are "closed" formulas. I need a term to cover all the modes of reference of singular terms (2.5–2.7). I shall use here (and in later truth characterizations in 5.8) the generic term 'refers' (1.3), rather than introduce a special term for that purpose. 'Refers$_s$' means "refers relative to the assignment of sequence s"; similarly, 'true$_s$'. 's_k' refers to the kth object in the sequence s. 'e_1', 'e_2', . . . are variables ranging over expression *tokens*. And, for example, 'e_1 is a singular term' says what we would more usually say using 'e_1 is a token of a singular term'. Ignore the complications caused by a designational term's failure to *apply* to its designatum (2.7), and by confusions of the sort to be discussed later (5.4, 5.6; most of these complications are taken account of in 5.8). Then the truth characterization for any language of that sort, "TC," is as follows:

(A) 1. If e_1 is a kth variable, then it refers$_s$ to s_k.
2. If e_1 is a designational term, then it refers$_s$ to a if and only if it designates a.
3. If e_1 is an attributive term, then it refers$_s$ to a if and only if it denotes a.

(B) 1. If e_1 is a singular term and e_2 is a predicate, then $\ulcorner e_2(e_1) \urcorner$ is true$_s$ if and only if (i) there is an object a to which e_1 refers$_s$ and (ii) e_2 applies to a.
2. If e_1 is a formula and e_2 is a negation symbol, then $\ulcorner e_2(e_1) \urcorner$ is true$_s$ if and only if e_1 is not true$_s$.
3. If e_1 and e_2 are formulas and e_3 is a conjunction symbol, then $\ulcorner e_3(e_1, e_2) \urcorner$ is true$_s$ if and only if e_1 is true$_s$ and e_2 is true$_s$.
4. If e_1 is a formula and e_2 is a universal quantifier under

the kth variable, then $\ulcorner e_2(e_1)\urcorner$ is true$_s$ if and only if, for each sequence s^* that differs from s in the kth place at most, e_1 is true $_{s^*}$.

(C) If e_1 is a sentence, then it is true if and only if it is true$_s$ for some (or all) s.

It is important to emphasize some features of this development of Tarski taken from Field. First, TC applies to *any* language having the specified structure; indeed, it applies to any sentence having one of the specified structures: it is in no way language specific. Corollaries of this are that it can apply to languages which have *ambiguous terms* in them, and that it can continue to apply to languages that allow for the introduction of *new terms* (as natural languages do). Furthermore, the language of TC, the language of the theory, does not need to contain *translations* of the nonlogical vocabulary of the languages to which it applies. Second, TC accommodates the demonstrative element in designational terms like 'this' without the complications of reference to the time, place, and so on. The problem of demonstratives is one for the theory of reference discussed in (iii) below. That theory tells us how to discover the designatum of each of the tokens that concern TC.

TC differs from the sort of definitions that Tarski offered in another way: it violates the constraint of "formal correctness" in its use of the semantic notions of *designation, denotation,* and *application*. However, as Field argued, Tarski's method of avoiding such notions has no real value and conceals the need for task (iii) below.

The focus of our concern in tasks (i) and (ii) is not on this or that natural language; it is on *the kinds of structure* to be found in the sentences of natural language. At the level of the canonical base we can expect many languages to have a lot of structure in common. We can even expect something in common in the method of generating the vernacular level, the "surface," from the base. However, our theory of sentences of a certain kind will be quite general even if such sentences appear in only one actual natural language: it will apply to any possible sentence of that kind in any possible language.

If we restrict ourselves to actual natural languages, then tasks (i) and (ii) could, in principle, be completed, for there are presumably only a finite number of different kinds of structure in these languages. However, without that restriction the task seems to be infinite, for there seems to be no end to the number of possible structures in natural language. So far as I can see this does not throw any serious doubt on our ability to explain truth.

Suppose that we were to complete tasks (i) and (ii) for actual languages, what would we have achieved? We would have explained the truth conditions of *any possible sentence token* having the structure of a sentence in one of those languages ultimately in terms of the referential properties of the simple parts of that sentence. We would have explained truth in terms of reference.

Since our concern is with natural language, it is convenient to see two tasks involved in explaining truth in terms of reference, for each such language seems to allow for the explanation of many kinds of "surface-sentence" in terms of the one kind of base-sentence. However, this is not important to the program. It would not matter if each kind of surface-sentence of a language had to be explained *directly* in terms of reference by the Tarski method.

(iii) Finally, we must explain the referential properties of each kind of simple part. This requires a theory of reference for each kind. The causal theory of proper names urged in this work is an example of such a theory. In chapter 7 I discuss the problems of giving theories of reference for other kinds of terms.

The kinds of words we need to distinguish for the purpose of (i) and (ii), *grammatical* kinds, may not be the same as those we need to distinguish for the purposes of (iii), *semantic* kinds. For example, names and demonstratives are treated grammatically as one by TC, but it seems we must distinguish them at the semantic level: they require different, though in my view closely related, theories of reference. That more than one semantic kind goes into a grammatical kind is of no significance. And there seems to be a certain amount of arbitrariness about determining kinds. A more interesting question, perhaps, is posed by the fact that a term like 'lamb', apparently one semantic kind, has a grammatical role as both a mass term and a general term.

My claim is that theories of reference explain not only reference but also word meaning. The meaning of a word is to be found in its *mechanisms* of reference. Thus, the only meaning that a proper name has is its underlying causal network (5.5).

Our tasks have covered *truth, reference,* and *meaning for simple expressions*. What about *meaning for sentences*? We cannot claim that the meaning of a sentence consists solely of the meanings of its parts together with its truth conditions in terms of those parts. Not all sentences seem to be in the right mood to have truth conditions. We must distinguish imperatives and interrogatives from indicatives. I go along with the common view that a theory of meaning comprehensive enough to take account of various moods will nevertheless be essentially truth-theoretical. I shall not venture an opinion on how the various moods are to be accommodated.

The theories we come up with in working on the three tasks will be completely general. I have already indicated that the theories in (i) and (ii) will apply to any sentence tokens having the appropriate structures, whatever language they appear in. Similarly, theories of reference in (iii) will apply to words of the appropriate kinds whatever language they appear in. All these theories, like any theory, will be *in* a language. In so far as that language contains sentences with those structures or words in those categories, then the theories will apply to that language too. This will not lead to paradox, so far as I can see.

I shall return to the question of the application of these semantic theories in 4.6.

3.2 The Language of Thought

What prompts the main problem of explaining *truth* is the human custom of emitting noises and making inscriptions in various circumstances. A big explanatory step is made in seeing these noises and inscriptions as having various semantic properties and hence being tokens of *language*. I go along with Jerry Fodor, Gilbert Harman, and Hartry Field in thinking that a further important explanatory step is the realization that there is a *language of thought*, a system of mental representations in which we think, that underlies the external tokens. I go along with Harman, but certainly not Fodor, in thinking that this language in humans is largely the spoken and/or written ("public") language of the thinker.[3] Drawing on these authors, I shall summarize why these views are plausible.

The intentionality of much of the mental poses a problem for a physicalist. Our beliefs, hopes, desires, and so on, have objects. What are we to make of these objects and of our relationship to them? The difficulty in answering this question might push us into denying that there are *really* any such objects; it might push us into instrumentalism (behaviorism). But instrumentalism is no more satisfactory here than elsewhere. The most plausible view is that these objects are mental representations, "sentences in the language of thought," to which we stand in believing, hoping, and desiring attitudes (Field 1978).

Consider the cognitive process of choosing one of many possible courses of action. A person has certain background beliefs and desires; he works out the likely consequences of this and that possible course of action; he weighs up the results and decides. The only psychological model of a cognitive process like this that seems plausible is one that sees it as computational. And "computation presupposes a medium of computation, a representational system" (Fodor 1975:27).

Why call this representational system "a language"? It is in many important respects *like* a natural language. There is no upper bound to the complexity of these mental representations just as there is no upper bound to the complexity of a sentence; we have the ability to represent entirely novel situations just as we have the ability to utter entirely novel sentences (Fodor 1975:31). Further, the system of mental representations has a logical structure just like a natural language (Harman 1973:54–56).[4] Finally, it has representational and referential properties just like a natural language: items in both can be about this or that object; they can be true or false (Fodor 1975:32; Harman 1973:56–59).

Why suppose that the language of thought for a person is largely the natural language he speaks, his public language? There are two basic alternatives here: either the language of thought is innate, as Fodor thinks, or it is learned. The view that it is innate is popular with linguists. Nevertheless it is wildly implausible, not least because it promises no reasonable account of the semantic links between thought and the world. I find Fodor's argument for this view (Fodor 1975:ch.2) quite unconvincing. My reasons are implicit in this section and elsewhere in this part. These reasons count also against the weaker view that *some* of the language of thought is innate. I shall not go into them but simply take it for granted that the language of thought is learned. It then becomes irresistible to conclude that this language in a human is largely his public language.

First, we have already noted the properties that the language of thought has in common with natural languages in general. Second, we learn our language of thought *at the same time as* we learn our public language. Third, parts of the language of thought we learn seem clearly correlated with parts of the public language: we get certain beliefs, desires, and so on when we get certain words. Fourth, there is a very close link between thought and speech: speech often seems to be, simply *thinking out loud*. Fifth, there is a familiar barrier we have to break through in learning a foreign language: we need to learn to *think in* the language. Before that we use the foreign language by translating back and forth in our minds into the familiar home language. When we have achieved the breakthrough we have learned *a new language of thought.*

In the light of all this it is plausible to claim that what we learn primarily when we learn a public language is a language to think in. In the case of learning our first public language, this involves a vast expansion in our ways of thinking. This is not to say that *all* thinking is in such a language. We ought to allow that the higher animals and human babies think, yet their system of representation is obviously not a public language. And some mature human thought is not in such a language either: consider our thought about music, for example.

Thoughts themselves are not "mysterious objects; they are just beliefs, hopes, suppositions, and so forth more generally described" (Harman 1974:10). Mysterious or not, it may be felt that such objects *could not* involve sentences of a natural language: whatever these thoughts are they are *nothing like* such sentences. But, what *is* a natural language sentence like? There seems to be no limit to the range of physical types that can yield tokens of such a sentence. In 1.4 we mentioned sound types and inscription types; we might also have mentioned flags, Morse code, sign language, braille, and so on. My stand on the language of thought simply requires that thought types have to be included in that list: tokens in the medium of thought, just like speech tokens and braille tokens, can be tokens of a natural language sentence; they can all be tokens of the one semantic type. Tokens of the semantic type 'Socrates' are to be found in our thought as well as in our speech and writing. Similarly, the English language is manifested not only in sounds and inscriptions but also in the medium of thought.

Considerations of the above sort do not, of course, *force* agreement that the language of thought is the public language. However, I suspect that disagreement on that score among people who grant the considerations may be merely verbal.

The view that thoughts are attitudes (believing, desiring, and so on) to sentences needs qualification. Dennett has pointed out that most of the things we believe about, say, New York or salt, we never actually entertain because they are too obvious and boring. Indeed, we have more beliefs than we *could* ever entertain, for we have an infinite number. The solutions is to claim that it is *core*-thoughts that are attitudes to sentences. Only they are represented in the mind. Thought in general is explained dispositionally. Thus a person believes all the *obvious consequences* of his core-beliefs (Dennett 1975:409–10; see also Field 1978:part 1). I shall ignore this qualification in what follows.

The word 'thought' is ambiguous in English between having an object of thought and that object itself. When I talk of thoughts as attitudes to sentences, I am using the word in the former sense. I shall also use it in the latter to refer to the sentences that are the objects of thought.

Two word tokens will be of the same semantic type if they share an appropriate semantic property. This applies to thought tokens as much as to sound tokens. What property? We must wait for the theories of reference that fulfill task (iii) to tell us. If our theory of proper names is right, your written and my thought token of 'Socrates' are of the same semantic type in virtue of having the same designational network underlying them.

Two sentence tokens, in whatever medium, are of the same semantic type if they consist of words of the same type in the same order and have the same grammatical and truth conditional structure. We must wait for theories fulfilling tasks (i) and (ii) to tell us about grammatical and truth conditional structure.

Ambiguity is a property of *physical* types: for example, the one type of inscription 'John' has many meanings (1.4). Can there be ambiguity in thought types? Consider the ambiguity of words first. It must be possible that the one physical thought type could yield tokens of different semantic types because of an ambiguous word: for example, it is possible, though probably unlikely, that mental representations of two different Johns could be the same. What removes the ambiguity (why does the token designate one John and not the other) is that underlying it is a d-chain grounded in one John and not the other (2.4).

Ambiguity is not the same as confusion. Ambiguity is a property of types; confusion a property of tokens. Confusion occurs when more than one meaning is involved in the one token (I shall consider cases with names in 5.4). Confusion can be deliberate, as in many puns. It can go unnoticed, leading to errors in argument—the fallacy of equivocation. (That we can equivocate in thought is further evidence that we think in our natural language.)[5]

There seems to be no good reason for ruling out the possibility of syntactic ambiguity in thought, ambiguity of structure. Presumably it is possible, though again probably unlikely, that the same physical type could yield tokens of different semantic types while containing no ambiguous words. Thus we could get in thought an ambiguity parallel to that in the written 'visiting relatives can be boring'. Since we think our thoughts "under analysis," there must be something in the psychological reality that removes this ambiguity. This will be something about the causal (or functional) roles of the token in our thought as a whole.

I think it appropriate to be skeptical of the claims philosophers of language and linguists make about the psychological reality of language. So I am concerned that the above claims should not be inflated. I am *not* claiming that the *mathematical* generation of a sentence by transformations from a base-sentence, discussed in (i) above, is in any way "mirrored" by the *causal* generation of the thought token in the thinker. And I am *not* claiming that the thinker knows *that* the token has a certain structure or *that* it has certain truth conditions. I am not claiming that he knows *that* a word means one thing and not another. Indeed, I am not claiming that he has any propositional knowledge of a semantic sort at all. Harman's analogy with perception is helpful here (1973:90–91). Just as we can perceive lines on a page as forming a certain three-dimensional structure without knowing any geometry, so also can we think a thought under a certain analysis without knowing any linguistics or semantics. What we have is not propositional knowledge but *a skill or ability*. At this stage in our knowledge we have very little to go on in determining the nature of this skill or ability. (I return to the issue of psychological reality in 4.4–4.5.)

3.3 Speaker Meaning and Conventional Meaning

My next step is to relate the acceptance of the language of thought to a Gricean distinction between speaker meaning and conventional meaning. (The acceptance of a language of thought may well be rather un-Gricean.)

Consider an utterance. In my view, *what the speaker means* by the token he utters is determined by the meaning of the thought that causally underlies his utterance. On the other hand, the *conventional meaning* of the token in a community is determined by what a member of that community using a token of that physical type would commonly mean and be taken to mean. What he would commonly mean and be taken to mean depends in some way on what people have commonly meant by words of that physical type and by sentences of that structure. In precisely what way it so depends is very difficult to say. Any attempt to say must, of course, be guided by such classical discussions of convention as those of David Lewis (1969) and Stephen Schiffer (1972:ch. 5).

Often there is not merely one thing that tokens of a given physical type would commonly be taken to mean: there are ambiguities of word and structure. These ambiguities have arisen because speakers have meant different things by tokens of the same physical type; or, we can say, because they have expressed thoughts with different meanings by tokens of the same physical type.

I explain conventional meaning in terms of speaker meaning and speaker meaning in terms of thought meaning. We are left then with the task of explaining the latter. Conventions play a role in that explanation. We must avoid an apparent circle. I shall make only a preliminary remark now, as more still needs to be said of my Gricean distinction.

The role of convention in explaining my thought tokens of the semantic type 'Socrates' has already been indicated. These tokens designate a certain ancient Greek philosopher because underlying them is a causal network grounded in him. This network was generated by conventions that linked a certain sound type and a certain inscription type to that philosopher. The network consists of (i) causally related tokens of those types, (ii) thought tokens, and (iii) Socrates.

Let us return to the Gricean distinction. According to me, linguistic conventions are regularities in actions—the actions of speakers in meaning something by tokens of a certain type and of hearers taking speakers to mean that by such tokens. It seems that David Lewis would not allow such a view, for he claims that the bestowal of meaning is not an action (1975:22–33). Why isn't it? Lewis himself sees the basic convention as one of truthfulness and trust in the language. It is hard to see why trying to be truthful in uttering x, and being trusting on hearing x, are actions, but meaning something by x is not.

It is a commonplace that speaker meaning may differ from conventional meaning. Consider a person in a foreign country unable to speak the language. He means by various pointings, actings out, perhaps even the odd foreign word or two, to convey quite complicated thoughts. The link between such an action and such a thought is not a conventional one. This is not to say that conventions play no role in any success an attempted communication of this sort may enjoy. The person makes use of conventions to do with acting and pointing (and, of course, to do with any foreign word he uses). However, there is "a large gap" between what he meant and what his actions conventionally mean.

This case is one of speaker meaning in the absence, near enough, of conventional meaning. There are other cases where a spoken token has a conventional meaning in a language, but the speaker means something very different by it. There is John Searle's now familiar case of the American soldier trying to get Italian troops to believe he is a German officer by reciting the only line of German he knows (1965:229–30). And Grice gives the case of the little girl who wrongly believes that a certain French sentence means "Help yourself to a piece of cake" (1969).

There are other more ordinary cases of speaker meaning differing from conventional meaning. Metaphor yields straightforward examples. Perhaps irony does too, but there do seem to be conventional ways of indicating that one means one's words ironically. The earlier claim (2.9) that a name can designate an object in the absence of any ceremony or custom linking it to the object might be put like this: a name can have speaker meaning in the absence of conventional meaning. Various confusions and mistakes in the use of names lead to a divergence between speaker meaning and conventional meaning (5.4).

I have said that what the speaker meant by x, its content, is determined by the meaning of the underlying thought. The Griceans have written extensively about the propositional attitudes that go into speaker meaning, a baroque structure of intentions. For me whatever attitudes are appropriate here are attitudes involving the thought token which determines the meaning of x. And it is those attitudes which cause x.

I shall not tackle the question of what attitudes *are* appropriate. There *need not* be any disagreement between me and the Griceans on that score (though I suspect there would be). My major disagreement with them is over the *content* of speaker meanings. Linguistic conventions have no role here for the Griceans; they have a radically nonconventionalist account of the essential nature of language.[6] I explain speaker meanings in terms of thought meanings. Although thoughts can exist independently of any conventions, the typical thoughts of a mature human are to be *explained by* conventions. I shall not be concerned here to *argue* for my view and against Gricean ones. My aim, rather, is to *set out* my view, a view that combines acceptance of a language of thought of the above sort with acceptance of a Gricean distinction of the above sort, and with causal theories of reference of the sort urged in this book. I discuss my disagreement with the Griceans in 4.9.

The Griceans claim that speaker meaning is "prior" to conventional meaning (e.g., Schiffer 1972). My view that the conventional meaning of an expression is to be explained in terms of common speaker meanings suggests that I agree. However, my view that conventions play a role in explaining speaker meanings undermines that suggestion. For me the main problem in semantics is not in the end to be solved by explaining external tokens in terms of internal ones or vice versa. Explanations of external and internal proceed together. However, I do think that speaker meaning is in some sense prior, for thought is prior to other linguistic activity. Bringing this out will throw more light on thought meaning and will show how I avoid the apparent circle in explanation.

We had thoughts before we were able to say anything and before we learned any linguistic conventions. This is true of us as a species and true of us individually. It is also true of the higher animals. These preconvention thoughts, primeval, babyish, or nonhuman, are very primitive, *so* primitive as to be quite unlike the thoughts of modern language-speaking adults. To say that these early thoughts precede the learning of conventions is not to say that they precede learning. Presumably we have innate predispositions to respond in different ways to different stimuli. These innate predispositions, together with the stimuli we receive, lead us to represent the external world in our thought. It is because the representations are *caused* by parts of the world that they are about (refer to) those parts. To say that these thoughts are primitive is not to say that they have no structure. One supposes that they have structures, albeit very crude ones.

84 *A Semantic Program*

Mental representations of the world come with theorizing about it. We feel a pressing need to understand our environment in order to manipulate and control it. The drive for understanding and control led our early ancestors, in time, to express a primitive thought or two. They grunted and gestured, *meaning something by* such actions: there was speaker meaning in the absence of conventional meaning. In time the grunts and gestures caught on and we had our first linguistic conventions.[7] What happened in that process, very likely, was that people came to have thoughts they had never had before: the desire to communicate and to understand had stimulated the capacity to think. What happened, certainly, was that people came to have new mental representations, based on those grunts and gestures, with which to have those thoughts. Different and more complicated noises were used to express an ever expanding range of thoughts. They caught on and became conventions, thus leading to new representations in the language of thought. This stimulated further expansion. And so on. The greatest expansion comes as we catch on to more complicated thought *structures*.

The picture is of a language of thought expanding with the introduction into it of a public language. The language is public because it has a conventional public form, the regular association of sounds with speaker meanings. The feedback goes both ways. No conventions can be established without the existence of the appropriate speaker meaning. But the drive to create conventions leads to new speaker meanings, a process that is facilitated by the introduction into the language of thought of mental representations which are causally based on, and have the same meaning as, the sounds that go into the conventions. The language of thought becomes more and more a public language, but it always remains a little ahead of it. Even now we have a capacity to think beyond the conventional established public language, as is shown by our ability to express thoughts using new words. We can now think thoughts which a century ago were unthinkable. We suppose that the development in human society of a public language with anything like the variety and complexity of ours was a very slow one. In contrast the development in a child of our culture is relatively quick. This is as we would expect, for the child gets the benefit of our past struggles: the stimuli he receives include sentences conventionally related to thoughts which are complicated in both structure and content; such stimuli make it much easier for the child to have these complicated thoughts than it was for those who first had them.

We might place the primacy of speaker meaning as follows. Speaker meanings create the conventional written and spoken forms of the language. But it is because we have learned those conventions that we are able to have the rich variety of thoughts, and hence produce the rich variety of speaker meanings, that we do. We often wish to convey these thoughts. We use whatever means seem appropriate. These will usually be means that rely largely, if not entirely, on the conventional forms of the language we have learned.

Conventions are explained in terms of speaker meanings. Speaker meanings are explained in terms of thought meanings. Thought meanings are partly explained in terms of conventions. We seemed to have a circle. What we really have is more like a spiral, a spiral that starts from crude thought meanings.[8]

The language of thought is not conventional though it is to be largely explained by conventions. Consider the convention for a word sound. We might express it like this: there is a convention in a certain population that sounds of that physical sort mean such and such. There can be no corresponding convention in the population that mental representations of a certain physical sort mean such and such. What sort? If there is anything physically in common between your mental representation 'Socrates' and mine, it cannot be the basis of any convention. This is not to say that words in the language of thought are independent of conventions. They are mostly brought about by sound and inscription conventions, and the explanation of their meanings involves reference to those conventions. Thus, my mental representation 'Socrates' means what it does because it was causally brought about by sounds and inscriptions conventionally related to that meaning. (I discuss this further in 5.1–5.3.)

Our semantic task is prompted by the production of sounds and inscriptions. To explain these I see them as the meaningful expression of a person's meaningful thoughts. To explain the meanings of these thoughts and expressions, I have to draw heavily on conventional meanings and hence to explain those. There is no denying, then, the importance of conventional meaning. However, the interest in it is derivative: we are interested in it because of its bearing on the meaning of thoughts which explains the production of sounds and inscriptions. As a consequence the interest in public languages (English, Japanese, and so on) is also derivative.

Despite these claims about the primacy of thought meaning and speaker meaning over conventional meaning, I see no objection, save possibly an uninteresting verbal one, to assigning semantic properties such as truth values to tokens in virtue of either. (Nor, indeed, do I see any objection to assigning such properties to *types*.) However, in light of these primacy claims, the semantic properties of a token that most concern me are the ones it has in virtue of what the speaker meant by it, and these are the ones I am usually referring to by such terms as 'true' and 'designates Socrates'.

This completes the description of the program into which I see my causal theory of designation fitting. In the next chapter, my defense of the program will add further details. Any reader who has found the present chapter uncontroversial has probably missed or been unimpressed by various views, particularly those of Donald Davidson, that are influential at present in semantics.

Chapter Four
DEFENSE OF THE PROGRAM

I start my defense of the program described in chapter 3 by rejecting various common views that suggest the program is faulty. First, I reject various conceptions of the task in semantics: that the task is to analyze (ordinary) semantic concepts (4.1); that it is concerned with particular languages (4.2); that it is to explain linguistic competence (4.3). I go on to reject the Davidsonian view that competence consists, in some sense, in semantic propositional knowledge, whether of semantic theory or of T-sentences (4.4): this leads to an account of what competence does consist in (4.5). A semantic theory must be testable. I set out the way evidence would bear on theories fulfilling the proposed program (4.6). I urge that neither *Convention T* (4.7) nor the *Principles of Charity and Rationality* (4.8) have a significant role. I conclude by defending both the need for, and the possibility of, theories of reference (4.9).

4.1 Semantics and Conceptual Analysis

A certain view of the nature of the semantic problem has been advanced in chapter 3 (also in 1.3 and 2.2). It is to explain the semantic properties of various sounds and inscriptions produced by humans, the properties that enable those items to play their roles in our lives. Other aspects of the view have been left fairly implicit. I shall fill out this view by rejecting some other views of the problem to be found in the literature.

First, there is the view that the semantic problem is the "analysis" of ordinary semantic terms expressing ordinary concepts. This view, I assume, is part of the theory of philosophy, once so popular at Oxford, according to which the philosopher's task simply *is* the analysis of ordinary language or "conceptual analysis." We have already seen signs in discussing Donnellan's distinction (2.7) of the view that our concern with singular terms is a concern with the ordinary term 'refers'. We shall come across it again later (6.1, 10.4). Similarly, some Griceans have seen the question 'What is meaning?' that concerns us as being a question about the sense, or one of the senses, of the English word 'mean' (and its cognates) (e.g., Grice 1957; Schiffer 1972:1–5).

This view seems to me completely mistaken. Philosophy is an area of knowledge, like others, concerned with theorizing about the world. Our concern here is to produce a *theory* about linguistic phenomena. The correct theory in semantics is no more likely to be discovered by examining ordinary semantic terms than is the correct theory in physics to be discovered by examining ordinary physical terms.

. This is not to say that our use of ordinary semantic terms is *irrelevant* to our task. Ordinary usage reflects ordinary theory. "What we would say" in this or that circumstance using ordinary semantic terms is a consequence of "folk" theory. In the absence of any other theory, that must be what we start from. It embodies such intuitions as we have had about linguistic phenomena, the wisdom of the ages in semantics. And realists have an interest in being conservative about past theories, as Putnam has pointed out (Putnam 1976:184).[1] However, it is an open question whether folk theory is right so far as it goes, and it is quite certain that it doesn't go very far. The task is not to study folk theory but to develop it into a scientific theory. (I return to this theme in 4.4.)

A sign of the inadequacy of folk theory is the paucity and vagueness of its vocabulary (think of 'refers', for example). So in starting on scientific semantics we have available to us an unsatisfactory vocabulary to mark the many distinctions that we soon find appropriate. It is tempting to coin new semantic words and even to abandon the ordinary words entirely because of their misleading connotations. I shall try to resist the temptation.

To say that someone has misconceived the problem is not to say that his proffered solution is necessarily irrelevant. However, misconceiving a problem is clearly a hindrance to solving it.

These remarks have methodological consequences. It is usual to test a semantic theory by considering "what we would say" in this or that circumstance. For example, would we say that a certain name "referred to," "designated," etc., Tom, Dick, or Harry? But we cannot uncritically rely on our answers to such questions, for they will be laden with undeveloped folk semantics. However, in the absence of a semantic theory which is both radically inconsistent with folk theory and a better explanation of linguistic phenomena than folk theory, we have nothing else to test out theories against but our ordinary intuitions embodied in folk theory. Clearly we must be guided by "what we would say" without accepting it uncritically. Further, I suggest, we can rely most confidently on our intuitions about the circumstances in which a statement would be *true*. For truth plays an important extrasemantic role in our lives (3.1). We have a great practical interest in establishing which of our neighbor's words are true and which of the theories offered us are true. Why? Briefly, because true theories correspond to reality, a reality we are all interested in understanding. This is not an idle interest. We are bent on the good life in a hostile world, and the more we understand of that world the better our chances of achieving it. By locating the true statements we place ourselves in the best position to explain the past, manipulate the present, and predict the future. So the test for a semantic theory of (definite) singular terms is this: which object *would* we say, or *should* we say, taking account of the role of truth, makes a statement containing such a term true or false (cf. 4.5.)? We should not assume that there will always be a determinate answer to this question (2.7, 5.4, 5.6, 5.8). We can look at Kripke's refutation of description theories (1.5) in this light. Folk theory gives us a view of what 'Catiline' refers to despite our ignorance of Catiline, of what 'Einstein' refers to despite our errors, and of what 'Jonah' refers to if certain historical speculations are correct. Kripke discovered that description theories, the received theory of the experts at that time, would not accommodate these apparently "irresistible" views of folk theory, but that another type of theory, a causal theory, would.[2]

4.2 Semantics and Particular Languages

The second view I should like to reject conceives of the semantic problem in terms of particular languages. One version of this view is obviously misguided. It sees the problem as the construction of *a theory of meaning for a given language*, and that requires *giving the meaning* of the sentences in the language. Thus Davidson claims:

there is agreement that it is the central task of semantics to give the semantic interpretation (the meaning) of every sentence in the language. (1967:308; see also 1970a:177)

Yet clearly we are not primarily concerned in philosophy with explaining meaning in any *particular* language nor of giving the meaning of any *particular* sentence. (Certainly if that is the task, philosophers, including Davidson, have done very little to fulfill it.) Our main interest is in language and meaning *in general*. We must take statements like Davidson's as loose statements of another version of the view.

This other version sees the problem as the construction of *a theory of* theories of meaning for particular languages. The view is well expressed by Brian Loar:

The leading question in the general theory of meaning is what the form of a theory of meaning for a particular language should be. (1976a:138)

The confusion of such a theory with a theory of the earlier sort is aided by the fact that terms like 'theory of meaning' and 'semantic theory' are used to refer sometimes to the one and sometimes to the other.

There is a remarkable amount of agreement among Davidsonians, Griceans, and others on some such conception of the problem (e.g., Foster 1976:4; Wright 1976:217–218). Yet, so far as I know, nobody offers any *argument* for the appropriateness of this conception.[3] Indeed, the question is hardly ever raised by those who favor this approach. Dummett does raise it but he frankly admits that he is unable to demonstrate that the conception *is* appropriate (1975:97). *Why suppose that the form of, or the constraints on, theories of meaning for languages will explain meaning in general?*

Perhaps the supposition would be reasonable if the theory of meaning for a given language *explained the meaningfulness* of all the expressions in the language. What is usually required of such a theory, however, is something very different: it is that the theory *give the meanings of, interpret*, all the expressions in the language. There is a perfectly ordinary sense in which we have given someone the meaning of an expression when we have told him a synonym for it that he already understands. And this ordinary sense seems to be just the one Davidson and others have in mind. Why suppose that a study of such theories will explain meaning? Indeed, what is the interest of such theories? A theory of meaning for a language in this sense will be of interest to someone who wants to *translate* the language into a language he already understands. Now, since all languages are understood by someone, a general theory of such theories will simply be a theory of theories translating one language into another.

I emphasize that my aim here is to criticize a certain conception of the semantic problem. Nothing follows simply from this criticism about the theories proposed by those who have that conception. However, I agree with Harman (1974) that a Davidsonian truth theory for a language tells us no more about meaning than is revealed by a method of translating that language into ours. For Davidson, a truth theory is distinguished from a translation theory by its *use* rather than *mention* of the translations in the home language. This seems significant to him because of his interest in competence (see 4.3). In my view the move from mention to use makes little difference in explanatory power.

I have a special reason for objecting to this conception of the problem. It is a conception that may seem to leave no place for theories of reference in explaining meaning. It is undeniable that we have *given the meaning* (in the ordinary sense) of a word when we have given an already understood synonym. It is also undeniable that we have not *explained its meaningfulness*; we have not said what its meaning consists in. That is what theories of reference fulfilling task (iii), like ours of designation, are intended to do. Our conception of the semantic problem should leave open, at least, the question whether such theories are appropriate and possible (4.9).

4.3 Semantics and Linguistic Competence

The third and final view of the semantic problem I should like to reject is also popular. It focuses on the *linguistic competence* of a native speaker of a language; "a theory of meaning is a theory of understanding" (Dummett 1975:99). The view usually accompanies the second view just discussed: the theories of meaning for particular languages whose form and so forth should interest us are seen as theories, in some sense, of the linguistic abilities of those who use and understand the languages.

This focus on competence seems to me misguided. In particular, it is a mistake to see the facts of competence as the only phenomena to be explained in semantics. What need explaining, basically, are the verbal parts of human behavior (3.1). In explaining these, we must attribute certain properties (for example, *being true* and *referring to Socrates*) to the sounds and inscriptions produced, and certain other properties (for example, *understanding 'Socrates'*) to the people who produce those sounds and inscriptions. I take semantics (or the theory of meaning) to be primarily the study of properties of the first sort, but I have no objection to it being taken to be also a study of properties of the second sort. I think it is very peculiar to take it as a study of properties of the second sort *only*. But this is little more than a verbal point (about what we mean by "semantics") and thus unimportant. *What is important is that, however we conceive of "semantics", we do not lose sight of the fact that there are these two sorts of property, prima facie quite different, to be explained.* An explanation of competence is not an explanation of truth and reference. The trouble with the focus on competence is that it misses a large part, in my view the main part, of what needs to be explained—the semantic properties of sounds and inscriptions.

Though my focus is on the latter properties, I certainly expect a semantic theory to throw light on competence. For, although the two sorts of properties are distinct, they are clearly related. I have already ventured some remarks on competence and will say more, particularly about the ability to understand names (for general remarks see especially 4.5, for remarks on names see especially 5.1).

So I think we can hope for something toward *explaining* competence. However, the problem is often seen as one of *describing* competence (Davidson 1965:387; 1967:310–11; Foster 1976:1). This difference would perhaps be innocent enough if competence were viewed strictly as *a skill*, knowledge-*how*, but it is not so innocent when it is taken, as it usually is, as knowledge-*that*. The main objection to this conception is to be found in the next section (4.4): competence does not consist in such propositional knowledge. Now I want to bring out two objectionable consequences of the conception. First, it is another conception that discourages interest in theories of reference. Consider my competence with

'Socrates'. If we regard my competence as a piece of semantic propositional knowledge which we must then seek to describe, we might well feel that we had done our work adequately by saying that the competence is knowledge that 'Socrates' designates Socrates. Yet clearly we have done nothing to *explain* that competence. (How, for example, does *Socrates* come to be the object of my knowledge?) Second, it leads to the constraint that the theory of meaning for a language should use no concepts beyond those in the language (e.g., Davidson 1977a:248). Stich finds this constraint uncontroversial (1976:203) yet it is surely extraordinary. Where else in science is any analogous constraint placed *by x* on a theory of *x*?

In his most recent writings, Davidson has been more explicit about psychological reality. The claim is not that a theory of meaning of the sort he is studying is what an actual interpreter of a language knows. Rather, knowledge of it *suffices* for understanding; if he did know it he would understand the language (1973b:313; 1974:309).[4] The main objection to this conception of the problem is also to be found in the next section: knowledge of a theory does not suffice for understanding in the relevant sense. Meanwhile, we should first note that this leaves the connection between a theory of meaning for L and the competence of a user of L absolutely mysterious. What light does a theory, knowledge of which suffices for understanding, throw on *actual* understanding? Perhaps the latter is completely different from the former. If the theory isn't psychologically real, what bearing does it have on the psychologically real? Yet it is clear that in some way the theory *is* supposed to be descriptive of that reality. *Why else impose the constraint that it not contain any concepts not in the object language?* Second, *why*, if our interest is in explaining meaning, should we be interested in the form of theories knowledge of which suffices for understanding languages?

A Davidsonian might reply (I have heard one do so) that the reason for seeing the problem in this way is that it focuses attention on the phenomena to be explained and away from abstract notions like *meaning* commonly used to explain them. This helps us to see what notions we really need for explanation. Anything that has such an effect is indeed desirable, but Davidson's conception does not seem to do so. The phenomena to be explained are certain sounds and inscriptions humans produce. The first step in explanation is to see them as meaningful. Related to this, we see them as understood by humans. Davidson's conception focuses neither on those phenomena nor even on that understanding, but on what *suffices* for understanding. Further, we don't need to reconstrue our problem in order to focus attention on the phenomena and avoid bad metaphysics: we can simply describe the phenomena to be explained and articulate as best we can any maxims of explanation we have found to apply generally, for they will apply here as elsewhere (for example, "Don't multiply entities beyond necessity").[5] Finally, the interest in competence seems to *lead to* bad metaphysics, for it seems to encourage the mistaken attribution of a large amount of semantic propositional knowledge to users of language. That brings us to the next section.

4.4 Linguistic Competence and Knowledge-That

Theories of language are littered with claims about psychological reality. Linguists claim that ordinary users of language know (tacitly) that a certain grammar fits the language. Philosophers claim that we know such things as theories of truth, T-sentences, and conventions. The claims of linguists have been well-criticized (without, interestingly enough, much effect on the linguists).[6] My main aim in this section is to criticize the claims of philosophers; in particular, to reject the claim that the competence of ordinary users of a language, their mastery, *consists in* any semantic propositional knowledge, that is, in knowledge that ____, where the gap is to be filled in by a sentence expressing something semantical about the language.

96 Defense of the Program

It has always been difficult to know precisely what propositional knowledge Davidson attributes to the normal person competent in a language. We might (uncharitably?) interpret some of his earlier remarks on the subject as suggesting that competence consists in knowing a truth theory à la Tarski, a "T-theory," for the language (e.g., Davidson 1967:310).[7] In his later works, with the insistence that a theory of meaning only *suffice* for understanding, the bearing of the theory on actual competence remains obscure, as we have said (4.3).

What is it that would, according to Davidson, suffice? It seems that it would suffice to know that *some T-theory states that* ___, where the blank is to be filled in by the clauses of a T-theory (a T-theory must meet the formal and empirical constraints Davidson outlines) (1973b:326–27; 1976:36; Foster 1976:20). I take it that if this is to have anything to do with *actual* competence, the view must be that *something like* that knowledge is possessed by the native speaker and constitutes his competence. At the very least, his competence is thought to include knowledge of all the T-sentences which are the theorems of the T-theory. So, if he speaks English, his competence consists in part of the familiar knowledge that 'snow is white' is true if and only if snow is white.[8]

Gilbert Harman has raised a very good objection to such a view of competence. To know the above T-sentence, the speaker must have some way to represent to himself that snow is white. If this is done in English, as Harman and I think it is for an English-speaker, then the theory seems clearly circular. If it is done in Mentalese, as Jerrold Katz would think, we still have to explain competence in Mentalese (Harman 1975:286).

My own position can be summarized as follows: Competence in, or mastery of, a language is a set of skills. Any semantic propositional knowledge we have is a semantic *theory* and is quite distinct from such competence. However, propositional knowledge of speaker meanings seems to have a role in *learning* our first language.

Defense of the Program 97

It is possible to isolate certain parts of a language from the main body. We could, for example, isolate the biological part, the economic part, or the semantic part. The isolation is achieved by identifying all the predicates and so forth that refer to entities in the appropriate area. The semantic part of English would include such words as 'true', 'refer', and 'mean' (in their semantic senses). I propose the following argument:

(1) It is possible to be competent in a public language L minus any isolable part.
(2) The semantic part of L is isolable.

So,

(3) It is possible to be competent in L minus its semantic part ("nonsemantic L").
(4) It is possible to be competent in nonsemantic L without being competent in the semantic part of any other public language.

So,

(5) Competence in nonsemantic L cannot consist in any knowledge that requires competence in the semantic part of any public language.
(6) Semantic propositional knowledge does require competence in the semantic part of a public language.

So,

(7) Competence in nonsemantic L does not consist in any semantic propositional knowledge.

So,

(8) Competence in L (as a whole) is not to be explained as semantic propositional knowledge.

How can this argument be resisted? An extreme holist might reject (1), but such extremism is not appealing. Perhaps we can reject (3) by rejecting (2). But then we need to be shown in what

98 *Defense of the Program*

respect the semantic part is different from the biological or economic part. The most likely place of resistance is (6). It will be claimed by some that one can have propositional knowledge of x without the means of representing x to oneself. This is to deny the necessity for a language of thought. I have already argued for that necessity (3.2). How, without a language of thought, can one's knowledge of x be explained? Alternatively, it may be claimed that we can have a means of representing semantic notions to ourselves in a *private* language of thought. In my view we do have such a private language; indeed, it is all we have before learning a public language and all that animals ever have (3.2), so I cannot dismiss this claim out of hand. In fact, I shall later allow that there may be some truth in it (4.5). However, given any such claim it is appropriate to ask some questions. What notions, precisely, are said to be represented? Where did the representations come from? What reason is there for supposing such representations exist?

We have seen that for Davidson and others the semantic propositional knowledge that is said to constitute our competence includes knowledge of T-sentences. We can be beguiled by the popular example of a T-sentence,

'Snow is white' is true if and only if snow is white,

into thinking that this knowledge is easier to come by than it is. What does the quoted sentence at the beginning of this T-sentence refer to? The quick answer is: a certain English sentence. An English sentence in what sense? A token, a semantic type, or a physical type (1.4)? It is clear that the intended referent is a physical type, usually a sound type. Now, sound types are not true *simpliciter* but true relative to a language. So our T-sentence should really be written:

'Snow is white' is true-in-English if and only if snow is white.

Defense of the Program 99

We still have a far from typical T-sentence. The demonstrative elements drive us to examples like this (Davidson 1973b:322):

'Es regnet' is true-in-German when spoken by x at time t if and only if it is raining near x at t.

Even this sort of T-sentence is too simple to deal with the problems of ambiguity, which are more widespread than might appear: for example, the sound 'Snow is white' can be true-in-English in appropriate circumstances if a person named 'Snow' is identical to a person named 'White', or if a person named 'Snow' is white-skinned.

So we see that a central semantic notion that appears in the Davidson account of competence in L is truth-in-L, a notion that finds its correct application in T-sentences of a complexity we have just hinted at. The rejection of (6) that will save this account must claim that we can have a means of representing truth-in-L in our language of thought without having learned any words in L (or another public language) which express that notion. How can we manage this? It is wildly implausible to suppose such a representation could be innate (*pace* Fodor). It is only a little less implausible to suppose we could gain the representation from experience that did not include the experience of learning L. So the claim must be that we could acquire a representation of truth-in-L while learning L without learning any words in L for truth-in-L, that is, while learning nonsemantic L. That also is implausible. Truth-in-L applies to complicated types of sounds in complicated types of situations. It seems to me unlikely that any such sophisticated concept could be grasped without learning a public language expressing theories that involve the concept. The attempt to resist the argument fails.

I suggest that each of the isolable parts of the language is learned in the process of *theorizing* about the entities in the area relevant to that part. Thus we gain the biological vocabulary in the process of theorizing about living things, and we gain the semantic vocabulary in the process of theorizing about language. My guess is that such sophisticated parts of the semantic vocabulary as 'true-in-L' come much later than the familiar vocabulary in areas of such burning interest as biology or economics. The little we have to say about semantics, the paucity and vagueness of our ordinary semantic vocabulary, suggests that folk semantic theory is, relatively, a very poor one (4.1). Most of us do seem to achieve such profundities as the belief (only roughly correct, as we have just seen) that 'snow is white' is true-in-English if and only if snow is white.[9] However, I doubt very much that everyone does. (Does every English-speaker have the concept *of* English?) Even if everyone does, the main point against Davidson and others is that these theoretical beliefs are not to be confused with our linguistic competence. Furthermore, I can see absolutely no reason for believing that we all achieve *anything like* such recondite pieces of knowledge, if knowledge it is, as the knowledge that some T-theory states that ____ and so forth. To claim at this point that though we cannot think or express such knowledge we nevertheless have it "tacitly" or "implicitly" is to obfuscate rather than clarify the issue.

Folk semantic theory does not go very far and, like any other theory, it may be wrong so far as it goes: our semantic *beliefs* may not be *knowledge*. Good semantic theories, if there are any, are in the heads of those experts who believe them. Everyone else neither has them nor anything like them. And to repeat, even if they did, such having would still not be competence.

Competence in a language, like competence on a bicycle, is a skill. We need to be given reasons for treating it differently from any other skill. Perhaps just as one can ride a bicycle without theorizing about such riding, one can speak a language without theorizing about such speaking. Do we need semantics for speaking any more that we need physics for riding?

To deny that competence in a language consists in semantic

propositional knowledge is not to deny that it is in some way propositional. Indeed, I think it is to be explained largely as the having of thoughts with the appropriate semantics. However, the thoughts are not semantic ones (except those for the semantic part of the language) and they may not be true.

Some of this may seem too obvious for it to be plausible that Davidson and others deny it. Indeed, there are plenty of signs of caution about psychological reality in some of the passages cited. The difficulty then is this: *if the views rejected here are not held by those who link theories of meaning to competence, what possible bearing can these theories have on competence?*

We can have great confidence in our attribution to Davidson and others of the view that knowledge of a theory of meaning *suffices for competence*. That view also seems false. The competence that concerns us is a set of skills in speaking, reading, and so on, but most importantly, thinking in, a language. It does not *follow* from the fact that one has a complicated piece of *theoretical knowledge about* a language that one has such *skills in* the language. It may be that the theory would enormously assist in acquiring the skills and that people who have the theory would tend to have the skills. In that respect the analogy with bicycle riding breaks down. Nevertheless, just as one could have a theory about riding without being able to ride, one could have a theory of a language without being able to use the language. We could imagine building a robot that knew the theory of meaning for L, yet represented that knowledge in L', and was completely incompetent in L. Of course, the robot would understand L *in some sense*, but not in the sense in which all native users of L understand it.

4.5 Linguistic Competence

I have rejected the view that the linguistic competence of native speakers should be the main object of semantic inquiry (4.3) and the view that linguistic competence consists in semantic propositional knowledge (4.4). In this section I take a more positive line, attempting to say what, from the perspective of my program, linguistic competence is, and whether any semantic knowledge goes into acquiring it. However, criticism continues.

Competence in L is not one competence but several:
1. Competence in thinking in L.
2. Competence in understanding spoken L.
3. Competence in speaking L.
4. Competence in reading L.
5. Competence in writing L.
. . . . .
. . . . .
. . . . .

The list is open-ended because there seems to be no end to the forms of L. To mention a few others: sign language, braille, Morse code.

What is the relationship among these different competences? My main claim is that 1 is primary. A person could not have any of the other competences in L without having the competence to think in L or in some other language, L', into which L can be translated. If we ignored the latter possibility, we could say that 2, for example, *consisted in* the ability to associate sounds with thoughts in L that are conventionally related to them. However, we cannot ignore that possibility. Suppose a person could already think in L' and was learning to understand and speak L. In the early stages he would be likely to do this by translating back and forth into L'. It is presumably *possible* that he could achieve complete competence in this way, though as a matter of fact nobody does. So *competence 2 consists in the ability to associate sounds with thoughts in L that are conventionally related to them or with thoughts in another language which are translations of those thoughts in L.* Similarly, *3 consists in the ability to put thoughts in L into sounds conventionally related to them, or to put thoughts in another language which are translations of those thoughts in L into those sounds.*

Return to our robot. *Provided he could speak and hear properly*, knowledge of some theory about L might suffice for competences 2 and 3. His competence would be very different from that of the ordinary users of L, for they don't go through a translation procedure. They don't go through it because they, unlike the robot, *think* in L. What the robot illustrates is that knowledge of some theory of L can't suffice for competence in thinking in L. In fact, the Davidsonian approach leaves our competence in thinking in L or in some other language completely unexplained (cf. Harman's objection in 4.4).

We have seen that all competences beginning with 2 are dependent (logically) on a competence 1. However, *those* competences are independent of each other. Not only could a person have one without any other, it is fairly common for people to do so. Finally, I suspect that, for humans, having competence 1 may be *causally* dependent on having one of the others. As a matter of fact, a human does learn to think in L in the process of learning to receive communications in L and to communicate in L (usually by means of speech). The reception of communications seems particularly important. Perhaps humans *could* learn to think in L only in this way. Even if this is so, this dependence is quite unlike the earlier one: thinking in L *does not consist in* anything that involves another competence on the list; one could still think in L even if one lost any other competence that helped to bring it about.

(According to me it is necessary that *all* thoughts about the external world have external causes: without external causes they would have no external reference. What I am supposing here is that the external causes for normal human thought must involve the gaining of another linguistic competence.)

In the light of our earlier discussion (3.2), competence 1—thinking in L—consists in the following closely related aspects. First, having mental representations of the semantic word types of L. Second, having the ability to put these representations together to form complex mental representations having the structures (grammatical and truth conditional) of complex semantic types in L. That we have this ability to combine simple representations to form any of an infinite number of complete thoughts is the only truth, so far as I can see, underlying Davidson's claims about competence.

Does this truth make Davidson's claims defensible? Consider first an analogous defense that might be made of the linguists' claims about the psychological reality of grammars. Their suggestions that grammatical skills consist in syntactic propositional knowledge must be regarded as an aberration. I reconstrue their remarks as the claim that grammatical skills consist in our minds containing a model of the grammar, a mechanism, which plays the central role in generating the sentences we utter. Provided this is amended so as not to imply that *the particular grammar linguists have come up with* (or hope to) is in the head rather than simply *some such grammar*, this seems to have some plausibility. Analogously, we might reconstrue Davidson's remarks about competence as simply the claim that our minds operate with some T-theory, even though we don't have any propositional knowledge of that T-theory and its outputs. (This is a considerable reconstrual, because it removes the rationale for the constraint on the concepts the T-theory may employ; 4.3.) However, there is a crucial dissimilarity between the two cases. Whereas the outputs of a grammar are the (idealized forms of) sentences we actually think, speak, and so forth, in demonstrating our ordinary syntactic mastery, the outputs of a T-theory are T-sentences. Our thinking, speaking, and so forth T-sentences does *not* demonstrate our ordinary semantic mastery. I can see no reason to suppose that we all have in our minds anything like a theory that generates such sentences. Indeed, if we were right in supposing that the generative mechanism is like a grammar, we have a good reason for thinking that we *don't* have a T-theory in our minds. That generative mechanism must take simple mental representations as inputs. So the picture of psychological reality in this supposition is of sentences built up out of simple representations by a grammar. This is nothing like a model of a T-theory. Davidson's claims about competence seem completely misguided.

A revisionist Davidsonian who accepts what I have argued here—that our linguistic competence does not consist in semantic propositional knowledge—is caught in what seems to be an inconsistent triad. He has to combine his acceptance with the view that a theory of meaning consists (largely, at least) in a T-theory, and with the view that a theory of meaning is a theory of competence. These three views seem incompatible.

Dummett sees very clearly that knowledge of a language is "a practical ability" but claims there is "no objection to its representation as propositional knowledge." This "theoretical representation" of our knowledge is "a theory of meaning for the language." Speakers of the language have "implicit knowledge" of the propositions in that representation (1976:69–70). These claims have a lot in common with the (orthodox) Davidsonian position, so far as it can be discerned. (Dummett's disagreement with Davidson is over the claim that the theory of meaning we seek here is a T-theory: his grounds are, roughly, that we do not have the propositional knowledge that this would require. Dummett is skeptical of truth-theoretic semantics.)

Now surely there often *is* objection to representing an ability as propositional knowledge. To think otherwise is to ignore the explanatorily important distinction between knowing-how and knowing-that. Consider the abilities of plants and lower animals, or our abilities to swim and ride bicycles. It is absurd to explain any of the behavior manifested in these abilities by attributing propositional knowledge to the organisms. Sometimes, of course, it is plausible to attribute propositional knowledge. It is plausible, for example, to explain a chess player's behavior *partly* by attributing to him knowledge of the rules of chess. Also *the particular quality* of his play may be explained partly by attributing to him propositional knowledge of certain strategies, but this is unlikely to exhaust the explanation. These attributions are plausible partly because it is plausible to suppose he has the requisite mental representations (for example, of the pieces and the possible moves). Each case must be judged on its merits. I claim that the correct judgment about linguistic ability is that it is not to be explained by attributing semantic propositional knowledge. So far as I can see, Dummett supplies no argument for the contrary view.

Let us return to our account of competence 2. To gain it one must come to know *the conventions* used for speaking L. Both Lewis and Schiffer seem to require that this knowledge be propositional (Lewis 1969:62–64; 1975; 6, 9, 25–26; Schiffer 1972:131), though Lewis's qualification that such knowledge "may be irremediably nonverbal knowledge" (1969:63) casts some doubt on this attribution. I reject this view for the reasons stated above: the knowledge of linguistic conventions we all have is a skill or an ability. One knows such conventions only in the sense that one *participates in* them. Clearly this raises a problem for our program. Is the requirement that the knowledge be propositional essential to the theories of convention offered by Lewis and Schiffer? If so, then we need a new theory of convention. However, I suspect that the requirement is not essential and that we could take over many features of the theories of Lewis and Schiffer.

Some of these points about competence can be illustrated by considering proper names, the main concern of this book. It may seem plausible that my competence with the sound 'Socrates' consists in my knowledge that 'Socrates' designates-in-English Socrates. Harman's objection shows that this can't be a sufficient explanation, for it presupposes an unexplained ability to represent Socrates to oneself. I claim that it can't be right because we could be competent with 'Socrates' without having the required semantic notion of designation at all. What we all know is *how* to designate Socrates with 'Socrates', *an ability or skill*. We come to know *that* 'Socrates' designates-in-English Socrates only as we advance into *semantic theory*. Perhaps nearly everyone who uses the name gains the knowledge in time. Description theories may attribute more profound semantic knowledge to us all: for example, where 'the *F*' is some identifying description of Socrates, we know that 'Socrates' designates the *F*. Kripke showed that we mostly don't have this knowledge. However, even if we did, our competence with the name could not consist in it. Our competences in making and understanding utterances about Socrates containing the name 'Socrates' *consist* partly in our competence to think thoughts about him containing the name. But we *gained* the latter competence in the course of gaining the former one (3.2, 3.3). Learning to make and understand utterances containing the name is learning conventions, yet it is learning skills for all that.

It may be objected that "we would not say" that someone was competent with a name, had "fully grasped its use," unless he could tell us quite a lot about its designatum. To a certain extent I think this claim is correct, but to that extent it is not inconsistent with the view I have urged. I shall claim that with the use of a name come beliefs about its designatum (5.1). This is something most of us have noticed (it has been absorbed into folk theory). It is to such beliefs, therefore, that we look for *evidence* of competence with a name. The failure to express common beliefs about the designatum using the name would count as good evidence for lack of competence. So, as the objector points out, "we would not say" of a person who exemplified this failure that he had the required competence. Yet the competence could exist without the common beliefs (though not, I think, without *any* beliefs). I *dis*agree with the claim to the extent that it suggests that what we would say, or should say, depends in any way on whether or not we think the beliefs expressed by the person are *true* (rather than merely common). (Cf. 4.1, 7.3.)

Competence in thinking in L is a skill and does not consist in any semantic propositional knowledge. However, if our earlier

108 Defense of the Program

suspicion is correct that we could only gain this competence while gaining one of the others, particularly one at receiving communications, then it *may* be the case that certain semantic propositional knowledge is necessary for us humans to learn to think in L. For, consider that process of learning; it would involve (3.3) many beliefs of the following form:

the belief that (person) x meant (thought) y by (token) z.

It seems plausible to say that such beliefs form a central part of the process of learning the conventions one must know to have, for example, competence 2. This is plausible because it seems that we would have to catch on to *the point* of language to learn one. This ties in with my earlier remarks about the semantic notions that should appear in our theory of people (3.1). I gave a central place to truth. The point of talking was often to convey information—things believed true—to an audience for mutual benefit. A listener was guided in his approach to reality by what a speaker said. He used his assessment of the reliability of the speaker, of how likely what he said was to be true, to form a view of the way the world was. Perhaps, then, we could not learn a language without having a notion of truth. Perhaps we also need to have opinions on what the speaker meant to refer to.

We must consider what I am allowing here in light of the earlier discussion (4.4). If we have such beliefs, we must have the appropriate means to represent them in the language of thought, including representations of the semantic notions mentioned. We must then reject the earlier (6) as it stands: to learn to understand public language, we need to be able to represent to ourselves a speaker *meaning something by* a sound token, perhaps also his *aiming for the truth*, and so forth. I have already considered the view that we could acquire a representation of truth-in-L while learning L without learning any words for truth-in-L. I found that view implausible. It seems to me much more plausible that in that process of learning we could come to acquire representations of a speaker meaning something by a token (something very crude to start with), representations that may involve notions of truth and reference for tokens. The difference is that whereas truth-in-L is a notion that applies to sound *types* in virtue of their conventional roles in a public language, these latter notions apply to sound *tokens* in virtue of their being expressions of a person's thought. The view is that language learning could not progress unless we could represent in our thought people and their actions in this sort of way; we have to advance quite a way in our theorizing about people. And that is perhaps the main reason animals can't learn languages: they are not smart enough to think such thoughts.

If this is right, we seem to have found a further dissimilarity between linguistic competence and bicycle riding. Some sort of semantic theorizing is required to gain linguistic competence, including some elementary theorizing about the point of language. It seems that no analogous theorizing is necessary to learn to ride.

These remarks about the role of semantic beliefs in language learning are meant to be tentative. Even if they are right, they do not undermine my claim that linguistic competence does not consist in semantic propositional knowledge. For (i) the beliefs may not be knowledge; and (ii) the way competence is *acquired* is one thing, what competence *is* is another.

Need *any* of the semantic beliefs necessary for learning a language be true? There certainly seems to be no reason to suppose that they *all* must be. Nevertheless, perhaps we have to get *some* speaker meanings right to learn the language. If so, perhaps our beliefs in those cases are knowledge. Even so, it would still be a mistake to make the requirement that we have some knowledge constitutive of our linguistic competence. We could *be* competent in understanding spoken L (competence 2) even if we misunderstood what all speakers of L meant by their words (though we would need to get some of them right to *become* competent); imagine a conspiracy among the speakers to mislead us. And it seems we could *think* in L without having any true semantic beliefs at all.

Our attention so far has been on competences in L. Those with these competences may exhibit other linguistic skills. A person may be skilled at understanding Tom, a particular speaker of L. This is just to say that when he believes that Tom meant *y* by *z*, he is usually right. This skill in believing truly is to be largely *explained by* his competence 2—a competence in understanding spoken L. Because of that skill at associating thoughts with sounds, he tends to be right about Tom. Generalizing, a person's skill at understanding speakers of L is his skill at getting their speaker meanings right, which is to be largely explained by his competence 2.

4.6 Testability

Davidson has rightly insisted that semantic theories must be testable. He finds virtue in his own on this score: he claims it is "empirical." How could theories fulfilling my tasks (i) to (iii) in 3.1 be tested against the evidence?

Consider what those theories would be like. For (i) there would be linguistic theories linking kinds of natural language sentences to kinds of canonical base-sentences. For (ii) there would be theories like TC explaining the truth conditions of kinds of base-sentences in terms of the referential properties of words of various kinds. For (iii) there would be theories of reference for kinds of words: for example, a theory for proper names like the one here.

The evidence that is *particularly* the concern of such theories is the production of sounds and inscriptions by people in various circumstances. Clearly the distance between the theories and this evidence is great. Much other evidence, and other theory, comes in when we try to bridge the gap.

From the theories for (i) and (ii) we predict that if a sentence token has a certain grammatical structure, then its truth conditions will depend on the referential properties of its parts in a certain way. To take a simple example, if a sentence consists only of a designational term and a predicate, then we can apply TC to get a statement of its truth conditions. Thus, if the sentence token is

Nana is a cat

we can get the following statement by universally instantiating on TC [in 3.1, see A(2), B(1), and C, particularly]:

(1) If 'Nana' is a designational term and 'is a cat' is a predicate, then 'Nana is a cat' is true if and only if (i) there is an object a which 'Nana' designates and (ii) 'is a cat' applies to a.

From theories for (iii) we predict that if a word token is of a certain semantic kind, then its reference is fixed in a certain way. Thus, adopting a simplified version of the theory of designation argued here (overlooking the difficulties in 5.4 and 5.6), we get the following statement:

(2) If 'Nana' is a designational term, then it designates the object in which the d-chain underlying it is grounded.

Now suppose that we are faced with an organism, Fred, producing a sound. Our hypothesis is that this sound has two parts: the first being a designational term, indeed a name, the second a predicate, and that the whole is a predication. We represent this sound, 'Nana is a cat'. Combining our hypothesis with (2) we predict that 'Nana' designates the object in which the d-chain underlying it is grounded. Which object is that? In the first instance this is a question of history, but answering it will immediately involve other theories including an ontological theory: the designatum must be selected from what exists. Similarly if we combine our hypothesis with a causal theory of natural-kind words of the sort discussed in chapter 7, we will have to look to history and other sciences, biology in particular, to determine what objects 'cat' applies to.[10]

Combining these findings with (1), we get a statement of the circumstances in which 'Nana is a cat' is true: it is true if and only if the object fixed by our investigation of 'Nana' is among the ones fixed by our investigation of 'cat'. Next we must decide, with the help of whatever theories are necessary, whether these conditions are met. Is the sentence as we interpret it true or not? Let us suppose we decide that it is. We are still some way from a test of our semantic theories.

At this point we must bring in our view of Fred. Our hypothesis about the sound he produced was influenced by another hypothesis: Fred is a person. We have a theory of people—of the sorts of things they desire, believe, do, and say in various circumstances. We apply this to Fred, considering such questions as the following: Is he intending to tell the truth by that sound? Is he likely to believe the truth about the subject matter of the sound (as interpreted)? Would he behave the way he does if he believed the truth about it? To answer these questions we call on our theory not only of people in general but of Fred in particular. We seek evidence of his life and times, of his history and of his society. Suppose we conclude our investigations with the view that he believes his sound to be true and that it is appropriate to suppose he believes what he would have to believe if we have interpreted him correctly. We have confirmed our semantic theories. Suppose, on the other hand, we conclude that though he believes his sound to be true he does not have the belief determined by our interpretation. We have disconfirmed our semantic theories. And clearly there are other possible confirmations and disconfirmations.

There is no simple connection between confirmations and disconfirmations and the proper fate of a theory anywhere in science. The connection here seems even less simple than usual. A wide range of theories, hypotheses, and evidence are required to get our test; we might be mistaken in many things apart from our semantic theories. For example, we might be wrong about the semantico-grammatical structure of Fred's sound: it has another structure which enables our theories (together with all the auxiliary information) to explain it perfectly. Or we are wrong somewhere in the history, ontology, or biology we used to determine reference; perhaps there are no such objects as we took 'cat' to apply to. Or we are wrong about the truth value of the sound. Or we are wrong in thinking Fred a person. Or our theory of people is faulty.[11] Or our application of this theory to Fred is faulty because of errors about him and his society. All of this casts no doubt on the empirical nature of our semantic theories. It shows only that they are like other theories that are remote from their evidence ("high-level").

Testing a semantic theory is not, of course, as difficult as might appear from the above discussion. We do not have to decide its fate in a series of *unrelated* tests. We have to explain not just one utterance of Fred's but *all* his utterances. The auxiliary assumptions we make in one case must fit in with those we make in others. Furthermore, we have to explain not only Fred's utterances but similar utterances of his fellows. This also puts considerable constraints on what we can assume: Fred's history, his language, his beliefs, his desires, his actions, and so on will have to be plausibly related to those of the people he associates with.

Two features of this discussion of the way in which evidence bears on semantic theory are "apt to shock old hands": there has been no mention of either *Convention T* or the *Principles of Charity and Rationality*. I shall explain why in the next two sections.

4.7 Convention T

I am uninterested in Convention T because I follow Field in his assessment of Tarski's achievement (1972). I seek, from an application of a Tarskian truth characterization not the following "T-sentence" (a substitution instance of the schema, "Schema

T," talked about in Convention T),

'Nana is a cat' is true if and only if Nana is a cat,

but rather,

'Nana is a cat' is true if and only if (i) there is an object *a* which 'Nana' designates and (ii) 'is a cat' applies to *a*.

And for the latter to test the truth characterizations, it needs to be supplemented by theories of designation and application, as indicated above. What we want is that our truth characterization be *correct*, and Convention T has no significant role to play in helping us to see if it is. Convention T is not false, of course; it is merely uninteresting.

Davidson exaggerates the methodological advantages of using Convention T as a criterion. It is said to lead us away from the talk of "facts" or "states of affairs" that is encouraged by the original vague and confused question, 'What is it for a sentence to be true?' (1973a:80). Furthermore, for a language with an infinity of sentences, Convention T demands a theory that explains "how the meaning of a sentence depends on the meaning of its parts" (1973a:81). I share Davidson's distaste for such entities as facts and his interest in an explanatory theory of the sort mentioned. Perhaps Convention T does encourage us in the right direction. However, if we do need its help, we shouldn't. Our task is to explain truth and meaning. We should approach putative explanations *with our usual standards of good scientific explanation whatever they may be* (and, of course, we know that we don't know how to say what they are). We don't need Convention T to keep us honest elsewhere, for example, to prevent the positing of dim entities, so why should we need it here? Furthermore, those usual standards show us, in my view, that *poor* explanations can satisfy Convention T: they would be poor because they do not include any genuine explanation of word meanings (4.9). And note that if the object language has only a finite number of sen-

Defense of the Program

tences, Convention T positively *dis*courages us from producing an explanatory theory: a list of T-sentences, one for each object language sentence, would satisfy Convention T.

4.8 Principles of Charity and Rationality

The Principle of Charity comes in various forms. A crude version, offered by Davidson, runs as follows:

> The linguist then will attempt to construct a characterization of truth-for-the-alien which yields, so far as possible, a mapping of sentences held true (or false) by the alien onto sentences held true (or false) by the linguist. (1967:313)

> We will try for a theory that finds him consistent, a believer of truths, and a lover of the good (all by our own lights, it goes without saying). (1970b:97)

This is not a mere pragmatic, methodological, or epistemic point for Davidson; it is a *constitutive* point. We cannot take the alien to be uttering meaningful sentences, to be interpretable; we cannot take him to have beliefs at all, unless we take him as having (so far as possible) only true beliefs, that is, beliefs that are in agreement with ours, From this constitutive point comes an epistemic one: it is evidence for a given interpretation of the alien's sentence that it places him in agreement with us.

Davidson's later statements of the Principle are more subtle: they allow the possibility of some explicable error (1973b:322–24; 1974:320–21; 1975:20–23; 1977a:244–45). However, they still remain too strong, in my view. Our task is to explain the alien's verbal behavior in a way that meshes with an explanation of his other behavior, his history, his surroundings, and his society. As always, we seek the best explanation. This explanation is likely to attribute to the alien many beliefs pretty much like our own. However, it is also likely to attribute many that are very different. He can be wrong about objects and yet still refer to them, as causal theories of reference show.

Consider my own situation faced with a "religious" alien.[12] If I interpret him charitably (by my own lights), I will not attribute religious beliefs to him. Overlook the appalling difficulties this is likely to bring me in explaining his language. What am I to make of the religious parts of his nonverbal behavior? They will seem inexplicable. Interpret him uncharitably, however, and that behavior falls into place. The *point* of attributing beliefs to organisms is to explain their behavior.[13]

It is surely common for many of us to expect *dis*agreement over vast areas of belief. I have just mentioned religion. Consider some others: politics, semantics, sexual morality, food, sport, child-rearing, beer, the weather.

The second passage quoted above also tells of finding the alien "consistent." This is an indication of another, related, principle that Davidson urges—the Principle of Rationality: we cannot take the alien as uttering meaningful sentences or having beliefs unless we take him as rational, or more or less so (1970b:96–97). People must not only get their beliefs mostly right but also get them right in a rational way. And insofar as they get them wrong, they are nonetheless rational. From this constitutive point comes an epistemic one: it is evidence for a given interpretation that it makes the alien rational.

The popularity of the Principle of Rationality is aided by its vagueness. I refer here not to the qualifications ("more or less," and so forth) which must accompany it if it is to have any plausibility, but to the vagueness of talk of "rationality" itself. People can be rational or irrational in various respects. In only one of these is rationality fairly obviously constitutive of having beliefs.

The respect in which rationality is constitutive is as follows: a person's *behavior* must be rational *given his beliefs and desires*. To give a belief-desire explanation of a person's behavior is to make that behavior rational in the light of his beliefs and desires. In this respect the Principle of Rationality has been presupposed in my discussion of the evidence for semantic theories (4.6).

Defense of the Program   117

However, there are two other respects in which the Principle has not been presupposed. First, I have not presupposed that a person's *beliefs* must be rational *given his experiences*; that even if his beliefs are wrong they must be ones it would be rational for him to have, given what he has been through. I see no reason to believe this version of the Principle. In my view many common views on religion, politics, sexual morality, and the weather are *ir*rational, even given the experiences that led to them. (I think this about a few views in semantics too.) Of course, one hopes that the views will be *explicable* given the experiences; but to explain a view is not to make it rational. And to hope for an explanation is not to insist on already having one.

Second, I have not presupposed that a person's *beliefs* must be rational *given his other beliefs*: that he must have arrived at his beliefs from other beliefs using good rules of inference; that he must have applied the rules as far as appropriate; that he must have unified his beliefs so that there are *no inconsistencies* in the total set. Davidson is expressing this version of the Principle in the passage quoted. I can see no reason to believe it. On the contrary, it seems that most people maintain emotional equilibrium by going against this Principle. Even some very bright ones do. I assume that some mentally ill people go against it a lot, yet they still have beliefs and utter meaningful sentences.

In rejecting various constitutive claims here, I am not denying certain epistemic, methodological, and pragmatic claims that might be made. For example, the most plausible explanation of an alien that looks and behaves like us, enjoys mostly success in its environment, and that we assume to have evolved as we did, is likely to be an explanation that attributes to the alien mostly true beliefs and roughly our degree of rationality (epistemic). So we should seek such an explanation (methodological). On the other hand if the alien is quite unlike us in its rationality and grip on truth, it may be very hard for us to explain it (pragmatic). These claims are sound enough (though unexciting), but they have nothing to do with the constitutive Principles of Charity and Rationality.

Davidson's position on Charity and Rationality has undoubtedly been heavily influenced by Quine's argument for the indeterminacy of translation (Quine 1960:ch.2). A difficulty is that Davidson indicates some differences with Quine's position, but gives us little in the way of argument to indicate the grounds for these differences (Davidson 1973b:327–28, nn.1, 3, 14; 1974:316, 321–22). Another difficulty is, of course, Quine's argument itself. Precisely what the steps are in that argument, and whether or not the steps are sound, are deep and dark questions. This is not the place to consider them. Suffice it to say that I am not convinced. The final difficulty is that Davidson often seems to be offering independent reasons for the Principles in the passages cited, yet it is quite unclear what these reasons are.

4.9 The Need for Theories of Reference

Throughout this chapter I have indicated a number of agreements and disagreements with Davidson, Grice, and Dummett. Perhaps my major disagreement with them, and with their respective followers, is over the role of theories of reference. In their various ways they give these theories no significant role. Davidson's opposition stems from his instrumentalism about reference, and Dummett's from his verificationism. The Griceans never seem to face the issue of reference squarely at all. It is no accident, as we shall see, that all these influential schools of thought tend to favor description theories of names. My aim in this section is to defend the need for, and the possibility of, theories of reference.

Right from the start Davidson has seen no need for theories of reference. His classical paper, "Truth and Meaning," begins by talking of "a satisfactory theory of meaning" giving "an account of how the meanings of sentences depend upon the meanings of words" (1967:304). Friends of reference might feel all is well at this point, for the implication is that there is the further task of explaining the meanings of words. However, by the end that task has completely disappeared; a Tarskian theory of truth is all that is required for a theory of meaning.[14]

Prima facie this is not all that is required. The theory of truth explains the truth conditions of sentences in terms of the referential properties of the words they contain [cf. tasks (i) and (ii) in 3.1]. If we are to complete the task of explaining truth, we must surely then explain reference: we must say something in nonsemantic terms about the nature of these links between words and the world [cf. task (iii) in 3.1]. In the absence of this, we do not seem to have explained how the whole structure of language is related to the world.

Davidson has recently acknowledged this *prima facie* case: "it seems that we can't live without the concept of reference." However, he goes on immediately to argue that "we should be reluctant to live with it" (1977b:251).[15] Why does he think this and how does he think he can manage without reference? I am not confident of the answers to these questions despite the article Davidson has devoted to answering them.

One reason for a lack of interest in theories of reference would be a thoroughgoing instrumentalism about semantic theory. There are many signs that Davidson's approach is instrumentalist (e.g., 1977b:255–56), but I don't think his position is the straightforward, and in my view false, one set out below. My difficulty is in understanding how his position differs from this.

We could sum up the discussion in 4.6 of the way in which nonlinguistic evidence bears on our semantic theories as follows: Suppose s is a sentence uttered by A. Our semantic theories, with the help of various pieces of background theory and information, predict that s is true if and only if certain truth conditions are met. Let us say that these are the conditions that p. So the prediction is the T-sentence,

s is true if and only if p.

Defense of the Program

With the help of a considerable amount of theory and other information, we can form an opinion on whether or not p; on whether or not A believes that p; on whether or not A is reliable in this area; on whether or not A believes that s is true. Thus we can test the prediction. Aside from some disagreements over which theories we need to call on in forming opinions and over the way our opinions bear on the prediction (for example, over the Principle of Charity), this is in accord with Davidson.

Now if we are thoroughgoing instrumentalists, we might say that the only semantic facts are those expressed by T-sentences like the one above; only they describe semantic reality; for only they are "tied to observation and experience." Semantic theory is merely an instrument for generating such T-sentences. It describes no reality beyond that described by T-sentences. Its "theoretical terms" do not refer and its "theoretical statements" are not true or false. Any theory that generates the right T-sentences is as good as any other. It would follow that if there were only a finite number of T-sentences, there would be hardly any point in having a theory. The only point might be as a convenient summary of the list of T-sentences. However, since there are an infinite number of T-sentences, we do need a theory. What theory do we need? We need go no further than a theory which contains axioms that assign referents to the finite basic vocabulary and which goes on to generate the right T-sentences, that is, we need a Tarskian theory of truth. We certainly do not need a theory of reference, for we can get the right answers without one. Indeed, a trivial device enables us to assign referents without using any referential notions like designation in our theory. Reference is not a real relationship, and so it does not need explaining.

It seems to me that the weight of evidence and argument in recent years has been strongly in favor of realism and against instrumentalism as a general doctrine of science. Why should we adopt a different view in semantics? In one respect instrumentalism here seems even less attractive than usual. Instrumentalism requires a sharp distinction between observational statements and theoretical statements; the former refer to reality, are true or false of it, and can be judged so, whereas the role of the latter is simply to generate such statements. A difficulty for this view is that there is no such sharp distinction: all statements are theory-laden. Even such an apparently pretheoretical statement as

Oscar is a black raven

carries a theoretical burden. How much worse is the situation for the observational statements of semantics! T-sentences carry such a vast theoretical burden that *they do not even appear to be pretheoretical*. We are not tempted to think that, looking at the world with an innocent eye, we can simply *observe* whether a T-sentence is correct or not.

If it could be shown that theories of reference were impossible, then we *would* have a good reason for being instrumentalist about reference. Davidson does seem to think that such theories are impossible.

The crux of Davidson's argument is that we cannot give reference "an independent analysis or interpretation in terms of nonlinguistic concepts." For this to be possible, reference must be a "place where there is direct contact between linguistic theory and events, actions, or objects described in nonlinguistic terms" (1977b:252). Yet it is "inconceivable" that one could explain the referential relation between a word and the world "without first explaining the role of the word in sentences" (1977b:253). Hence, reference does not involve such direct contact.

We start by observing the production of sounds. Semantic theorizing begins when we see them as true or false, meaningful, referring to this or that, expressing meaningful thoughts, and so forth. It may be that our very first move is to see the sounds as true or false according to the way the world is. But the *order* of speculation does not seem important.

The important point is that if we see sounds as true or false, we need to explain truth and falsity. In virtue of what does a sound have the property truth? Clearly it does so because it stands in some relationship to the world (or else why does it matter how the world is?). The explanation is a complicated one involving Tarskian theories and theories of reference. This shows that there is ultimately no question of explaining truth without explaining reference, or vice versa. A sentence cannot be true unless it consists of words that refer; a word cannot refer unless it plays certain roles in sentences that may be true. For example, central to the explanation of reference for any proper name is that it *is* a proper name and hence suited for the role marked out for proper names by Tarskian and other theories.

I have agreed that the *evidence* for our explanation is at the level of sentences because the sounds that prompt our investigation are sentences. And truth is a property of sentences, and reference a property of words. However, I do not understand the link between this and the mysterious claim that truth is, but reference is not, a place of "direct contact" with the nonlinguistic world. The whole semantic theory including talk of truth and reference is tested at once by the evidence, and rather indirectly tested at that, for there are many other theories involved as well.

My stance here, as always, is a thoroughly realist one. I have assumed throughout, although it is controversial in some quarters, that the notion of truth we need in semantics is a realist (correspondence) one rather than, say, a verificationist one. In my view the everyday notion of truth, central to our ordinary theorizing, is a realist one. We need an argument to talk us out of the very plausible theory that the truth values of our sentences depend on the objective referential relations their parts have to an independently existing reality. We need an argument to talk us out of such "full-blooded" realism. I take it that Davidson's remarks about reference are intended to be an argument. They seem to me to fail.

Davidson's analogy with physics does not help:

> we explain macroscopic phenomena by postulating an unobserved fine structure. But the theory is tested at the macroscopic level. (1977b:254)

Analogously we explain the truth values of sentences by postulating the reference of words, but we test the theory by testing the truth of sentences. One problem with the analogy is that physicists *are* interested in explaining the nature of that unobserved fine structure; similarly, we are interested in explaining the nature of reference. At least, we are if we are realists. Another problem is that it is sentences, *not their truth values*, which are the observed macroscopic phenomena: a vast amount of theory, including theories of reference, goes into assigning truth values.

I have mentioned Quine's influence on Davidson (4.8). It is probably operating here. Once again it is hard to know what precisely is being taken from Quine and what the grounds are for any differences. Quine's argument itself does seem to suggest that certain referential questions are indeterminate. However, it does not, in my view, show that the whole notion of reference is suspect, nor does it throw any doubt on questions of *partial* reference.[16] And it is to partial reference that I turn in the final analysis (5.4). We must concede that reference may often be an idealization of partial reference and what we really need are *theories of partial reference*, but that concession is not serious.

At the beginning of this part I mentioned the interdependence of theories of names and semantic programs. This is nicely illustrated by Davidson. He himself points out that his view of reference is naturally associated with a description theory of names (1977b:252–54);[17] and he seems to favor such a theory (1975:20–21). This association is not surprising when we notice that *a description theory of names is not a theory of reference at all* in the sense intended here: it does not relate names directly to the world but explains their reference in terms of the reference of descriptions.

From our point of view, that still leaves the very considerable task of explaining reference for descriptions.[18] The interdependence is also illustrated by Dummett. He urges a description theory of names, claiming that a causal theory *could not form part of a theory of meaning* (1973:146–48)[19] Why not? A theory of meaning must explain what a speaker's grasp of the name consists in. This is, of course, an application of Dummett's thesis that a theory of meaning is a theory of understanding (4.3). The difficulty for the causal theory comes from Dummett's insistence that the grasp of a name consists in *knowing how to recognize* the situations in which sentences containing it are true or false. Because a causal theory alludes to matters quite outside our ordinary knowledge, it is irrelevant to this process of verification and so cannot be part of a correct theory of meaning. Dummett's position on names reflects his verificationism in semantics. Conversely if the arguments against description theories and for causal theories (1.5) are sound, they count against verificationism in semantics; people who use a name properly may well lack the recognitional capacity that interests Dummett.[20]

Opposition to verificationism in semantics does not have to rest, however, on the plausibility of causal theories. Recent philosophy has produced a host of reasons for thinking that verificationism is, in general, a bad doctrine. Dummett's version seems particulary bad, for it requires that truth values be established *conclusively* (1975:123; 1976:111) and *with certainty* (1973:148). This is not the place to present arguments against verificationism in general and Dummett's version in particular.[21]

Dummett's long and intricate discussion of Davidson's truth-theoretic approach to semantics (1975 and 1976) can be seen as an argument for his verificationism and against realist semantics. However, the argument rests on the assumption that a theory of meaning is a theory of understanding. Given that assumption, it is hard to see how truth can feature centrally in a theory of meaning because, as Dummett shows, we do not seem to have the knowledge of truth conditions that this would require. Davidson agrees with the assumption and so is open to this criticism. I do not (4.3) and so am not. Once rid of that assumption we can feel free to continue to give truth pride of place in our semantic theory. And giving it that place promises the best overall explanation of people and their language (3.1).

In 3.3, while making extensive use of a Gricean distinction between speaker meaning and conventional meaning, I indicated a disagreement with the Griceans. We *agree* on explaining conventional meaning in terms of speaker meaning. How then is speaker meaning, for example, my meaning in writing

Socrates is wise,

to be explained? According to me, this is to be done by explaining the meaning of the underlying thought, an explanation that talks of a causal network linking me to Socrates. It was in virtue of that link that my thought was *about Socrates*. For the Griceans my meaning is a complicated intention. What makes it an intention about Socrates? So far as I can see, such questions about the link between thought and the world are never squarely faced by the Griceans. Given their radically nonconventionalist view of speaker meaning, I doubt very much whether they *can* offer plausible answers to these questions.

Once again we find an interdependence between a theory of names and a semantic program. The question of the relationship between Socrates and my intention would surely seem pressing to someone with a Millian view of names. It is no accident, therefore, that Griceans tend to favor description theories of names (Loar 1976b; Schiffer 1978): the question then seems much less pressing. On the other hand, adoption of a causal theory would not only press the question but also lead to serious revisions in Gricean doctrine in answering it. For the causal theory shows that conventions *do* play a role in explaining speaker meaning.

In sum, I have two objections to the Gricean program. First, it seems committed to a description theory of names and such theories are false (1.5). Second, though a description theory makes the question of the relationship between Socrates and my intention seem less pressing, the question still remains. The associated descriptions must be linked to the world. What, for example, relates 'ancient' to ancients, 'Greek' to Greeks, and 'philosopher' to philosophers? I see no hope of an adequate Gricean answer.

Finally, it may be asked, why do we stop at asking for explanations of proper names, general terms, and so on? The explanation TC gives of negation and conjunction symbols (3.1) is quite as trivial as the list-style explanations of proper names in a standard Tarskian theory. If there is a need to go further and explain reference for proper names, then surely there is a need to go further and explain reference for truth functional connectives. Perhaps there is. Explanation must stop somewhere, but it is not obvious where it must stop. A good indication that explanation has not gone far enough is that we have in prospect theories that go further. We have such for proper names and some other terms. It is not clear that we have such for the connectives.[22]

To conclude, the *prima facie* case that we need causal theories of reference in our semantic theory seems strong. None of the popular reasons for being skeptical about this is convincing.

III

Chapter Five
A CAUSAL THEORY OF DESIGNATION (2)

Singular terms are semantically linked to the world by relations of designation, denotation, and application (2.5, 2.6). Designation is the important relationship for all designational terms (2.7). The great majority of name tokens are in that category. Most other singular term tokens probably are too. In chapter 2 I started to bring this out and to give a theory of designation. In this chapter, I continue this development against the background of the discussions in Part II. In the next chapter I consider the bearing of the theory on empty singular terms. I finish this part of the book by considering the problem of giving a similar theory for other terms (chapter 7).

5.1 Abilities to Designate

I am explaining designation in terms of d-chains. There are three different types of link in a d-chain: groundings which link the chain to an object; abilities to designate; communication situations in which abilities are passed on or reinforced (reference borrowings). My aim is to distinguish (in nonsemantic terms) the semantically significant d-chains from other causal connections between singular terms and the world (2.1). Can we say more about the links that make up a d-chain than I did in chapter 2?

To say more about any of the links, we must first say more about abilities to designate. I have already indicated that, if the theory is correct so far as it goes, we cannot expect too much more at this time (2.1, 2.2, 3.1). Nevertheless we can make use of our discussion of the language of thought in 3.2 to advance a little further. What the discussion suggests is that we should see a person's ability to designate with a term as, basically, his having thoughts that include mental representations which are both of the object and associated with the term. This is the proposal I shall develop. I shall not attempt to be comrehensive, for such an attempt would lead to details that are tedious for both writer and reader. My aim is, rather, to give sufficient details to make the proposal plausible.

My strategy is to tie an ability to an object and a term in virtue of their role in bringing about the relevant mental representations. The causal path starts with the object at a grounding and runs through patterns of thought and reference borrowings. Groundings are discussed in 5.2 and reference borrowings in 5.3.

An ability to designate is part of our linguistic competence. Just as we can divide linguistic competence in general into distinct but related competences (4.5), so can we an ability to designate. We can distinguish the ability to designate *in thought* (the ability to think *about* the object in a certain way), the ability to designate in speech, in writing, and so forth. And there are various abilities to *understand* designations which also need to be distinguished. I shall focus on abilities to designate in speech, as I did implicitly in chapter 2. Nevertheless, *the ability in thought is basic.*

Consider my ability to designate our cat with 'Nana'. If this is a speech ability, it is the ability to use tokens of a certain physical type (1.4)—a sound type—to designate Nana. I have a set of thoughts "associated with" that type in that those thoughts dispose me to utter sentences containing tokens of it; they dispose me *to speak it.* This is not sufficient, of course, because I am likely to have the ability to designate several objects with the sound type 'Nana'. It is only the thoughts that are *about our cat* that are relevant to the ability in question.

A thought consists of an attitude to a sentence in the language of thought. I continue my former practice of ignoring the fact that most of the thoughts we have we never entertain; also of using the word 'thought' to refer to the sentence only (3.2). Now a thought token will be "about our cat" in the appropriate sense if it includes a token—a mental representation—that designates her. That token in thought will designate her if she is in fact the object in which the token is grounded.

A person cannot have a speech ability if he has lost the power of speech. Yet he might still have thoughts that dispose him to speak in certain ways. I might lose the power of speaking 'Nana' yet still have thoughts prompting me to speak it.

We can say then that *for a person to have an ability to designate an object with a sound type is for him to have (a) the power of speaking that type, and (b) a set of thoughts including tokens which are grounded in the object and which dispose him to speak the type.*

I give a precisely analogous explanation of all the other abilities to designate, covering the making and receiving of communications in the various media. However, an ability in thought is different. An ability in thought is involved in all other abilities. Indeed, an ability in thought binds other abilities together to make them all abilities with the one *semantic* type (1,4, 3.2). Thus a certain sound type and a certain inscription type are used in English for the one semantic type in virtue of the fact that they play the same role in expressing the same thoughts for English speakers (3.3). Finally, abilities in thought do not consist in abilities to use or understand public and external physical types (4.5).

An ability to designate an object in thought poses no new problem: to have it is *to have thoughts including tokens which are grounded in the object*. However, we want to make distinctions within such an ability. For example, we want to distinguish an ability in thought to designate a certain object associated with the sound (or inscription) type 'Tully' from that associated with the sound (or inscription) type 'Cicero'. These two abilities have different causal histories; they involve different "modes of presenting" the object. A striking difference in the histories is that tokens of the sound (or inscription) type 'Tully' form the central part of one, while those of 'Cicero' form the central part of the other. As a result a person with the two abilities expresses some of his thoughts about Tully (Cicero) using the type 'Tully' and some using the type 'Cicero'. This difference in mode of presentation, in causal history, leads to different ways of representing the object—one associated with the physical types of 'Tully' and the other with those of 'Cicero'. These different ways are different abilities. (This bears on our handling of identity statements in 5.5.) *For a person to have an ability in thought to designate an object, an ability associated with a physical type, is for him to have a set of thoughts including tokens which are grounded in the object and which dispose him to use the type.*

Return to abilities with sound types. I have earlier considered what feature of the context determined that one object and not another was the designatum of an ambiguous name (2.4), of a demonstrative (2.6), and of an "imperfect" description (2.7). We can bring the present discussion to bear on that question. A person designated one object and not another by a sound token in virtue of the fact that underlying it was a token in thought—a mental representation—grounded in the one object not the other.

A person who has an ability to designate an object with a sound type may lose it (2.3) even though his powers of speech remain unimpaired. This loss occurs when he ceases to have any thoughts which include tokens grounded in the object and which dispose him to speak the type.

Description theorists claim that users of a name associate descriptions with it. On my "centralist interpretation" of description theories (1.4), this association consists in the holding of beliefs which the user would express using the name and the descriptions. And it is because those beliefs have a certain causal role in an utterance containing the name that the name designates what it does. Overlook the fact that not all thoughts are beliefs (and this is probably not much to overlook since it seems that we cannot have thoughts about x without having beliefs about x). Then in all this description theorists are right. *Where they are wrong is in thinking that the designatum is the object of which (the weighted) most of the beliefs are true. The designatum is the object in which the beliefs are causally grounded.*

This explanation of abilities to designate will be filled out by the discussion of groundings and reference borrowings in the next two sections.

5.2 Groundings

In a grounding a person perceives an object (2.2, 2.3, 2.5, 2.6, 2.9), preferably face to face (2.5), correctly believing it to be an object of a certain very general category (2.10). *The grounding consists in the person coming to have "grounding thoughts"*[1] *about that object as a result of the act of perceiving the object.* A grounding thought about an object includes a mental representation of that object brought about by an act of perception. The thought is one which a speaker of a public language would express using *a demonstrative* from that language; for example, "that cat is friendly." Or perhaps, since descriptions can play a role like demonstratives (2.7), he would use a description; for example, "the cat is friendly." However, I see no reason to deny that beings which do not speak public languages could have grounding thoughts. If they do have them, then they must have appropriate mental representations. Call all these representations of the object in grounding beliefs "demonstrative representations." The act of perception leading to these representations defines a mode of presenting the object. It leads to an ability to designate made up of these grounding thoughts. Underlying the demonstrative representations in those thoughts is a d-chain grounded in the object in virtue of which they designate the object.

All groundings involve grounding thoughts. All other singular terms become grounded in objects by taking advantage, directly or indirectly, of grounding thoughts. Advantage is taken by coming to hold *identity beliefs* (beliefs we would express using identity statements). In order to take direct advantage, this identity belief will include a demonstrative representation. Nevertheless, *that belief is not to be classified as a grounding thought*. Its role is to pass on the benefit of grounding thoughts to the *non*demonstrative representation it includes: that representation will subsequently be grounded in the object via this belief, which links the representation to grounding thoughts (cf. 5.4).

A singular term can take *direct* advantage of a grounding. The person in our example might come to have, or already have, the name 'Nana' for the object perceived. That name will be grounded in Nana as a result of that act of perception if the person comes to hold the identity belief, *that cat* is Nana, a belief containing a demonstrative representation arising out of the same mode of presentation (the act of perception) as his grounding thoughts on that occasion. As a result of that act of identification, the person is likely to come to have many thoughts containing representations associated with 'Nana' (that he would express using the speech or inscription type 'Nana'); for example, if he had the belief, that cat is hungry, he is likely to come to have the belief, Nana is hungry. All these thoughts arising out of the one act of identification form the one ability. They are all grounded in Nana via the identity belief that led to them. The identity belief links the set of these thoughts associated with 'Nana' to the set of grounding thoughts and thus to Nana.

Direct advantage is taken of grounding thoughts by an identity belief containing a demonstrative representation like those in the grounding thoughts. A definite description can take such advantage too. Thus, a person might come to ground 'the Devitts' cat' in Nana in the situation mentioned by holding the identity belief, *that cat* is the Devitts' cat. Furthermore, those who borrow their ability to designate Nana with 'Nana' or 'the Devitts' cat' will also be taking direct advantage of the grounding. (We shall say more on reference borrowing in 5.3.) As before, many thoughts may arise from taking advantage. These thoughts form an ability to designate grounded in Nana via the identity belief that led to them.

When a person has *non*demonstrative representations of an object, for example, the above person's representation associated with 'Nana', he is in a position to use it to gain others. This is to take *indirect* advantage of grounding thoughts. Such advantage is taken by an identity belief that includes not a demonstrative representation but an already grounded nondemonstrative one. Thus, someone who already had the ability to designate Nana with 'Nana' or 'the Devitts' cat' could come to have the ability with 'the F' on the strength of the belief, Nana is the F, or the Devitts' cat is the F. The set of thoughts resulting from this identification will be linked to the set of thoughts including the nondemonstrative representation in question and ultimately to grounding thoughts and Nana. As before, these resulting thoughts form an ability grounded in Nana via the identity belief that led to them.

In this way we can *introduce* a designational use by taking indirect advantage. Can we similarly *reinforce* a use we already have? Suppose we have independent use of two names 'a' and 'b' and come to believe that $a = b$. Does this identity belief transmit the benefits of the groundings for each term to the other? This question is similar to one I considered in 2.8, and again our later consideration of certain confusions suggests that groundings are not transmitted in this way (5.4). Abilities with different names are kept distinct (5.5).

I talk of acts of perception and identification leading to thoughts which, as a result, contain representations grounded in an object. This is not to say, of course, that they *alone* lead to the thoughts: many other thoughts, particular and general, may play a role.

Conversely these acts may lead to thoughts, particular and general, that are not about the object. The thoughts which concern us are the ones that take place only because they make use of the way of representing an object in the particular act in question. It is because the thoughts are of this sort that they are grounded in the object.

Among the other thoughts that influence the thinking process following an act of identification that grounds a term are likely to be some associated with the term and grounded *independently* in the object. In this way abilities become *multiply* grounded in an object (2.8). The person already had thoughts about the object which he would express using the term. By bringing these thoughts to bear on what the act of identification prompts, the person *unifies* his thoughts associated with the term and about the object. This modifies his old ability. Furthermore, it binds together the groundings, and the d-chains they gave rise to, into the one causal network. Underlying the modified ability is a mode of presenting the object which involves all the groundings in the object that influenced the unified thoughts.

A person may have thoughts containing representations of an object even though none of these thoughts is a grounding thought or identity belief. He may have thoughts arising out of identity beliefs that he has long since forgotten (cf. description theories).

I have used the notion of a *semantic type* in an intuitive way (1.4, 3.2) and have rested nothing on it. Nevertheless, it may be of interest to relate the present discussion to the intuitive notion. We can identify a semantic name type with a type of d-chain, exemplified in a causal network involving many people's abilities and grounded in an object (cf. 5.5), for two tokens of an ambiguous physical name type are intuitively of different semantic types if they designate different objects. This is not the case with demonstratives and definite descriptions: tokens of 'that' or 'the book' are intuitively of the same semantic type even though they designate different objects; the one semantic type is involved in representing different objects.

5.3 Reference Borrowings

In reference borrowing *the act of perceiving a designation of the object by the term* plays the role for the borrower that the earlier act of perceiving the object played for a person present at a grounding: it grounds the term in the object (2.3, 2.5, 2.6, 2.8).

Consider first the passing on of an ability. A person hears the expression of a thought containing what is in fact a designational term. He comes to have thoughts as a result, thoughts including representations based on the designational term he heard. For them to be so based, they must, of course, play the grammatical role in thoughts appropriate to a designational term. Since the speaker's term was in fact a designational term, it had underlying it a representation grounded in an object. The reference-borrower, by coming to have these thoughts on the strength of this utterance, gains the benefit of that grounding. He gains an ability to designate that object associated with the physical type of which the designational term was a token. He has mental representations which are of the object in virtue of being causally linked via his act of borrowing to the object. Underlying them are d-chains grounded in the object in virtue of appropriate grounding thoughts and identity beliefs.

A person who borrows his reference may already have an ability to designate the object with the term. If the thoughts about the object associated with that ability influence the thoughts about the object prompted by the act of borrowing, then the person is *unifying* his thoughts, as before (5.2). He has reinforced his ability which becomes thus *multiply* grounded in the object.

A person in a position to unify his thoughts may fail to do so: he wrongly treats the use of a term as a new one for him. This mistake has no serious consequences for reference. The person will simply have two abilities associated with the term to designate the object where he could have had one.

What does have serious consequences is the incorrect assimilation of one use of a term to another. A person comes to have thoughts, including mental representations, that are grounded in two objects. I consider this in the next section.

It is tempting, and I think correct, to say that when a person uses a name he (mostly) intends to designate whatever was designated by the person from whom he borrows his reference (Kripke 1972:302). Such intentions seem as much in need of explanation as designation itself. I do not talk of these intentions but capture the intuitions in another way: the tokens of the name a person produces are tied to the token from which he borrowed his reference by causal links (of the sort discussed) between his mental representations of the object. Similarly, I have often been guided by ordinary semantic intuitions involving the vague notion of *having a particular object in mind* (2.4–2.7), but the notion does not feature in the theory.

I have not attempted to be comprehensive in this account of d-chains. I hope to have avoided two defects: on the one hand, that of making the discussion tediously long by working out many of the minor details; on the other hand, that of making it so short as to render it implausible that the details can be worked out along the lines indicated.

Finally, I emphasize that we look to d-chains not merely to discover how a word came to designate an object but to discover the nature of designation (1.3). Understanding designation is understanding groundings, thoughts (of a certain sort), and reference borrowings.

5.4 Partial Designation and Designation Change[2]

The picture presented so far has been briefly as follows: When a designational term occurs in a statement, there is underlying that occurrence a causal network grounded in an object. In virtue of this the term designates the object. This is an idealized picture.

Many things can go wrong and, typically, some will go wrong. One problem is that the causal chains underlying a term may be grounded in more than one object. (Another is that the chains may not be grounded in *any* object; see chapter 6.)

First, two objects can be involved in the gaining or reinforcing of an "ability," one mediately and one immediately. The discussion of the way in which an ability can be doubly grounded in an object (2.8, 5.2) makes this apparent. Suppose, for example, my statement (ii), "This is Nana," is *false*; it is actually Jemima. I am mistaken, or perhaps I am lying. Any ability gained or reinforced as a result will be grounded in Nana via my use of her name, and in Jemima via the demonstrative. Underlying a later use of 'Nana' arising from this would be d-chains grounded in both cats.[3] Would that use designate Nana or Jemima, neither, or both? Or suppose that the object *im*mediately involved in the use of 'Nana', as a result of her presence, is not Nana (as we supposed in 2.8), but Jemima. In a sense, the speaker has *both* cats in mind in using the name. What is designated by that use, and hence will be designated by someone who uses the name as a result of it?.

These examples concern names but they could as easily have concerned descriptions. And it is even possible to invent examples that concern demonstratives.

We have seen so far how two objects can be involved in one causal network in the gaining or reinforcing of an ability. Second, more than one ability, and hence more than one network, may have an immediate role in the production of a designational term. When this happens, we have slips of mind or tongue, cases of "crossed wires." A classical example of such an occurrence was supplied, appropriately enough, by Canon Spooner. He once delivered a sermon that included many uses of 'Aristotle'. He was leaving the pulpit when suddenly he stopped, returned, and announced to the congregation, "When in my sermon I said 'Aristotle' I meant St. Paul." We are inclined to say that Spooner had St. Paul in mind but ended up referring to Aristotle. Two abilities had a role in the production of the tokens of 'Aristotle': the St. Paul-ability set the mechanism in motion, but the Aristotle-ability intervened in the process, substituting its token.

Third, we note that *misunderstandings* can lead to the involvement of more than one object in a causal network. On hearing a designational term, we must associate it with an ability (or form a new one) to understand it. We can do this wrongly and hence *mis*understand (2.4, 5.3).

Consider the following situation: Joe has a number of politically well-informed friends who frequently discuss the history of socialism. They often use the name 'Liebknecht', sometimes to designate Wilhelm, the father, and sometimes Karl, the son. Joe, who knows little of politics, finds himself on the edge of these discussions and takes all these uses of the name to be about the one person. Later he uses it in a statement. Does he designate Wilhelm or Karl?

Joe is not only confused himself, he spreads confusion. He spreads it most obviously among those to whom he passes the name. But he seems to spread it also among those who already have both uses of the name. Whichever way they interpret Joe's remarks (unless they are aware of his sorry state), they seem tainted by his confusion. Instead of reinforcing an ability by establishing new linkages to one of the objects, each such remark damages the ability by bringing both objects into one network.

My initial solution to the problem of the ambiguity of proper names was qualified (2.4). The need for such qualifications is now clear: my causal approach to determining reference in various cases (2.4, 2.7, 5.1) was based on the idealized assumption that the d-chains underlying a term would be grounded in one object.

Cases of mistake and confusion are, naturally enough, the sort that critics of causal theories of reference have singled out.[4] I claim that they can be dealt with satisfactorily with the help of the Gricean distinction between speaker meaning and conventional meaning (3.3), and of Hartry Field's notion of *partial reference*.

The clearest motivation for introducing partial reference is supplied by the Liebknecht example. Suppose Joe's utterance was

(1) Liebknecht was German.

Did this token designate Wilhelm or Karl? There is no determinate answer to this question. We are inclined to say that, in some sense, Joe was talking about *both* men, yet designation is a one-one relation. The problem is not, of course, the familiar one of ambiguity (1.4, 2.4, 5.1). That problem is the one of saying *what determines which of* two possible interpretations of a sound type applies to a particular token of that type. Our problem is that there seems to be *no fact of the matter about which* interpretation of 'Liebknecht' applies to Joe's particular utterance. What meaning does that token have then? How can it be *true*, as it seems to be?

The case is parallel to the main example Field uses to introduce the notions of partial reference, the example of the Newtonian term 'mass' (1973). He argues that many scientific terms are *referentially indeterminate*. In particular, he claims (in the light of the special theory of relativity) that there is no matter of fact about whether Newton's 'mass' denoted "relativistic mass" (= total energy/c^2) or "proper mass" (= nonkinetic energy/c^2). Furthermore, the term does not denote anything else, yet it is not *straightforwardly* denotationless. This poses a problem. How can we make sense of the common assumption that many of Newton's statements have perfectly determinate truth values (from a relativistic viewpoint)?[5] According to the usual "referential semantics," the truth value of a sentence is determined by the referential properties of its parts (3.1). Field's solution is to introduce various notions of *partial* reference which are intended to serve instead of the usual notions of reference in our semantics. Thus, the Newtonian term 'mass' partially denoted *both* relativistic mass and proper mass. He then suggests a Tarski-style truth definition in terms of partial reference along the following lines:

> ... introduce the term 'structure'; a *structure* for a sentence is a function that maps each name or quantity term of the sentence into some object or quantity, and maps each predicate into some set. The structure *m corresponds* to the sentence if each name or quantity term of the sentence partially denotes the thing that *m* assigns to it, and each predicate partially signifies the set that *m* assigns to it. Now for each structure *m*, we can apply the standard referential (Tarski-type) semantics to determine whether the sentence is *m-true* or *m-false*, i.e., true or false *relative to m*. (To say that the sentence is *m*-true is to say that it *would* be true if the denotations and extensions of its terms were as specified by *m*.) We can then say that a sentence is *true* (false) if it is *m*-true (*m*-false) for every structure *m* that corresponds to it. (Field 1973:477)

Making use of this and relativity theory, we are able to justify assigning intuitively desirable truth values to Newtonian utterances. For example, the following one comes out true:

> To accelerate a body uniformly between any pair of different velocities, more force is required if the mass of the body is greater.

Others come out false. Some come out neither true nor false: they *would have been true* if their use of 'mass' had denoted relativistic mass, say, and *would have been false* if their use had denoted proper mass; they *are partially true and partially false*.

Similarly, to explain the meaning of Joe's utterance, we need to see the token of 'Liebknecht' it contains as *partially designating* both Wilhelm and Karl. The utterance will then come out *true*, as it intuitively should, because it would have been true if it were about either person. On the other hand,

> (2) Liebknecht was a Swiss

and

> (3) Liebknecht was the proto-martyr of German communism

come out false and only partially true, respectively. [(3) is only partially true because the predicate is true of Karl but false of Wilhelm.]

I suggest that this treatment in terms of partial designation gives the most plausible solution to our problem. Note that the distinction between speaker meaning and conventional meaning is irrelevant here; the conventional associations of 'Liebknecht' with both Wilhelm and Karl, consisting according to me in causal networks grounded in those two people, bear as much on the speaker meaning of (1) as on its conventional meaning.

Let us now apply this to our earlier difficulties with 'Nana'. Consider the following statements:

(4) That cat is Nana;
(5) Nana is a cat;
(6) Nana is a Persian;
(7) That cat is black;
(8) Nana is black.

Suppose these utterances are made by someone misled by my false assertion, "This is Nana." Suppose, further, that he had, prior to this misintroduction, a perfectly good ability to designate Nana by 'Nana' though not one based on his own acquaintance with her. Now Jemima, who is before his eyes, is black. Nana, who is absent, is not. Both are cats but neither is Persian.

It is uncontroversial that (4) is false and (7) true in these circumstances. That is how they come out on the theory. (7) expresses a grounding thought and (4) an identity belief of the sort that passes on the benefit of a grounding (5.2). Any thought associated with 'Nana' resulting from this identification will contain a token grounded in the object designated by 'that cat', that is, in Jemima. So the thoughts expressed by (5), (6), and (8), hence, those statements themselves, contain tokens grounded in Jemima. However, since the tokens of 'Nana' in (5), (6), and (8) result partly from the person's earlier ability, they are also grounded in Nana.[6] So they partially designate both cats; (5) comes out true, (6) false, and (8) only partially true.

A further word is appropriate on the token of 'Nana' in (4). Unlike those in (5), (6), and (8), it is grounded only in Nana (unless there were earlier confusions), whom it therefore designates. This must be so to avoid the absurdity that an identity statement like (4) *could not* be (completely) false, as we supposed it was, because it would contain a name that partially designated the object demonstrated as well as the object in which it had, to that moment, been grounded. I avoid this because of *the special role* I give identity beliefs in passing on the benefits of groundings (5.2). (4) expresses the link *in virtue of which subsequent tokens of 'Nana'*, like those in (5), (6), and (8), come to be grounded in Jemima. The token of 'Nana' in (4) itself is not thereby grounded in Jemima.[7]

What I have been talking of here is, of course, the *speaker meaning* of (4)–(8). This is in line with my view of the primacy of speaker meaning. Our interest in *conventional meaning* is derivative: we are interested in it because of its bearing on the meaning of thoughts and hence speaker meaning (3.3). It is worth distinguishing the two notions of meaning here because the conventional meanings of (5), (6), and (8) differ from the above speaker meanings. There is, presumably, only one convention concerning 'Nana' in question here, one that links the name to Nana. So she alone is the conventional designatum of the name in those statements: there is no question of partial designation. Hence, in its conventional meaning, (8) will be simply false. What (4) makes possible is another convention; and if that misidentification catches on, that is what we shall have, as we shall see.

My view of the conventional meaning of (8) is uncontroversial. However, many may want to disagree with my view of its speaker meaning, particularly with the talk of partial designation and partial truth. It may be claimed that the speaker of (8) straight-forwardly designated Jemima by 'Nana' and hence that what the speaker meant was *simply true*.⁸ I think there is some intuitive support for this claim but, on examination, this support turns out to be flimsy. Furthermore, the theoretical explanation of this situation and others shows the claim to be false.

Consider our basic intuitions, the reflections of folk semanticists. I suggest that there is only one strong one: the "total performance" involves elements of truth and falsity. I capture this: in its speaker meaning (8) is partially true and partially false; in its conventional one it is false. Does this accord with intuitions enriched by the Gricean distinction? According to the above claim, it does not. That claim may seem to be supported by the fact that the speaker would agree that he designated *that cat* (pointing at Jemima). But, of course, he would *also* agree that he designated Nana. The problem is that (8) expresses a belief that comes with *two* others, the true one expressed by (7) *and the false one expressed by (4)*.⁹ The speaker is confusing the two cats, and we have no clear intuition that he meant the one and not the other. Our talk of partial designation captures the confusion and explains the lack of a clear intuition.¹⁰

It may be felt that the opposing claim is supported by what the speaker would do if he discovered that it was not Nana but Jemima before his eyes: he would withdraw (8), replacing it with "Jemima is black." Suppose he would, so what? He has just learned something new and significant in this area which has led him to *change his views*. What significance has this for what he meant before? His new belief *differs* from the one that led to (8), just as it also differs from the one that led to (7). Furthermore, he may not make the replacement. Perhaps if he were to discover that it was Jemima and not Nana, he would not believe it was black. His background beliefs about the two cats might have considerable influence on what he would assert on the evidence of his eyes in those circumstances. "Observation statements" like (8) are theory-laden.¹¹

These low-level intuitions are not decisive on this question.

What is decisive, in my view, is the theoretical explanation of them and others. Suppose that the speaker had asserted a sentence containing 'Nana' in her absence and before the misintroduction. Clearly we want to say, in this normal situation, that the speaker "meant," "intended to refer to," and so forth, Nana. Such talk requires explanation. My explanation is that there is a causal link of the sort we have specified between name and object. The first point in favor of my present view is this: *such a link also exists between the token of 'Nana' in (8) and Nana.* So Nana must have *something* to do with the speaker's meaning. The second point arises from considering the link between the token of 'Nana' in (8) and *Jemima*. The opposing claim was that the speaker "meant," "intended to refer to," and so forth, Jemima, the cat in front of him.[12] I have conceded that there is *some* intuitive support for this. How is this link to Jemima to be explained? It also is a causal link. Indeed, for me it is a significant one constituting *a grounding*. Such groundings play a crucial role in the general theory of names: they are the ultimate link between *all* (designational) names and the world. *So the speaker is linked to Nana and Jemima in similar ways.* There is no basis for picking out Jemima as the sole object of the speaker's thought. Both cats are relevant to his meaning.

Canon Spooner's confusion does not seem to call for partial designation. The conventional meaning of his utterances containing 'Aristotle' clearly involve Aristotle and not St. Paul. What about their speaker meaning? There seems no reason to deny the intuition that they concerned St. Paul and not Aristotle. His *thoughts* were grounded in St. Paul, but somewhere in the process of articulating them irrelevant factors pertaining to Aristotle intruded.

So far we have stayed close to initial confusions. As we move away from them we see the need to complicate the theory. All those who *gain* an ability with 'Liebknecht' or 'Nana' from the confused person will obviously inherit his confusions, but what about all those who already have *un*confused abilities? Consider Joe's well-informed friends. It is implausible to say that their abilities would be affected in any way if they should hear his (1) and misinterpret it as about either Wilhelm or Karl. Yet the situation seems to be one where the "benefits" of the confused groundings underlying Joe's remark are passed on (5.3).

What seems to be the case is not the case however. For *only thoughts that result from a grounding, directly or indirectly, gain the benefit of that grounding* (5.2, 5.3). Joe's friends will not be led to any new thoughts by such a humdrum statement as (1). Suppose, however, that Joe shows some originality: he makes a statement that leads a friend to a new thought associated with 'Liebknecht'. I must say that such thoughts *are* grounded in both Wilhelm and Karl. This seems intuitively correct.

How affected will the friend's thoughts be? We should like to say that a thought inherits the confusions underlying Joe's remark *to the extent that* it arises out of that remark. More generally, we should like to say that a thought is grounded in Wilhelm (Karl) *to the extent that* groundings in Wilhelm (Karl) underly it. This is the natural application of the earlier discussion of multiple groundings and unification of thought to the present case of confusion (5.2, 5.3).

I need, therefore, to refine the notions of partial designation and partial truth into notions of *degrees of designation* and *degrees of truth*. However, I had this need quite apart from the consideration of the last paragraph. In some cases of confusion more than two objects may be involved. This will make it necessary to draw distinctions between partially true statements that I cannot yet draw: some will be "more true" than others. I shall need to talk of degrees of designation in order to assign degrees of truth. A fairly straightforward development of Field's approach makes this possible. Instead of saying merely that 'a' partially designates b, I say that it "designates b to degree n," or that it "n-designates b." I can then explain the degree of truth of a sentence containing '*a*' in terms (partly) of this degree of designation using a method like the one quoted earlier.[13]

This refinement *enables* us to make distinctions between the truth values of statements when they are called for, but it *does not force* us to make them when they are not. It does not force us, for example, to conclude that a token of 'Liebknecht' designates Karl to some small degree because Joe's confusions underlie it to some small, but intuitively insignificant, degree. We can assign the degree zero, thus allowing the statement containing it to be completely true or false about Wilhelm. What is important to the theory is not the precise degree to which a token designates an object *but that the decision on that question is based on the relative importance of groundings in that object in the causal explanation of the token.*

This discussion suggests that the earlier decision about Joe himself may have been too hasty. Suppose that when he uttered (3) he was expressing a belief he had come by *solely* on the basis of a similar statement made by one of his friends. Although confused groundings underlie many of his thoughts associated with 'Liebknecht', this one is grounded simply in Karl. So the name in (3) designates Karl and the statement is true. It is perhaps unlikely that many of Joe's thoughts will be simply grounded in this way. Joe will presumably try to *unify* his thoughts associated with 'Liebknecht', for he takes them all to concern the one man. This unification will tend to spread his confusion.

We have not considered two sorts of cases which may seem to involve confusion. Suppose that instead of falsely saying (ii) "This is Nana" in Jemima's presence (as above), I falsely say (iii) "Nana is our cat" in her absence, where 'our cat' designates Jemima. Any ability with the name 'Nana' reinforced by this may then seem to involve d-chains grounded in both cats. Similarly, suppose we have the independent use of two names '*a*' and '*b*' and come to believe, mistakenly, that $a = b$. It may seem that this identity belief transmits the benefits of the groundings for each term to the other and hence results in abilities with the terms grounded in both of the objects involved.

These suggestions must be resisted because they would lead to counterintuitive results. If the person I address with (iii) goes on to say

(9) Nana is Siamese,

on the strength of (iii) and some overheard remarks about a cat, then he has said something *simply true or simply false* according as things are with Nana; Jemima is irrelevant. Similarly, if a person says

(10) a is F

because b is F and he has come mistakenly to believe that $a = b$, he has said something simply true or simply false.

We must disallow that the groundings of one term can be transmitted to another in this way. Although an identity belief involving a nondemonstrative representation can be used to *introduce* the designational use of a term, it cannot *reinforce* that use. It was for this reason that I suggested in 2.8 that the truthful assertion of (iii) did not lead to a doubly grounded ability, and in 5.2 that the belief that $a = b$ did not transmit the benefits of groundings.

My motive in ruling out transmission of benefits in these cases is simply to get the intuitively right answer at the level of truth values. There is no cost to the approach if I can do this by making distinctions in the causal background of utterances. This is what I have done. For the approach is to describe which of the many causal links between an utterance and the world are the semantically relevant ones.

It is clear that we ordinarily concede that reference is confused only when we are forced to: when there are no good reasons in the circumstances for taking one object and not another as the designatum. This is understandable given our interest in truth as a guide to the way the world is. A theory of designation should be similarly reluctant to concede semantic confusion.

Realization of confusion can affect developments; here knowledge does play a role. Suppose a person misled by my false statement about Nana, (ii), realizes his mistake soon afterward. He will amend his thoughts and it will be as if that confusion had never been, provided he has not passed it on. He can start again with 'Nana', using it for Nana, Jemima, or both (two distinct semantic types). Any of his dependents can have a similar realization and also start again, though the further the confusion spreads, the more difficult this becomes. However, it is each person for himself here: others can get no benefit from a person's realization alone (unless he brings it to their attention).

Although knowledge can help to remove confusion, it is important to notice that knowledge is not necessary to remove it: given later groundings in only one of the objects, confusion will disappear anyway. Let us say that the person I misled about Nana walked away able to .5-designate Nana and .5-designate Jemima with the name 'Nana'. This is the ability he will pass on to others. Now suppose there are later groundings of this new network by that person or his dependents. If the groundings are sometimes in Nana and sometimes in Jemima, thus reinforcing the confusion, we would continue to assign roughly the above degrees of designation. *A new and confused convention has been established.* However, it is much more likely that later groundings will be in only one of the two cats. If they are in Nana, there will be a rapid increase in the degree to which those who get the benefit of these groundings designate Nana by 'Nana' along with a corresponding drop in the degree to which they designate Jemima with it. The convention of designating Nana will remain established. The opposite process will occur, on the other hand, if the later groundings are in Jemima. This will lead to *designation change, a species*

of reference change. A new unconfused convention, the convention of designating Jemima with the name, will become established.
Reference change for names differs from that for other terms. If, for example, Einstein adopts a term like 'mass' from Newton's theory to use in his own, while fully aware that the two uses are distinct, we may say that the reference of the term has changed (as indeed it has in this case). However, if I adopt the name of Zola's courtesan for my cat, while fully aware that the two uses are distinct, we would not regard this as an example of reference change: we have simply created a new semantic type. It seems that there has to be *confusion at the beginning* of the sort just illustrated with 'Nana' for it to seem appropriate to talk of reference change with names.

There are two possibilities with designation change: either the name continues after the change to have its old designatum as well as the new, or it does not. In the former case one semantic type splits into two; in the latter one semantic type changes into another. If the community that uses 'Nana' for Nana remains largely unaffected by my false statement, "This is Nana," while the network arising from that statement becomes thoroughly grounded in Jemima, we have an example of splitting. If, on the other hand, Nana is switched with Jemima and then destroyed, the switch never being discovered, we have an example of one semantic type changing into another.[14]

A strength of the account offered here, making use of multiple groundings and partial reference, is that it enables a plausible account of the gradual transition from one convention with a name to another.

My earlier discussion of criterion of identity (2.10) has bearing on designation change. For there to be designation change, a network originally grounded in one object must become grounded in *another*. To settle whether there is designation change, therefore, we must settle whether or not the object in later groundings is *the same as* that in the earlier ones. The truth values of statements containing the name in question will depend on how we settle this matter. It will often be very hard to settle. What, for example, are the identity conditions of a restaurant? Must it be in the same building, have the same decor, the same cook, or what? However, it seems we would require at least that the object be of the same very general category. If we require for a successful grounding of a name that there be an object present satisfying some categorial predicate, we must require that if another grounding is to be in the *same* object, it must satisfy the same predicate.

In 5.8 I shall consider in more detail the truth and falsity conditions of statements arising out of confusions like those considered in this section.

5.5 Identity Statements[15]

I have not yet treated the problem of identity statements, a problem that loomed very large in the development of description theories (1.2). The problem arises from what Frege called the differing "cognitive values" of '$a = b$' and '$a = a$'.

One way in which the statements have been thought to differ turns out to be illusory. It has been thought that whereas '$a = a$' is *necessarily* true, '$a = b$' is only *contingently* so. We must sharply distinguish the term 'necessary' in its metaphysical sense from the epistemic term '*a priori*', as Kripke has pointed out (Kripke 1972:260–263). If 'a' and 'b' are designational names, then they are what Kripke calls "rigid designators": If a is b, then a is necessarily b; it is b in all possible worlds (1972:303–11). This is not likely to seem plausible to someone committed to a description theory of names, but once such theories are abandoned it does seem plausible.[16] So, whatever their epistemic differences, '$a = a$' and '$a = b$' are alike in being necessarily true if true at all (and if anything is "necessarily true").

That '$a = a$' and '$a = b$' differ epistemically seems undeniable, however dubious we may feel about using the controversial *a priori/a posteriori* distinction to describe the difference: we seem to have different ways of knowing that the two statements are true. This difference must be accommodated by my theory of names.

A related difference between the two statements is the difference in their *conceptual roles*. More accurately, the beliefs that underlie these statements seem to have different conceptual roles—one a trivial one and the other a significant, unifying one. This difference must also be accommodated.

It may be thought that the difference between the two statements can be put more simply: they differ in *meaning*. The trouble with this as a starting point is its vagueness, a vagueness arising from its reliance on the ordinary notion of meaning. This notion is even less helpful than the ordinary one of reference (1.3, 4.1). It is important to realize that any notion of meaning that is to carry weight in a semantic theory must be a technical one.[17]

My explanation of the differences between '$a = a$' and '$a = b$' briefly is this. Frege rightly saw that the solution to the difficulty lay in the different "mode of presentation" of the object associated with 'a' from that associated with 'b'. Frege's mistake was to embody these modes within "senses." For me the modes are types of d-chain exemplified in the networks.[18] Underlying 'a' will be a very different network from that underlying 'b'. It is this difference which explains the differences between the statements.

Consider first the alleged difference in "meaning" between the statements. We need to be careful to see whether we need any notion of meaning beyond designation for (designational) names. However, suppose we do. I claim that the only such notion (notions) we need is one (are ones) of synonymy for tokens and that *any such notion is to be defined ultimately in terms of similarities between d-chain networks*. For there are no semantic differences between names without differences in networks.

Similarity between networks is a matter of degree. As a result there are various notions of synonymy we might define in terms of such similarity. At one extreme *any* two (designational) name tokens have underlying them "mechanisms of reference" which are in certain respects similar, for those mechanisms are both d-chain networks. In this respect the two tokens "differ in meaning" from a general term or a mass term. We might use this similarity to define a notion of synonymy.[19] However, there seems to be no need for this: we can simply say that the two tokens are both *designational names*.

Two networks become more similar when they are grounded in the same object. This could be the basis for defining another unnecessary notion of synonymy[20]—unnecessary because it is sufficient to say of the two name tokens in question, as we can say already, that they are *codesignational*. In fact a notion of synonymy here is worse than unnecessary; it is misleading: it may encourage the interpretation that the two "synonymous" tokens "have the same semantical content," thus making Frege's problem with identity statements insoluble.[21]

At the other extreme even two tokens out of the one mouth which are intuitively "of the same semantic type" may have semantic differences in their underlying d-chain networks: further groundings and consequent development of thought may have taken place between the time of one token and the time of the other. However, once again, we seem to have no need of a notion of synonymy that would make this a difference in meaning.

If we have a need for a notion of synonymy, it is, I suspect, to capture the above intuitive idea of sameness-of-semantic-type that has featured before in our discussions (1.4, 3.2, 5.2) and implicitly will again (9.7). Certainly that seems sufficient to capture any felt difference in meaning between '$a = a$' and '$a = b$'. Two tokens will be synonymous if the d-chain networks underlying them are linked together in the one overall network (2.3). We may need to distinguish synonymy for a speaker from conventional synonymy here. Thus, two tokens of the same physical type from the same speaker will not be speaker synonymous if they do not arise from the one unified ability (5.2–5.3), but they might be conventionally synonymous if, despite the speaker's ignorance of this fact, his two underlying abilities arose from the one convention, a network of interconnected d-chains grounded in the one object. Tokens of 'a' and 'b' will never be synonymous using these notions of synonymy, for our practice with names is to keep the networks for such physically distinct types separate (5.2, 5.4).

Consider next the undeniable epistemic difference between '$a = a$' and '$a = b$'. In the situation Frege has in mind (but see below), '$a = a$' arises from exercising the one ability with the physical type 'a' twice. The belief expressed is one of such massive triviality as to be hardly ever entertained. To believe it, it is sufficient to have caught on to identity and to have gained the ability with the name. On the other hand, '$a = b$' arises from exercising two distinct abilities, one with 'a' and one with 'b'. To have these abilities and to have caught on to identity is *not* sufficient to have the belief expressed: a further step has to be taken, one probably requiring significant other beliefs about a and b that provide the *evidence* for the identity belief. Given the semantics of names that I have described and the nature of identity, there is bound to be an epistemic difference of the sort observed. And anyone who has caught on to names and identity is bound to be aware, however dimly, of that difference.

This epistemic difference is related to a difference in conceptual role which is also striking. Whereas the belief that $a = a$ leads to no new beliefs, the belief that $a = b$ may lead to many: for someone who believes that a is F should be led by that identity belief to believe that b is F.

Despite this discussion it is not the case that '$a = a$' *does* always have a trivial cognitive value. A difficulty here is that an utterance like '$a = a$' is seldom heard. It might occur out of a simple desire to give support to the law of identity (as assumed above). However, it is more likely that, if it is ever uttered, it will have similar epistemic and conceptual significance to '$a = b$'. Sometimes a person fails to recognize that a token is of a semantic type he already has: he comes to have two abilities where he should have had only one (5.3). When he comes to realize his mistake, we can imagine, with a little effort, him registering his discovery by uttering, for example, '$a = a$', "meaning that" this $a =$ that a. Certainly he will register his discovery by *believing* that $a = a$. Doubtless we hardly ever entertain a belief of this form except when it is significant in this sort of way. That a belief that $a = a$ may not be trivial is vividly demonstrated by the fact that it can be *false*: consider, for example, Joe's earlier confusion of the Liebknechts (5.4).

Gilbert Harman has urged that "meaning depends on role in conceptual scheme rather than on truth conditions" (1974:11). Hartry Field, in a regrettable moment of ecumenicalism, has recently urged that meaning depends on *both* conceptual role *and* truth conditions (1977). Furthermore, he has offered a conceptual-role semantics to supplement the earlier discussed truth-theoretic semantics (3.1) in order to make this possible. It seems to me that Field provides insufficient reasons for his ecumenicalism and that it is not really called for, at least as far as names are concerned; and Field relies largely on names and their role in identity statements to motivate an interest in conceptual-role semantics.

My claim is not that conceptual role is irrelevant to the meaning of a name. And I agree, of course, that we need to talk of more than truth and reference to explain the phenomena here. However, a complete truth-theoretic semantics *does* talk of more, for it must include *theories of* reference (as Field was the first to point out). Such theories talk of *mechanisms* of reference, in the case of my theory for names, of d-chains. My claim is that we have no need for any notion of meaning for names that cannot be defined within this semantics; I have discussed this above. Any notion of meaning so defined gives significance to conceptual role, for the way the name is treated conceptually appears in the account of d-chains in the theory of reference (5.1–5.3). However, we have no need to go further than this; in particular, we have no need to add a special conceptual-role semantics.[22]

5.6 The Distinction between Designational and Attributive Terms

Although most names are designational, some are attributive. Underlying a designational name is a network grounded in an object (assuming that it is not empty), perhaps by a designational description. Underlying an attributive name is a network linked to the object denoted by the attributive description used to introduce the name (again assuming that it is not empty) (2.5).

There is a class of names that seem to blur this distinction: what seems to be one semantic type has a double role—sometimes as a designational name, sometimes as an attributive name. This occurs most commonly with the names of authors.[23] Gareth Evans has an example which brings out the problem vividly.

An urn is discovered in the Dead Sea containing documents on which are found fascinating mathematical proofs. Inscribed at the bottom is the name 'Ibn Kahn' which is quite naturally taken to be the name of the constructor of the proofs. Consequently it passes into common usage amongst mathematicians concerned with that branch of mathematics. "Kahn conjectured here that . . ." and the like. However suppose the name was the name of the scribe who had transcribed the proofs much later; a small '*id scripsit*' had been obliterated. (1973:203)

We are inclined to say that the remarks by the mathematicians concern *whoever it was* that made those mathematical discoveries. The truth values of the remarks are unaffected by the fact that the name is that of the scribe. The mathematicians have nobody in particular in mind and the name seems to be attributive. Yet there are clearly other remarks, by historians perhaps, in which the name seems to be designational: "Ibn Kahn was no mathematician but a scribe." The problem is that in my theory, all these uses may seem to have underlying them d-chains grounded in the scribe: they all may seem to borrow his reference (to himself) with the name. How am I to explain its apparent role as an attributive name? More seriously, how am I to distinguish the two roles?

In the case of 'Ibn Kahn' the causal network arose out of one token of the name. We have no "fix" on the scribe except via that token which led us to the mistaken belief that he was responsible for the proofs. Problems arise also when we have a multiply grounded name. Consider 'Shakespeare', for example. This name is multiply grounded in a certain person who lived at Stratford-upon-Avon. It seems to have an orthodox role as a designational name in discussions of Shakespeare's life; also in matters of his authorship of the famous works. However, it seems to have another role as an attributive name; our interest then is in Shakespeare *qua* author.[24] Now suppose that Bacon was in fact the author. The truth value of many statements containing 'Shakespeare' will depend on whether the name is designational or attributive. What determines whether a particular token is one or the other?

The existence of a few attributive names is not troublesome for the theory: our concern is to explain the semantics of the many designational names. The first problem here is to explain how a name that seems to have underlying it a network grounded in an object can be attributive. This can happen when *we decline the opportunity to borrow a reference*. Consider the mathematicians faced with the urn. There is nothing about the situation that *compels* them to borrow the reference of 'Ibn Khan' from the urn in the way indicated in 5.3. Rather than borrowing the reference from the urn, they can be stimulated by it to introduce the semantic type 'Ibn Khan' for *whoever constructed those proofs* (just as Zola's use of 'Nana' stimulated the naming of our cat). This would be, implicitly at least, a naming ceremony.

So there is no difficulty explaining how a name *can* be attributive "despite the opportunity to be designational." Nor is there any problem about there being both a designational and an attributive semantic type associated with the one physical type; indeed, there is no problem in there being several (2.5). *The problem with cases like 'Ibn Khan' and 'Shakespeare' is in distinguishing the two types in practice.* It is simply not plausible to suppose that the mathematicians *did* introduce a new type for 'Ibn Khan' in the way (described above) that they *might have*. Believing that Ibn Khan constructed those proofs, the mathematicians are unlikely to have had the required thoughts. Of course, once doubts about authorship arise it is plausible to say that we distinguish the two types. But what are we to say about tokens of the name before any such doubts? And even after the doubts, do we always distinguish the two types?

A causal theory of names pushes us toward saying the following in answer to the first question: unless and until there has been, implicitly at least, a naming ceremony introducing the attributive name, the tokens are designational. That is one way of seeing what Kripke was arguing for in his example of 'Gödel' (1972:293–294). After the introduction there are two distinct uses. I am not *absolutely* convinced that we should move from that position to accommodate these examples. However, perhaps we should. Given that a name '*a*' can be used attributively in a way that ties it to an identifying description 'the *F*', and given that the users of '*a*' believe that *a* is the *F*, it is possible that we sometimes do not bother to distinguish the attributive from the designational use of '*a*'; we muddle up the two uses. Perhaps our present examples are actual cases: we have not clearly introduced an attributive use but rather have started to run the attributive with the designational. And, moving to the second question, perhaps even after doubts have been raised about whether *a* is the *F*, we do not always bother to distinguish the two uses where the distinction seems irrelevant to what we want to say.

What I am contemplating here is that there may be nothing in reality to determine whether some name tokens are attributive or designational. Two "meanings" are run together. In such a case we must say that the token *partially designates* the object to which it is linked by a d-chain and *partially denotes* the object picked out by the identifying description (cf. 5.4).

I have talked so far of names, but clearly the problem may arise elsewhere. If a person is in a position to designate a and believes that a is the one and only F, he might use 'the F' without it being a determinate question whether he was using it attributively or designationally; it may be partially used both ways (cf. 2.7).

The qualifications contemplated here to my version of Donnellan's distinction diminish the elegance of the theory. However, they do not lessen the significance of the distinction for the vast majority of singular terms. The qualifications also concede a little more truth to description theories than I conceded earlier (2.5, 5.1). It is only a little more truth, for Kripke's arguments should have persuaded us that if there are names of the sort described here they are the exception, not the rule.

5.7 The Fundamental Notions

My explanation of d-chains, and hence of designation, rests on various notions which remain largely unexplained.

First, there is the notion of *perceiving an object*. I have committed myself to some sort of causal theory of this and have talked briefly of the importance of face-to-face situations (2.5) and of the application of categorial predicates (2.10). However, it is clear that what I have said falls far short of an account of perceiving an object. More needs to be said to pick out that object from others causally involved in the act of perception.

Second, there is the notion of *thought*. On this I have said only a little in chapter 3. What I *have* attempted is to explain what distinguishes certain thoughts which are *about x* from others which are *about y*: roughly, it is *about x* in the requisite sense if experience of *x* (not necessarily the thinker's experience) played a certain causal role in bringing about the thought.

Third, I have relied on the notion of *cause*. I have offered no explanation of this notion, nor could I in a work like this even if I had one available. My reliance on the notion is a defect only if it seems likely that cause will be shown to be a thoroughly objectionable notion that has no place in science. Given the central importance of cause in our conceptual scheme, I suggest that each of the following is more likely than this: (i) that cause is essential to our world view though incapable of explanation (explanation must stop somewhere); (ii) that explanation will show cause to be acceptable; (iii) that cause will be shown to be defective in certain respects but that there are other related notions that should replace it and which will serve the same purposes in science that cause was thought to; in particular, notions that can replace cause in our theorizing about language and mind. So I do not think a reliance on cause is a defect in a theory.

Causation is of course pervasive. As a result there is a danger that a theory that makes much of causal links will have a spurious plausibility. I have tried to avoid this in my theory of designation by showing the very *special* place that one object, the one designated, has in the causal explanation of a designational term: other objects are causally related to the term but *not in that way*.

5.8 Truth Value Conditions

In this section I shall consider the bearing of designation on truth, part of the problem of explaining the semantics of complex expressions in terms of that of simple expressions. The task is largely to bring together earlier remarks and to make explicit what has been implicit. The contexts we consider will all be transparent. Opaque contexts will be treated in chapters 8 to 10. I shall assume that a designational or attributive term may fail to refer, but postpone discussion of such "empty" terms until the next chapter.

In 3.1 I gave a simplified truth characterization, TC, for a simple language. The language was simple in that it had only a few constructions: predication, negation, conjunction, and universal quantification. Less interestingly, it was simple in not allowing terms that are partially designational and partially attributive (5.6). I shall not try to complicate the language. TC was simplified in that it ignored (i) the fact that a designational term may fail to apply to its designatum (2.7) and (ii) the fact that a designational term may partially designate more than one object (5.4). In this section I shall take account of (i) and (ii) to give a modified truth characterization, TC*. (TC was simplified also in that it ignored the fact that terms may *apply* only partially, but that fact does not bear closely enough on our interest in designation to justify attention.)

To take account of (i) we need to revise

(A) 2. If e_1 is a designational term, then it refers$_s$ to a if and only if it designates a.

My firm position was that no question of *denotation* arises for a designational term. However, I adopted rather tentatively the view that, for designational descriptions at least, a question of *application* did arise (2.7). As a result, if such a description failed to apply to its designatum, I concluded that it did not identifyingly refer and that, for this reason alone, the sentence containing it was not true: 'the F is G' is not true if the object 'the F' designates is not F. Application must be similarly relevant to any anaphoric demonstrative or pronoun that depends on a designational description. Further, it seems appropriate to extend what we say for 'the F' to the complex demonstrative 'that F' and to deictic pronouns like 'he' and 'she' which have a descriptive element (2.6); so 'that F' identifyingly refers only if its designatum is F, and 'he' only if it is male. However, it seems that no question of application arises for the other designational terms. Consider these other terms. In 2.10 I made the application of a certain categorial predicate necessary for a name to designate, but since that is a *condition on* designation it does not have to be mentioned *in addition to* designation in giving our truth characterization. In other respects my theory for names made application semantically irrelevant to them. A name is linked to its object by grounding thoughts and identity beliefs (5.2). Whatever descriptive elements appear in these thoughts is irrelevant to the future semantics of the name. An appropriate way of putting this would be to say that no question of the name's *application* arises, just as no question of its *denotation* arises. Similar remarks would be appropriate about the deictic demonstratives 'this' and 'that' and the deictic pronoun 'it'. However, we will get a neater truth characterization if we say of this group, not that no question of application arises, but rather that they *apply to everything* (a "merely verbal" difference, of course). Our first step then toward a modified truth characterization is to replace (A)2 with:

If e_1 is a designational term, then it refers$_s$ to a if and only if it both designates and applies to a.

The next step is to take account of (ii): a term may partially designate more than one object (5.4). Field has shown how the standard Tarski-type semantics can be used to determine *m-truth—truth relative to a structure m which maps terms onto the world* (5.4). Here m must map each designational term onto an object that it "m-designates" and a set of objects that it "m-applies to" (the set of all objects if the term is a name or a deictic 'this', 'that', or 'it'). It must map each attributive term onto an object that it "m-denotes." Finally, it must map each predicate onto a set of objects that it "m-applies to." *The structure m "corresponds" to a sentence if each of the sentence's designational terms partially designates the object it m-designates and* applies to the objects it m-applies to; if each of its attributive terms denotes the objects it m-denotes; and if each of its predicates applies to the objects it m-applies to. (A designational term fully designates if it has only one partial designatum. We are ignoring problems of partial application and hence of partial denotation.) A sentence is true if and only if it is m-true for every structure that corresponds to it.

TC*, my modified truth characterization that takes account of both (i) and (ii), is as follows:

(A)* 1. If e_1 is a kth variable, then it m-refers$_s$ to s_k.
2. If e_1 is a designational term, then it m-refers$_s$ to a if and only if it both m-designates and m-applies to a.
3. If e_1 is an attributive term, then it m-refers$_s$ to a if and only if it m-denotes a.

(B)* 1. If e_1 is a singular term and e_2 is a predicate, then $\ulcorner e_2(e_1) \urcorner$ is m-true$_s$ if and only if (i) there is an object a to which e_1 m-refers$_s$ and (ii) e_2 m-applies to a.
2. If e_1 is a formula and e_2 is a negation symbol, then $\ulcorner e_2(e_1) \urcorner$ is m-true$_s$ if and only if e_1 is not m-true$_s$.
3. If e_1 and e_2 are formulas and e_3 is a conjunction symbol, then $\ulcorner e_3(e_1, e_2) \urcorner$ is m-true$_s$ if and only if e_1 is m-true$_s$ and e_2 is m-true$_s$.
4. If e_1 is a formula and e_2 is a universal quantifier under the kth variable, then $\ulcorner e_2(e_1) \urcorner$ is m-true$_s$ if and only if, for each sequence s^* that differs from s in the kth place at most, e_1 is m-true$_{s^*}$.

(C)* If e_1 is a sentence, then it is m-true if and only if it is m-true$_s$ for some (or all) s.

(D)* If e_1 is a sentence, then it is true if and only if it is m-true for every structure m that corresponds to it.

Suppose that a sentence is m-true for some structures that correspond to it but not for others. We should like to characterize its *degree of truth*. Clearly this degree will be some sort of *average* of the sentence's m-truth-values for all corresponding structures.

However, the average may have to be *weighted* because some corresponding structures are more important than others. This is so because a designational term may (partially) designate one object *to a greater degree* than another (5.4). We can capture this with the following:

(E)* If e_1 is a sentence, then its degree of truth is the sum, for each structure m for which it is m-true, of the product of the degrees to which its terms refer to the objects m assigns to it.

Take an m-true sentence the predicates and designational terms of which apply to the objects they m-apply to and the attributive terms of which denote the objects they m-denote. According to (E)*, the m-truth of that sentence counts toward its truth to the extent that its designational terms designate the objects assigned by m. Clearly if the sentence is m-true relative to *each* corresponding structure, its degree of truth will be 1. So (E)* entails (D)*.

TC* illustrates the way in which truth depends on designation. It is a relatively simple example, of course, but more complicated examples are difficult to come by, given the level of our knowledge here.

TC* will apply to any language of the required form. It will apply to tokens in speech, thought, or whatever. I have speaker meaning rather than conventional meaning primarily in mind (3.3). However, it can be applied to either by interpreting the semantic vocabulary appropriately; for example, "conventionally designates" or "speaker designates" (5.4).

Chapter Six
EMPTY TERMS

6.1 The "Tough" and the "Tender"

Opinions on empty names seem to be surprisingly divided. On the one hand there are the "tough" philosophers. For them, empty names like 'Pegasus' "fail to name anything" (Quine 1950:198); they have only "the superficial grammar" but not "the use" (Anscombe 1959:41) of a proper name. Further, an empty name gives rise to "truth value gaps" (Quine 1950:220; 1953:165; 1960:176): "nothing has been ascribed to any object by sentences in which it occurs; and so nothing has been said, truly or falsely" (Anscombe 1959:41).[1] On the other hand there are the "tender" philosophers. For them, empty names "refer" in just the same way as nonempty names; they are "about" characters like Mr. Pickwick and James Bond—"fictitious beings."[2] Further, assertions are "true and false in the same way that ordinary empirical assertions are true and false" (Crittenden 1966:317).[3]

On a related question, that of the status of singular existence statements, we find a similar division of opinion. Traditionally, the issue has been the far from clear one of whether or not 'exists' is a "predicate." The tough view is that it is not:

To say that [the actual things in the world] do not exist is strictly nonsense, but to say that they do exist is also strictly nonsense. (Russell 1956:233)[4]

For the tender, on the other hand, 'exists' is a predicate: it distinguishes those objects that are real from those that are fictitious; fictitious objects don't exist.[5]

There is a further difference between the tough and the tender, a difference of interest rather than opinion. The tender are interested in investigating the ordinary meaning and role of empty names. The tough are sometimes tempted by the problem of empty names into a description theory of names (1.2), but mostly they have little interest in the problem, for empty names are defective and have no place in the language of science.

Of course, not all writers on empty names can readily be classified as belonging to one of these two camps. But surprisingly many can be.

My concern is with natural language and not just with scientific. So the semantics of empty singular terms must be investigated, at least to the point where I have shown that they cause no trouble for my theory of designation. For obvious reasons I shall focus attention on empty *names*. I take my point of departure from the views of the tough which are, for the most part, unassailable. However, much more needs to be said.

For the tough, semantics must be scientific. There is no place in science, hence none in semantics, for talk of nonexistent fictitious characters; it lacks all explanatory power. Any proper explanation of the semantics of empty names must link them to *reality*. Theories which include talk of what is admitted to be unreal show "a failure of that feeling for reality which ought to be preserved even in the most abstract studies" (Russell 1919:169).

Further, such understanding as we have of the truth conditions of 'a is F' leads us to require for its truth that there *exists* something which 'a' refers to whether by designating it or denoting it (5.8). Talk of "fictional existence" at this point is, as Russell said with characteristic vigor, "a most pitiful and paltry evasion " (*Ibid.*). So if 'a' is empty, the statement (taken straightforwardly) cannot be true.

In this, the tough are surely right. What, then, lies behind the views of the tender? First, the tender are in accord with "ordinary" (pretheoretic) semantics. The person in the street would agree that 'James Bond' refers to or designates a fictitious character; that 'James Bond does not exist' denies existence of that object; and that such statements as 'James Bond is virile' are true. Put this another way. The tender usage of semantic terms like 'refer' and 'true' is in accord with "ordinary usage" (usage reflects theory). And, to the "champions of ordinary language," the task of semantics is the analysis of these ordinary semantic terms.[6] I have already rejected this view of semantics (4.1).

Second, the tender rightly see (or so we may charitably suppose) that the institution of empty terms requires an explanation that is simply not given by the tough view. For, if statements containing empty terms are *really* not true, what are we to make of everyone stating them (cf. 3.1)? People assert such statements quite sincerely. Others listen and take them quite seriously. Generally people are aware that the terms in question are empty; thus, they are aware of something that is alleged to be a sufficient condition for the statements' not being true. Yet it is pointless, in general, to assert a statement that has no chance of being true. We are in danger of dismissing the whole institution of empty terms as an aberration. We should be reluctant to do this, far more reluctant than we were above to dismiss the ordinary semantic *theory* of this institution. There is ample motive here for finding a semantic theory that would make some of these statements true.

Names are hardly ever dropped because of emptiness, as we shall see. But suppose it were always the case that as soon as we discovered that a name was empty, we ceased to use it. Then there would not be a great deal more to be said about empty names than had already been said by the tough. The main problem is posed by our habit of using empty names with full knowledge of their emptiness.

The task is therefore to find a semantics of empty terms that *explains* the institution, one that explains the role those terms play in our lives, while at the same time remaining within the tradition of scientific semantics established by the tough.

Given my stand on the disagreement between the tough and the tender, I can now say what it is that makes a singular term "empty": it is empty because it does not (identifyingly) refer; that is, it does not designate and apply to an object, and it does not denote an object. This is, of course, the view implicit in TC* (5.8). (I have ignored the fact that a term may only partially refer to an object. In discussing empty terms, I shall continue to ignore this and will also ignore failures of application.)

The empty names that give rise to the main problem are the ones that arise out of fiction,[7] for their use seems unaffected by their emptiness. I will call such names "fictitious names" and will roughly distinguish them from others with a different origin, which I will call "failed names." In sections 6.2 and 6.3 the semantics of sentences containing fictitious names will be discussed. My concern to this point is with the effect of empty names on sentences. In 6.4 and 6.5 I will consider the semantics of empty names themselves in the light of the theory of designation. In 6.6 I will return to the semantics of sentences containing empty names, considering more complex sentences than those considered before. Pseudonyms are discussed briefly in 6.7. The final section, 6.8, deals with singular existence statements.

6.2 Fictitious Names within Fiction

Fictitious names "arise out of fiction," I have said. In fact they (normally) occur first *within* fictional works. It is important to distinguish these occurrences of fictitious names from other occurrences *outside* fictional works. A consideration of the former use points the way to an explanation of the latter.

Some stories for children begin, "Let us imagine that . . ." or "Let us pretend that. . . ." Stories as a whole are best viewed as being implicitly preceded by such an operator. For, as Peter Strawson has pointed out, a storyteller is not making a statement

(1954:221). His sentences have no truth value and do not claim to have any truth value.[8] A storyteller imagines that a world of a certain sort containing entities of a certain sort exists and goes on to "describe it." Or, a storyteller pretends that a world of a certain sort containing entities of a certain sort exists; the pretence will involve both the imagination and the "description."[9] Because this is what he is doing, he may say about this "imagined world" any of the sorts of things we say about the actual world. He takes over the full vocabulary and uses it in the same sense, but his sentences are in a different form.

It has often been felt that the user of an empty name is involved in "pretense" or "make believe." This is an insight into the use of a name *within fiction*. The context of storytelling is one of pretense, and while that context is preserved, while the storyteller (perhaps with the assistance of his audience) is "giving structure to the imagined world," questions of truth or falsity do not arise. However, once we stand back from the story and discuss it, they do seem to arise; we are making statements; pretense has ceased; criticism has begun. Some of these statements will use the names of "imagined entities"; hence, the main problem of empty names.

Empty names introduced in fiction in this way are the ones I call "fictitious names." It is possible, though not common, for those of us who wish to talk about a fiction to go through some "naming ceremony" for a previously unnamed character. Suppose, for example, that we have watched a silent film without titles and say, as a preliminary to criticism, "Let us call that character who got the bucket of paint on his head, 'Charlie'."[10] It seems best to see us here as *adding* a little to the fiction: our remark, like the author's, is implicitly preceded by the storytelling operator. The name so introduced is a fictitious one.

6.3 Fictitious Names outside Fiction

Consider now the first uses of a fictitious name outside a work of fiction. Typically all those who use it are fully aware of the ontological situation. People all *knew* that Tom Jones, Mr. Pick-

172 *Empty Terms*

wick, and so forth, did not exist. No sooner is a story spun than we are off, speculating about *a*'s moral growth, *b*'s courage, *c*'s villainy, and so forth. What is the explanation?

The above discussion of the use of names within fiction suggests one. I have claimed that statements *in* fiction are implicitly preceded by a storytelling operator roughly paraphrasable by "let us pretend that." When we talk *about* fiction we are making reference to this pretence, to this imaginative act. So the suggested explanation is that a statement about fiction is (usually) implicitly preceded by a fiction operator roughly paraphrasable by "it is pretended that" or "in fiction." Let us use 'S' for the storytelling operator and 'F' for the fiction operator.

Take as an example the name 'Tom Jones'. Suppose that Fielding's novel includes the sentence,

(1) Tom Jones is illegitimate.

That token of (1) is paraphrasable by

(2) S (Tom Jones is illegitimate)

and is neither true nor false (because it is not a statement). On the other hand suppose I assert (1), then my token is paraphrasable by

(3) F (Tom Jones is illegitimate)

and is true. Similarly,

(4) F (Tom Jones is chaste)

is false. These are just the results we want. By introducing these operators we have taken the first step in giving point to statements using empty names and explaining the institution.

Clearly (3) is true because of Fielding's use of (1), and (4) is false because of his use of various other sentences. Now consider the following:

(5) F (Tom Jones likes raspberry jam),
(6) F (Tom Jones does not like raspberry jam).

Empty Terms 173

The novel has nothing to say one way or the other about Tom's attitude toward raspberry jam. Typically there are many such "gray areas" in any fictional work. Neither (5) nor (6) is true. And given our paraphrases of 'F', it is most natural to treat them both as false: it is not pretended that. . . . Alternatively, we could treat them both as neither true nor false. I shall remain neutral on this question.

An occasional feature of fictional works is that they play fast and loose with the laws of logic and with other fundamental laws of nature. "Fictional worlds" are sometimes not "possible worlds." The above account enables us to explain our talk about such fiction without semantic strain.

(7) F (Donald Duck circled the earth so fast he met himself before he left)

poses no special problem. If that is what was pretended, it is simply true. If not, it is simply false.

Sometimes there is pretense *within* fiction; there are plays within plays (for example, within *Hamlet*). Here we have *double* operators. And that is not the end of it; in principle there is no end of it: we can have triple operators, quadruple operators, and so on. Every level of fiction in the story requires an operator for us to talk about it.

There are other more difficult sentences to consider but these are best set aside for the moment. They are taken up in section 6.6.

These remarks on the "logical form" of some statements about fiction do not take us very far into the semantics of such statements: they are only a first step. We need to know *how* the truth conditions of F-sentences depend on the referential properties of their parts. How can they be dealt with in a truth-theoretic semantics like that outlined in 3.1? The most I can claim for this first step is that it makes the task of accommodating our intuitions about the truth conditions of these statements within such a semantics seem promising. [These intuitions are exemplified in the brief discussion of (3) to (7) above.]

Some may feel that the task does not seem promising. Since Frege it has been common to think that the truth conditions of a sentence are a function of *the referents* of its parts. Indeed, my earlier TC (3.1) fits that view. Yet my claim is that 'Tom Jones' in (3), for example, has no referent; it neither designates nor denotes. How then can (3) be true? In claiming that it is, even though 'Tom Jones' has no referent, I do seem to be abandoning the Fregean principle. However, I do want to maintain, as I did (3.1), the principle that the truth conditions of a sentence are a function of *the referential properties* of its parts. The difference between these two principles seem largely verbal, as we shall see. It seems that the more restrictive Fregean principle can be applied to sentences like (3) to (7) and various other difficult sentences (6.6, 9.7), but at the cost of introducing some unusual referential relationships.

Given the view that truth conditions are a function of referential properties, the present approach will seem promising so far as singular terms are concerned if we can show that their underlying mechanisms of reference involve the parts of reality that seem relevant to the truth conditions of the containing F-sentences. I shall claim that they do in 6.6.

Acceptance of the idea of an operator on a sentence should not be difficult. It seems that a semantic theory will have to allow such operators to explain, for example, irony and metaphor; perhaps also to distinguish assertions, questions, and commands. The one sentence can be used literally, ironically, metaphorically, and, we now say, to tell a story or to talk about one.

6.4 Empty Names and the Causal Theory

The most puzzling feature of the institution of empty names is our practice of using names in full knowledge of their emptiness.

In most contexts the names so used will be fictitious. However, there is another sort of empty name. Names are introduced for entities *wrongly assumed to exist*: a posited planet is named 'Vulcan', a posited god 'Zeus'. There is no element of pretense here. Subsequent statements containing these names aim straightforwardly to describe reality; they involve no fiction operator. I call such names "failed names." The statements containing them pose less of a problem, for they are (mostly) simply untrue (5.8).

In this section I consider how the causal theory offered here applies to fictitious and failed names. Let us start with fictitious names, which constitute the great majority of empty names.

Part of what needs to be said is clear enough. (a) Our present uses of a fictitious name depend on earlier uses, including first uses, in the same way as do our present uses of nonempty names: there is a causal network stretching back via various uses of the name to first uses. (b) The first uses are not linked to the object designated (for there is none such) but rather are linked to an imaginative act, the act of creating a fictional work. The first uses are in fact *within* fiction in S-sentences. This imaginative act, and the causal network arising from it, is all there is in reality underlying the use of a fictitious name.

Suppose that we are gathered round a storyteller. In the course of his story he introduces a character by the name 'Jum Eli'. At the end of the story one of us says, "Jum Eli is sinister." My picture of this is as follows: The storyteller's imaginative act is in the form of a series of S-sentences. Among these are many that use the name 'Jum Eli'. These uses of the name are heard by the audience. On the basis of this causal link to the imaginative act (strictly, to these parts of the imaginative act), one of the audience uses the name in the above statement, an F-sentence. This statement will be true or false as the case may be with the imaginative act that gave rise to it.

It is tempting to say that the causal network for a fictitious name is "grounded in" an imaginative act. However, that would introduce too much vagueness into the term 'grounding'. I shall say simply that the network "arises out of" the imaginative act. The network for a nonempty name, on the other hand, "arises out of" the object in which it is grounded. The causal chains that constitute the network for a fictitious name are not d-chains, for they are not grounded in an object.

The causal network for a nonempty name is typically grounded in the designated object on more occasions than the first use of the name (2.8). Similarly, the network for a fictitious name arising out of a fiction is typically linked to that fiction on more than one occasion.

This is the account for fictitious names. How must it be varied to account for failed names? Here there are no imaginative acts, simply mistaken assumptions. The causal network for a failed name begins with what is intended to be a naming ceremony (or a suitable substitute therefore as in 2.9), involving a naming sentence: "Let us call that planet 'Vulcan,'." However, the ceremony fails because, unbeknown to those involved, there is no object to be named. The singular term used to pick out the object for naming, for example, 'that planet', is empty. The subsequent causal network arises out of this failed ceremony; more accurately, it arises out of the naming sentence token, particularly the use or mention of the name. If the token has a long existence (if it is written, for example), it is likely that the network wll be linked to it on more than one occasion. Furthermore, if the situation prompting the original ceremony (an experiment perhaps) is recreated, other sentence tokens may occur which function like the naming sentence in "generating" the network.

Underlying all names there are causal networks. If the network is grounded in an object, the name is nonempty and designates that object. If the network is linked to reality by an attributive description which denotes an object, the name is nonempty and denotes that object. If the network arises out of a failed naming ceremony, the name is empty and does not designate or denote; it is a failed name. If the network arises out of fiction, the name is empty and does not designate or denote; it is a fictitious name.

The success or failure of a naming ceremony settles whether a name is nonempty or failed. The ceremony fails if there is nothing there of the appropriate category to be named (2.10). For the ceremony to yield a name that designates, it must meet the conditions for a grounding (5.2).

Kripke suggests that it may be the case that our present use of 'Santa Claus' is causally linked to a certain historical saint (1972:300). Even if this were so it seems unlikely that 'Santa Claus' would designate that saint; it is unlikely that the causal network underlying the name would be grounded in the saint in the required way (5.1–5.3). Objects can be involved in the causal explanation of a name in various ways without being the object the name designates (2.4, 5.6).[11]

The distinction between a failed and a fictitious name is not a sharp one. What was once a theory (and may still be to some) may now appeal as a myth. Consider, for example, the name 'Zeus'. We may suppose that the network for this name arose out of ceremonies (or substitutes) that were serious attempts to name something. Since the attempts failed, the name should be a failed name. However, many of us now treat all these early uses of the name as part of the creation of a myth; we treat the name as fictitious. We need not try to draw a clear line between the failed and the fictitious. What is theoretically important is to distinguish both from nonempty names and to explain the fact that many names, the paradigm fictitious ones, are used in full knowledge of their emptiness.

6.5 The Distinction between Designational and Attributive Empty Terms

I have talked of names being empty because they fail to designate or denote. The first failure is significant for designational names, of course; the second for attributive ones. We need to consider the application of that distinction to empty names. And it is time to consider other empty terms.

Intuitively we marked the distinction between attributive and designational terms in this way: if the speaker has a particular object in mind in uttering the term, it is designational; if not, it is attributive (2.5–2.6). Clearly if having-in-mind is construed transparently, as I said it should be (2.4), this can't be the intuitive mark of the distinction for empty terms: there is no object to be had in mind. Nevertheless having-in-mind still seems relevant to our intuitions here. I shall show how it can be later (9.8). We should now look at the theoretical basis of the distinction.

The across-the-board distinction among (definite) singular term tokens arises because there are two conventions associated with deictic definite descriptions, two modes of identifying reference. One is a Russellian convention in which the mode is denotation. The other is a convention in which the description functions like a (deictic) demonstrative: its mode of reference is designation (2.7). Denotation is successful only if the description applies to one and only one object. Designation is successful only if there is a certain sort of causal link to an object, a d-chain. Which mode of reference is relevant to a particular description token depends on which convention the speaker in fact employed. If he employed the former then denotation is relevant: the token is attributive. If he employed the latter then designation is relevant: the token is designational.

We can see then that the distinction applies to deictic description tokens quite independently of whether or not they are empty. And all deictic demonstratives are designational independently of whether or not they are empty (2.6). Such a demonstrative is empty if it is not prompted by an object of the appropriate category (2.10). Anaphoric demonstratives and descriptions borrow their semantic properties from the terms on which they depend (2.7). So also do names. Generally names depend on demonstratives and designational descriptions and so they are designational. Sometimes, however, they depend on attributive descriptions and are attributive (2.2, 2.5). All empty singular term tokens seem, therefore, to be covered by the distinction (but cf. 5.6).[12]

This is too swift. How could a *fictitious* name be designational? Such a name arises out of fiction. It is never part of a naming ceremony the success or failure of which depends on whether or not a demonstrative or description designates. Yet such a name is like other designational terms in "having a particular focus." And it is unlike some descriptions, stimulated by fiction and appearing in F-sentences, which seem attributive. Here we are simply airing part of the earlier mentioned intuition: sometimes when we use an empty term "we have a particular fictional character in mind," sometimes when we use one we don't. Our theoretical distinction can cover these cases as follows: The parts of a work of fiction that "mention a character" stand in for a grounding. A token is designational if its network arises out of such a "mention"; if not, it is attributive.

6.6 Truth Value Conditions

I have distinguished theoretically between empty terms and nonempty terms. In particular I have distinguished between empty and nonempty designational terms, which are especially interesting to us. Next we must return to the question of the contribution empty terms make to the semantics of the sentences that contain them (6.3).

Suppose an empty designational term appears in a straightforward assertion about reality; the sentence is not an F-sentence. Its emptiness poses no special problem in stating the truth conditions of the sentence. They are of the sort set out in 3.1 and 5.8. These truth conditions cannot be met if the term is empty (I am, of course, ignoring opaque contexts here); see, for example, (A) 2 and (B) 1 of TC. The term is meaningful, for it has mechanisms of reference (5.5). However, the term is empty because these mechanisms are not grounded in an object. The sentence has perfectly good truth conditions but is not true.

This treatment may be too simple. TC does not distinguish between untruths. Some may want to distinguish between those that are *truth-valueless* ("a truth value gap") and those that are *false*. Others may want to make a distinction in the scope of the negation sign which TC also does not countenance: whereas 'Pegasus does not fly' is false (truth-valueless), 'It is not the case that Pegasus flies' is true. However, these refinements are beside my main purpose.

Given their truth conditions, it is not surprising that literal assertions of '*a* is *F*' are seldom made by anybody who knows that the contained singular term is empty: the sentence has no chance of being true. Our problem was that many sentences, *apparently* of that form, are uttered in full knowledge of the term's emptiness (6.1). The first step in solving this problem was to recognize that these sentences are implicitly governed by the operator 'F'; such sentences can be true even though the contained singular terms are empty (6.3).

To go further with F-sentences, we need to specify the way in which singular terms contribute to their truth conditions. Intuitively F-sentences are true if there are fictions "having the appropriate form" out of which they arise. Consider a designational fictitious name. According to the theory this will have underlying it a causal network arising out of certain parts of a fictional work. Those are just the parts to which we would look to see if the fiction is of the appropriate form for an F-sentence containing the name to be true. Just how these truth conditions are to be worked out in detail is, of course, quite unclear. However, I claim that the parts of reality from which fictitious names arise are the parts to which the F-operator directs us to determine the truth of F-sentences. The truth conditions of an F-sentence depend on the referential properties of its contained name. I shall not attempt to go into this more.

It seems that if we had the complete answer here we could rephrase it to preserve the Fregean functionality principle (6.3). Although the fictitious name does not designate, we could say that it stands in some other referential relationship to the world: it "F-designates" those parts of the fiction which appear in its underlying network and which bear on the truth conditions of the F-sentence. It seems that we could then state its truth conditions using F-designation: the F-operator directs us to look not for the designatum of a name but for its F-designatum. If this is so, the difference between my functionality principle and Frege's is merely verbal here.

What determines which way a given sentence token should be construed? What determines, for example, whether or not it is an F-sentence? *That is determined by what the speaker had in mind, meant, or intended.* This is a factual matter concerning the underlying processes leading to the production of the token. It is a matter on which, in all usual circumstances, we can depend on the speaker for information. However, circumstances can be unusual: a speaker can be wrong about his own mental processes.

It is important to note that the choice of appropriate semantics for a sentence is *not* determined by whether the name in it is failed, fictitious, or nonempty. The speaker may be wrong about the name. He may mistakenly think that a fictitious name is nonempty or that a failed name is fictitious; in the former case the statement is to be taken literally, though the name is a fictitious one; in the latter the statement is to be taken fictionally, though the name is a failed one. What counts is whether or not the speaker employs the F-sentence convention. Generally, of course, speakers know which of the names they use are fictitious and so generally the fictional treatment will be appropriate when they use fictitious names.

There are other statements which merit a few words of discussion here. Some can be treated in one of the two ways we have been considering; others cannot.

Consider a libel case arising out of what is presented as a fictional work. What the prosecution attempts to prove, and the defense to deny, is an identity statement. There is no question of it being an F-sentence: the statement is to be taken literally.

No interesting new problem arises if we suppose that the defense is right. The identity statement is not true because one of its singular terms is empty.

However, suppose that the prosecution is right. It is well established that Dryden wrote the poem *MacFlecknoe* to defame his enemy Shadwell. So neither name in

(8) Shadwell = MacFlecknoe

is empty and the statement is *true*. This can be accommodated into the theory without problems. What makes such a statement worthy of note here is that one of the names in it is introduced in what is presented as fiction and may largely be fiction. In these respects the name, though nonempty, is just like a fictitious name. This raises the whole question of the appearance of real entities in fiction. I shall return to this shortly.

The truth of (8) licenses substitution *salva veritate* of 'MacFlecknoe' for 'Shadwell' in transparent contexts. So the statement

(9) MacFlecknoe was a writer,

containing a name introduced in fiction, is true (taken literally). This may seem counterintuitive on the ground that we do not normally use a name like this, introduced in fiction, when our discussion has nothing to do with the fiction. Such usage may indeed be largely inappropriate, but that is insufficient ground for denying the truth of (9). There can be all sorts of *pragmatic* reasons for it to be inappropriate to use an expression that is perfectly in order semantically. In particular there can be pragmatic reasons for not using one of the many available devices for designating an object on some occasion: perhaps it is offensive, as are many nicknames; perhaps it is out of keeping with the occasion; perhaps it is misleading; and so on. The best explanation here seems to be that such a use of 'MacFlecknoe' is misleading. Certainly there are problems in *denying* that (9) is true: either we must also deny that (8) is true, which is implausible, or else we must put what seems to be an ad hoc restriction on substitutivity.[13]

Leonard once pointed out that predicates

may be classified according as they entail existence, entail non-existence, or neither entail existence nor entail non-existence. (1964:30)

My discussion so far has, implicitly, concerned predicates that entail existence, predicates like 'planet' and ' = '. 'Fictitious' is one that entails nonexistence (if we grant that it is a predicate at all). I discuss this predicate in the section on singular existence statements (6.8). 'Ralph worships . . .'' is a predicate that entails neither existence nor nonexistence. So also is 'Tom believes that . . . flies'. I discuss such predicates in sections 9.4, 9.7, 9.8, and 10.4.

Names are seldom dropped from our language because of their known emptiness. If they are fictitious, they have a place in statements governed by the fiction operator. Even if they are failed, they may still have a role with predicates that do not entail existence.

We have seen with the example of MacFlecknoe that real entities can appear in fiction. Indeed, it would be unusual for there to be no real entities in a fiction. Consider, for example, the novel *Tom Jones*. It contains many references to London. As a result,

(10) F (Tom Jones visited London),

which is governed by the fiction operator yet contains a nonempty name, is true. That 'London' is nonempty is irrelevant to the truth of (10). What is relevant is what is imagined in *Tom Jones* using the names 'Tom Jones' and 'London'. Or, continuing the attempt to preserve the Fregean principle, what the names F-designate is relevant to the truth of (10), what they designate is not.

Fielding's use of 'London' brought the capital city of England into his fiction because he had it in mind; his tokens of that name designated the city because it was the object in which the underlying network was grounded. A similar account applies to 'MacFlecknoe', with the difference that a *new* name was introduced for the real entity in question: the poem, in effect, *bestowed* the name 'MacFlecknoe' on Shadwell.

A statement that is interestingly different from (10) is

(11) Oscar is more indecisive than Hamlet.

Like (10) it contains both an empty and a nonempty name. However, unlike (10), the use of the nonempty name does not arise from a reference to a real entity in fiction. (11) relates the actual attributes of something to the imagined attributes of something imagined. We might attempt to paraphrase it by:

(12) The indecisiveness of Oscar is greater than the indecisiveness in fiction of Hamlet.

Clearly neither of the two ways we have considered for treating sentences containing empty names can be straightforwardly applied to the likes of (11).

I shall not attempt to say anything more about the truth conditions of statements like (11). The problem does not arise from the use of empty names as shown by the following:

(13) The real Brutus was less noble than Shakespeare's.

Indeed, much the same problem arises when there is no reference to fiction at all:

(14) Oscar is not as smart as he thinks he is.

The problem is beyond the scope of this book.

6.7 Pseudonyms

The pseudonym adopted by a single author poses no difficulty: it functions as an ordinary nonempty name (2.9). However, some other pseudonyms are difficult. Consider 'N. Bourbaki'. It is the name under which several French mathematicians publish their work. There is, I believe, much doubt as to whether there existed one man named 'Homer' who was the author of the *Iliad*. We might suspect that the situation here is somewhat like that with 'N. Bourbaki'.

A pseudonym like 'N. Bourbaki' does not seem to fit the account I have given. It seems to be an empty name, yet we use it as if it were nonempty.

Consider the statement,

(15) N. Bourbaki has made great mathematical advances.

We want to say this is literally true: there seems to be no fiction operator implicit. However, perhaps there is some pretense here: perhaps it is pretended that one person did what, in fact, many did. Thus, (15) is true if and only if the many who publish under 'N. Bourbaki', according to the pretense that they are one, have made greater mathematical advances. [Note that (15) does *not* require for its truth that any *one* of the persons in question made great mathematical advances but simply that, *as a whole*, the group did.]

Another way of treating (15) seems more plausible. We take 'N. Bourbaki' not as an empty name but as *the name of a group*, the group of mathematicians using the name. In this way the name would be comparable to 'The Australian team' in

(16) The Australian team lost to New Zealand in the hockey finals.

This interpretation of (15) has the advantage of raising no special semantic problem: group names function like other names. How-

186 Empty Terms

ever, there is a problem, for what is a group? It is not a set: it was no abstract object that lost to New Zealand. Nor is it a mere heap: what lost the match had to be an organized group of people. Once again we have struck a problem we must set aside.

6.8 Singular Existence Statements

Consider the truth conditions of the singular existence statements: ⌜e_1 exists⌝ and ⌜e_1 does not exist⌝. There is no problem in following our usual practice (3.1) of stating these conditions in terms of the referential properties of words. The rough idea is that ⌜e_1 exists⌝ is true if and only if e_1 designates or denotes, and ⌜e_1 does not exist⌝ is true if and only if e_1 does not. However, we can state the conditions much more precisely, even taking account of partial designation, by simply adding an axiom to TC* as set forth in 5.8:

> (B)* 5. If e_1 is a singular term, then ⌜e_1 exists⌝ is m-true$_s$ if and only if there is an object a to which e_1 m-refers$_s$.

'Refers' here covers all the modes of reference of singular terms. ⌜e_1 does not exist⌝ is dealt with, of course, by the negation axiom (B)* 2.

In thinking that we need to *add* an axiom here, I am implicitly conceding that 'exists' is not a predicate. If we treat it as a predicate, albeit one that applies to everything, TC* will handle singular existence statements as it stands, for it includes the following:

> (B)* 1. If e_1 is a singular term and e_2 is a predicate, then ⌜$e_2(e_1)$⌝ is m-true$_s$ if and only if (i) there is an object a to which e_1 m-refers$_s$ and (ii) e_2 m-applies to a.

At this level, at least, the difference between the two views of 'exists' is "merely verbal."

These remarks do not, of course, offer "an analysis" of ⌜e_1 exists⌝ in the sense of a synonym or translation of it. I see no prospect of an informative one, any more than I can see one for an ordinary predication like 'Nana is a cat'. However, in each case we can *explain* the semantics of the sentence. Why do we need "an analysis"?

Hankering after "an analysis" may well go with finding the following plausible:

If e_1 is a proper name, then ⌜e_1 does not exist⌝ can be meaningful only if e_1 refers.[14]

The plausibility of this assumption stems, I suppose, from an oversimple application of the Fregean functionality principle. The Russellian way of removing that plausibility was to offer "an analysis" showing that ⌜e_1 does not exist⌝ means the same as another statement that does not seem to require that e_1 refers (1.2). I am suggesting another way. Names can be introduced in naming ceremonies that fail, or in fiction. Such names do not refer; nevertheless, they have mechanisms of reference ("are meaningful") and can contribute to the truth conditions of sentences in many ways, some of which I have indicated (I will discuss further ways in chapters 9 and 10). Many of these sentences can be true in perfectly explicable ways, as we have seen. Negative existentials are among these. Perhaps some ordinary negative predications are, too; perhaps these are true when the scope of the negation is wide and the name empty (6.6). There is no special puzzle here.

The Russellian way of treating singular existence statements was, of course, part of a description theory of names (1.2). A consequence of the refutation of description theories (1.5) is that all such views of singular existence are mistaken. Thus, when we are investigating whether or not Jonah existed, we are *not* investigating whether a certain associated description, or a substantial part of it, is true of one man. Jonah may have existed and yet not have had those properties; someone with those properties may have existed and yet not have been Jonah.

Consider briefly now such predicates as 'exists in fiction', 'is fictitious', and 'is a fictional character'. Clearly, for predications using such predicates to be true, the singular term in question must have underlying it a causal network arising out of fiction. If the predicate is 'exists in *Tom Jones*', then the network must arise out of that work. And there are other predicates that can be similarly treated.

To conclude, empty terms and the institutions associated with them can be accommodated within the theory of designation offered here.

Chapter Seven
OTHER TERMS

I have argued for a causal theory of designation; the mechanism of identifying reference for many singular terms is, I claim, a causal network of the sort I have begun to describe. Designation is only one mode of reference. some singular terms, notably definite descriptions, have other modes. So do the terms in other grammatical categories. My suggestion is that we should seek causal theories for these other modes of reference. In this chapter I shall expand on this suggestion. My remarks will be only programmatic; they do not pretend to be a full-blown theory.

7.1 "Observational" Natural-Kind Terms

Natural-kind terms stand for natural kinds. "Observational" terms stand for things that can be perceived. So the terms that are the concern of this section are those like 'tiger' and 'raven' that stand for certain kinds of *object*, and those like 'water' and 'gold' that stand for certain kinds of *stuff*. The former are general terms; the latter mass terms. I put the word 'observational' in "scare-quotes" because I do not give the distinction between observational and theoretical terms the epistemic and semantic significance that the positivists (and others) have given it. Nevertheless, the distinction has some theoretical significance for my sort of causal theory, as we shall see.

Saul Kripke has again shown the way for observational natural-kind words (1972:particularly 314–331). A similar view has been

190 *Other Terms*

urged by Hilary Putnam (1975:196-290). Drawing on these views, I suggest a theory along the following lines: Each use of a general term (of this sort) is linked to each object in its extension in virtue of the fact that the object is the same sort of object as the ones involved in the causal network underlying that use, the ones in which the network is grounded. Two objects are of the same sort if they have the same sort of internal structure. The involvement of objects comes from their being perceived. The causal network grows as the word is passed from person to person (reference borrowing).

The account of a grounding is similar to the one for singular terms in 5.2. It consists in a person coming to have a "grounding thought" as a result of the act of perceiving the object. The appropriate grounding thought for, say, 'cat', includes a demonstrative representation of the object perceived and a mental representation of the semantic type 'cat'. An example is a thought that might be expressed, "That is a cat." It is in virtue of the causal link to that particular cat that the term 'cat' appearing in the thought is grounded in cats.

Baptisms constitute the first grounding for a term: "Let's call animals of this sort 'grugrus'." Usually, however, these groundings are only the first among many: terms are typically *multiply* grounded in objects of the appropriate sort. This sort of multiple grounding differs from that for names. When all is going well for a name, it has underlying it a network multiply grounded in that there are *many groundings in the one object* (2.8). When all is going well for a natural-kind general term, it is likely to have underlying it a network multiply grounded in that there are *groundings in many objects of the one kind*.

When do two objects have the same sort of internal structure? The objects that form a natural kind are grouped together initially because of their perceptible similarities which are thought to have a common explanation in terms of underlying mechanisms. If the grouping is right, there must be something common to their internal structure that makes them all look and behave alike. Objects have the same sort of internal structure if they have a structure with that property, the property that is explanatorily significant.

Internal structures alone do not explain superficial properties: change the diet or the climate or, more broadly, the environment (including that before birth), and the superficial characteristics may change. A relatively insignificant change in the "normal" life of a tiger can make it three-legged. However, the characteristics of an abnormal member of a kind are explained just as much by its having an internal structure with the appropriate property as are the characteristics of a normal member. In both cases the explanation is in terms of that structure together with features of the environment.

Our talk so far has been of general terms. A similar story is told of mass terms. Each use of a mass term (of this sort) is linked to all the stuff in its extension in virtue of the fact that each bit of stuff is of the same sort as the bits involved in the causal network underlying that use, the bits in which the network is grounded. Two bits of stuff are of the same sort if they have the same sort of internal structure. The involvement of bits comes from their being perceived. The causal network grows as the word is passed from person to person (reference borrowing).

The theories outlined in this section are clearly restricted to observational terms, for they require perception of the object in a grounding. I shall consider what difference it makes if this requirement cannot be met, in 7.4.

7.2 Mistakes and Reference Change

Arthur Fine (1975: part 4) has criticized Putnam's causal theory of natural-kind terms on the ground that it makes reference change *impossible*: reference is independent of theory and so can't change with theory. This "trouble at Harvard" arises in the following way: A term is attached to its object at an act of introduction.

Thereafter, the term refers to that existent to which it was originally attached. (Fine 1975:23)

When we trace back our use of a term to fix its referent, we always arrive at the historical act of its introduction. That act cannot change. So reference cannot change.

There does seem to be reason to suppose that Putnam is too conservative about reference change (Putnam 1975:197). This conservatism seems to arise, however, not from his commitment to a causal theory but from his commitment to his Principle of Benefit of Doubt (1975:281), a principle I shall not adopt. A straightforward causal theory is open to Fine's objection only if it overlooks the fact that terms are *multiply grounded* in objects. The theory must not give all the responsibility for grounding a network to a baptism. If it does not, then it can hope to explain reference change by finding *changes in the pattern of groundings over time*.[1]

Consideration of some mistakes with natural-kind terms shows that it will not be easy to fulfill this hope, nevertheless. Suppose that the network for a natural-kind term, say, 'grugru', has been grounded in objects which our best scientific theory now tells us to be of two different kinds; so there are two different sorts of underlying structure that explain the common characteristics that led us to call all those objects at some time "grugrus." Situations of this sort must be common. What are the consequences of it for the referential properties of 'grugru'?

Two possibilities immediately occur. First, we might conclude that objects of only one of the two kinds were "really grugrus"; the other objects were wrongly classified in that way: they were "really mumus," perhaps a newly discovered species, perhaps an old one. To conclude this is to treat the groundings in these other objects as mistakes having no effect on the referential properties of 'grugru'. Sentences containing the term will depend for their truth values on the objects of the kind we now consider grugrus.

Second, we might conclude that the reference of 'grugru' has *changed* from the one kind of object to the other: once we applied it to objects of one kind; now we apply it to objects of the other. We conclude this because we have found a change in the pattern of groundings away from one kind of object toward the other, as we suggested above. As a result of this conclusion, we will think that sentences containing the term before the change depend for their truth values on the objects of one kind, and sentences using the term after the change on objects of the other kind.

This suggests a third possibility. if the reference change is made deliberately, we can expect it to take place immediately: before time t all groundings were in objects of the one kind and so reference was to those; after t, groundings were in objects of the other kind and so reference was to those. However, suppose that the change is not made deliberately: it takes place because of a gradual change in the pattern of groundings. Perhaps up to a certain time t all groundings were in one kind of object and after another time t' they were all in the other kind of object, but in the period between t and t' they were in both kinds of objects. What are we to say of the referential properties of 'grugru' during that period of change, the period of muddle? Perhaps what we should say, guided by our earlier discussion of names (5.4), is that during that time 'grugru' *partially referred* to both kinds of objects. In that case, sentences containing the term will depend for their truth values on the objects of both kinds.

We can vary this third possibility slightly by putting our moment of awareness of muddled groundings during the period when the muddle is still occurring: *we discover* that what had been thought up to that moment to be one kind is in fact two. Our view of the referential properties of the term during the muddle is, presumably, as before: it partially refers to both kinds of object.

In this case we face a decision. Having discovered the muddle we cannot allow it to continue, but there are various ways in which we could clear it up. Each constitutes a reference change. We might decide to reserve the term 'grugru' for one of the kinds and call the other 'mumu'. And, of course, we might do this in one of two ways. Or we might decide to drop the term 'grugru' altogether and introduce two new terms. Our choice here seems largely, if not entirely, arbitrary.

This variant suggests a fourth possibility. In Australia there are a number of different species of tree having the term 'tea-tree' as part of their common name, for example, 'coast tea-tree', 'woolly tea-tree', 'common tea-tree', and one called simply 'tea-tree'. All of these species except the last mentioned are members of the genus *Leptospermum*; the last mentioned is a member of the genus *Melaleuca*: it is *Melaleuca ericifolia*. Now, given that *all* species of *Leptospermum* have been commonly called "tea-trees" but *only one* species of *Melaleuca* has been so called, we are inclined to say either that "only *Leptospermum* species are really tea-trees"—*Melaleuca ericifolia* was *wrongly* classified in that way (the first possibility above)—or that the term 'tea-tree' partially referred to both *Leptospermum* and *Melaleuca ericifolia* (third possibility). And given knowledge of these facts about what have been called "tea-trees," we would not expect the term to continue to be applied to trees from two different genera; at least we would not expect this if 'tea-tree' were a natural-kind term covered by our theory. The difficulty is that *'tea-tree' is still applied to both sorts of trees* years after we gained knowledge of these facts. It seems hard to deny that the term refers (fully) now (as always?) to *both* kinds of trees and hence is not a term covered by the theory at all. Perhaps we should say that, despite appearances, it is not a natural-kind term at all.

The differences between the first, third, and fourth possibilities can be brought out by considering the truth value of the statement,

"This is a tea-tree," said of a *Melaleuca ericifolia*. According to the first possible conclusion, the statement is *false* because the object indicated is not a *Leptospermum*. According to the third, the statement is *partially true and partially false* because the object is a *Melaleuca ericifolia* but is not a *Leptospermum*. According to the fourth, the statement is *true* because the object is either a *Leptospermum* or a *Melaleuca ericifolia*. The reason that it is hard to deny the reality of the fourth possibility is that, intuitively, the truth value it yields is the correct one.

There is no surprise in discovering that there are terms which my outline of a theory does not fit. It is a theory for natural-kind terms, which obviously won't fit a term like 'bachelor', for example. What may be a little surprising is that there are terms which seem to be so much like paradigms for the theory such as 'tiger', and yet the theory does not fit them. With 'tiger' our use depends on the scientific facts about underlying structures, whereas with 'tea-tree' it does not.

It can be seen then that the problem of reference change raised by Fine is part of a larger problem. A causal theory of natural-kind terms must distinguish each of these four possibilities (and very likely others) and explain the first three. This is not the place to attempt to solve this larger problem, but there is no reason to suppose it is insoluble.

7.3 Knowledge of "Meaning"

Assuming that this outline of a theory is correct, what is "the meaning" of a natural-kind term? I suspect that it would be sufficient for our theoretical purposes to define only a notion of *synonymy* (cf. 5.5 on names). However, suppose we do need to talk of "the meaning" of a term here; what would it be? It would be the relevant sort of internal structure together with the causal network by which it is presented. That seems sufficient to accommodate the truth conditional, epistemic, and conceptual role phenomena. How then would we *tell* what a term means? It would be a judgment involving many theories.

Take as an example a particular token of 'grugru'. Central to judging its meaning is judging what it refers to. Which objects are there that *could* be referred to by that token? This is an ontological question requiring scientific and philosophical theories to answer. Insofar as it concerns living things, it is, in particular, a biological question. A decision about the meaning of our particular token of 'grugru' will require knowledge of the causal network underlying it, a matter of history and psycholinguistics. We must determine *which* of the objects it is grounded in. Then we must determine what sort of internal structure those objects have, a further matter of biology.

If this is so, then most of the people who use a natural-kind term quite successfully, who understand it, do not know much about its "meaning." Such semantic propositional knowledge as they have does not constitute their understanding of the term. That understanding is a skill or ability which they have in virtue of being correctly linked into the causal network for the term. The view here is like that for names (5.1) and reflects my stand on the psychological reality of language (4.4–4.5).

Just how ignorant can someone be and yet still succeed in referring with a natural-kind term? Certainly the person must have caught on to the syntactical role of the term. Perhaps something more is required, but I suspect not much more. Our theory suggests an answer to this question like the one given earlier for the analogous question about names (2.3). Consider my use of 'echidna'. Until recently I knew next to nothing about echidnas and could certainly not pick one out in a crowd. Yet, given my place in the causal network for 'echidna', there seems to be no reason to deny that I could make true or false statements about them, ask questions about them, give orders about them, and so forth, all the time using 'echidna'.

Just as description theories of names are rejected partly because we may not have the required knowledge of the objects referred to, so also are "description theories" of natural-kind terms, for these theories claim that the extension of such a term is fixed by the descriptions associated with it.

It may be felt that I have gone too far in my move away from description theories. "We would not say that you knew the meaning of 'echidna'." Interestingly enough, that would be the opinion of one causal theorist, Hilary Putnam. He rejects description theories in that he thinks it is not "analytic" that tigers are striped; he thinks reference is determined not by associated descriptions but by causal links. Nevertheless, he claims that the set of descriptions (or properties) commonly associated with a term, what he calls "the stereotype," is *part of the meaning* of the term and that knowing the meaning requires knowing the stereotype. A person who does not know the stereotype for 'echidna' would *not* succeed in referring to echidnas with it (Putnam 1975, esp. pp 148, 205-6, 246-52).

What are the phenomena leading Putnam to his conclusion? First, there is "what we would say," as illustrated above. Second, he claims that we wouldn't think there was any point in using a term to someone who did not know the appropriate stereotype. Third, if we want to teach someone a term nonostensively, we tell him the stereotype. In my view these phenomena are better explained quite independently of our semantic theory.

These phenomena are undoubtedly linguistic and so there is a *prima facie* suitability in using a notion of meaning to talk about them and in including such talk in a semantic theory. Nevertheless, they seem to me best explained *pragmatically*. It is easy to slip into "merely verbal" issues here about what you *call* "meaning" and what you *call* "semantics" (4.1, 5.5). In my usage, pragmatic linguistic phenomena are those linguistic phenomena left unexplained after semantic theory has ceased. And semantic theory is the theory that commands the center of the stage in explaining linguistic phenomena. (So there is no "theory-neutral" way of settling disagreements here.) I have given the main role to *truth, reference*, and the mechanisms of reference, in that theory (3.1). If I am right in that, then the issue here becomes whether Putnam's phenomena are best explained within that theory by adding the notion of *stereotype* to it or best explained elsewhere. The addition not only is inelegant but also forces an otherwise unmotivated modification in the theory: my use of 'echidna' no longer refers. So it seems to me that we need powerful reasons for making the addition. Putnam does not supply them.

Consider "what we would say." I have discussed a similar point before and have made two sorts of response. First, I have emphasized how "what we would say" about semantic questions reflects folk semantic theory and so cannot be accepted uncritically (4.1). Second, I have pointed out that what we would say may indicate what we would regard as *good evidence* of knowing the meaning (4.5). The present discussion suggests an addition to the first point. It may be that there is a perfectly acceptable, though vague, ordinary notion of *knowing the meaning*, such that a person can be said to instantiate it with respect to a term only if he can produce the stereotype. From our theoretical perspective this notion is not semantic at all. (The mere fact that it involves *the word* 'meaning' certainly does not *show* that it is; cf. 5.5.) We have an interest in distinguishing those of our fellow English-speakers who have the basic information about echidnas from those who don't. One way of doing this is to say the former "know the meaning of 'echidna.'" Another way is to say they "know what echidnas are." The fact that there is this other way gives support to the idea that this is not a semantic matter.

The second phenomenon mentioned suggests why we have the above interest. Those who do not have the basic information about echidnas are simply not worth talking to using 'echidna'. However, this does not show that if we did talk to them, their contribution to the discussion would not be about echidnas. Whom it is worthwhile for x to talk to using y is *clearly* a question with many pragmatic aspects as well as a basic semantic one; note, for example, how much the answer depends on the value of x. There is no pressing need to make knowledge of the stereotype part of the semantic aspect.

The third phenomenon is explained accordingly. Teaching someone a term by giving him the stereotype is giving him the most basic and useful information about its extension, the sort of thing that would help him to recognize a member. However, it is not necessary to teach him this for him to use the term meaningfully. We have no need to see what is conveyed to him by the teacher as "the meaning" in any theoretically interesting sense.

I claim, therefore, that Putnam's phenomena can be explained, and are best explained, independently of our semantic theory. Whereas *truth* and *reference* are central to a theory of language, *stereotype* is peripheral. These disparate notions should not be lumped together. If they are kept apart, what we *call* "meaning" becomes a verbal question. However, if we call stereotypes "meanings," then *meaning* will not be a semantic notion.

7.4 "Theoretical" Natural-Kind Terms

The theory outlined in 7.1 will not serve for "theoretical" terms because they do not refer to perceptible parts of reality and so cannot be grounded by perception of those parts. The general term 'electron' is one such natural-kind term; another is 'electricity'—what Putnam calls "a physical magnitude term" (1975:198).

There are various views of the semantics of theoretical terms which commit the same error as description theories of names: they require the language-users to know too much about the referents of their terms (1.5). For example, terms are often introduced by descriptions, and so it is tempting to say that a term refers to whatever its introducing description fits. However, the people who introduce the term are often *wrong* about the entities they seem to be referring to, sometimes *very wrong*. A variant of this view, open to a similar objection, gives the task of determining reference to *all* the descriptions (not just the introducing one) that the theory associates with the term.[2] Another approach, analogous to "cluster" theories of names (1.3), claims that the term refers to whatever *best* fits its associated descriptions. But the theory may be so mistaken that the wrong objects best fit the associated descriptions; or perhaps there are no objects that are clearly the best fit, even though the term seems to refer.

It is worth remarking that, aside from the defect noted, these description theories, like those for names, suffer the defect of transferring the problem of linking language to the world onto the descriptions that are alleged to determine reference (4.9). How do *they* refer? Indeed, in what respect are they semantically any different from the terms whose reference they are supposed to determine?

The correct account of theoretical terms must allow for the fact that theories can be *wrong* and yet their terms still refer. Putnam wants to allow for this. He thinks, for example, that a term like 'electricity' can refer even though it may be introduced by something that *mis*describes electricity. How is that possible? Putnam claims that the term refers to electricity because the term's introducer *intended* that it do so (1975:200–202–77). Putnam offers a methodological maxim, "The Principle of Benefit of Doubt," to use in *judging* the introducer's intention, but says nothing about what *constitutes* that intention.[3] In virtue of what was it an intention to refer to electricity?

I suggest that we can hope to answer this question only by adapting the usual causal approach. That approach links a term causally to its referent via the perceptions of those in grounding situations (one of which will be the baptism). It is because of the special role of the referent itself in leading to the use of the term that speakers intend to refer to it and do refer to it. Our problem with a theoretical term is that its referent cannot be perceived.

We need some substitute for perception in our adaptation. However, not any old causal link will do: we do not want 'phlogiston' to refer to oxygen because it was in fact oxygen that caused people to come up with the phlogiston theory. Our substitute must be *very like* perception: quasi perception. I suggest that what we seek here is a relation consisting of an instrument "perceiving" the referent and our "reading" of the instrument: we are "perceiving the referent through the instrument." It would, of course, be difficult to fill out the details of this suggestion. I shall not attempt to do so.

According to this suggestion, then, what counts in fixing the referent of a theoretical term is what, in reality, *prompted* (in the required way) the theorists to conjoin it with various descriptions (*not* what those descriptions are true of). We have to be prepared for two eventualities. First, there may not be only one aspect of reality, one sort of thing, that prompted the use of the term; there may be several. However, by making use of the notion of *partial reference* (5.4), we can cope with this fact.[4] We take the term to partially refer to *each* of the sorts of object which prompted its use. The sorts may not all be tied for first place, of course: the term may refer to one sort *to a greater degree* than to another. Second, there may not be *any* aspect of reality that prompted the use of the term. We must conclude that the term is empty; for example, 'phlogiston'.

If the suggestion is correct, we should *judge* the referent of a term in the following way: Armed with our present best theory of that area of reality, we try to determine what aspects of that reality those who used the term were reacting to in using it; we examine the history. The most helpful evidence here will be the descriptions that the theory associated with the term. However, we will also be interested in the experimental situations, including the reports made of phenomena. We are interested not only in what the theorists said but also in what prompted them to say it. We may conclude that they were referring to x's, even though most of what they said about *x*'s was wrong. We may conclude this because it may be *the best explanation* for their saying those things. (*In general*, the best explanation *often* involves interpreting people uncharitably; see 4.8. So I do not agree with Putnam's "Principle of Benefit of Doubt.")

Nothing in this section should be taken to imply that *all* theoretical terms can be treated in the way suggested. The terms I have discussed are analogous to Donnellan's *referential* terms. Presumably there can be theoretical terms analogous to Donnellan's attributive terms. (Perhaps some of these can lay claim to being *natural-kind* terms, in which case my terminology would have to be modified.) Even some *names* seem to be both theoretical and attributive. Consider, for example, a name introduced for an unobserved planet that causes certain previously unexplained irregularities in the movement of other planets.

7.5 Other Terms

It has been clear from the start that not all terms can be given a straightforward causal semantics: the possibility of "attributive" theoretical terms reminds us of this. What our program suggests, however, is that, wherever it seems plausible, we should seek such a semantics. [Putnam has argued ingeniously that even artifact terms like 'pencil' and 'chair' can be treated causally (1975:242–45).] I shall conclude this chapter with a few words on those terms like 'bachelor' for which a causal theory in any way like those so far discussed would be quite unsuitable.

What our program suggests is that we should seek a theory for terms like 'bachelor' that shows their semantics to be tied *ultimately* to other terms which are to be explained causally along the suggested lines. Suppose that people are right in thinking that 'bachelor' "means" *adult unmarried human male*. Then one of the words it is tied to is the natural-kind term 'human', for which a causal theory seems promising. Perhaps 'adult' and 'male' are not too distant from a causal explanation. Clearly, a lot of work needs to be done before 'unmarried' can be explained causally: it will need to be tied to other terms.

If this approach to 'bachelor' is right, then there is a good deal of truth in description theories for such terms. Perhaps there is some also in the analyticity doctrine for them: the mechanisms of reference for 'bachelor' really are linked to those for the other four words. However, it seems unlikely that anything significant will remain of the closely related doctrine of *a priority*. The investigation of mechanisms of reference, "meanings," will be an empirical one like all others.

There can be no question of the immensity of the tasks mentioned in this chapter. We have only the beginnings of a causal theory for "observational" natural-kind terms. In particular, the theory does not tackle the problems of error and reference change. Those problems will also face a causal theory of "theoretical" natural-kind terms, and such a theory is not yet available. Finally, there is the vast problem of the many terms for which a straightforward causal theory seems quite inappropriate. Nevertheless, it seems to me that a program along the lines suggested here offers the best hope for the semantics of terms, the best hope of linking words to the world.

IV

Chapter Eight
MODAL CONTEXTS

A singular term in a modal context is troublesome. It seems often to be used there not "as a means simply of specifying its object, or purporting to, for the rest of the sentence to say something about"; it seems not to be in "purely referential position." If it is not, the context that gives rise to this is "referentially opaque." As a result we cannot "quantify into" that context.[1]

In 5.8 I considered the bearing of designation on truth for transparent contexts. Modal contexts seem to be opaque and hence not to fit that approach. In this chapter I shall consider the ways in which the truth conditions of (nonepistemic) modal statements depend on the referential properties, particularly designational ones, of the singular terms they contain. In the remaining two chapters of this part I continue the discussion of referential opacity by considering singular terms in propositional attitude contexts.

My discussion of modal contexts will be brief because the theory of designation has only a minor explanatory role here. However, my view of the differing semantic properties that singular terms have is important. And Kripke has made the discussion more necessary by associating causal theories of names with his popular idea that names are "rigid designators."

8.1 Substitutivity and Essentialism

The trouble associated with singular terms in modal contexts is indicated by failure of "the law of substitutivity of identity." The traditional example concerns the number 9: designated by '9', it seems true to say of it that it is necessarily greater than 5; designated by 'the number of planets', it does not. Some restriction on the law of substitutivity is called for. The position preceding 'is necessarily greater than 5' is not purely referential.

If the number 9 is an object, it is an abstract one. I am not concerned here with modes of referring to such objects. So let us consider another example of failure of substitutivity. Whereas

(1) Mary's husband is necessarily married

seems true,

(2) Joe is necessarily married

does not, even though Joe is Mary's husband. The position occupied by the singular terms is not purely referential. Because of this we cannot always quantify into modal contexts:

(3) ($\exists x$) (x is necessarily married)

is not true, even though (1) is.

For statements like (3) to be true, an object must have some of its properties "essentially." These properties are distinguished from the others which it has "accidentally."[2] The necessity in such cases as (3) is necessity *de re*. In contrast, the sort of necessity which makes (1) true is necessity *de dicto*. In the first case the necessity lies *in the object*; in the second, *in our way of speaking about the object*.[3]

It seems that each object has at least one property essentially, the property of being self-identical. But this is not an exciting *de re* necessity. Excitement comes with the suggestion that an object has other less trivial properties essentially. Kripke has gone against a common philosophical opinion in suggesting just this. He suggests, for example, that a person has such essential properties as coming from a certain sperm and egg, being human, being of a certain sex, and being of a certain race. Similarly, it is an essential property of a certain table that it is made from the material it is made from (Kripke 1972:268-69, 311-14). For the sake of argument I shall assume here that Kripke has made a doctrine of essentialism both intelligible and plausible. Necessity *de re* lies in the object and so it should make no difference to the truth value of a statement that asserts such a necessity how the object is referred to: substitutivity should hold. Necessity *de dicto*, on the other hand, lies in our way of speaking about the object; here we would expect failure of substitutivity. Thus, when we substituted 'Joe' for 'Mary's husband' in (1), we turned a truth into a falsehood. If this is so, our first task is to distinguish statements of *de dicto* modality from statements of *de re* modality.

8.2 Distinctions of Scope

It has often been noted that modal statements containing definite descriptions are syntactically ambiguous. They can be interpreted so that the scope of the modal operator is the whole sentence, or they can be interpreted so that its scope is only the predicate. In the first case the statement asserts a *de dicto* modality; in the second a *de re* one.

A statement like (1) naturally suggests the *de dicto* reading, for this reading makes it seem true. We can make this interpretation more obvious by paraphrasing (1):

(4) Necessarily, Mary's husband is married.

The necessity is thought to arise from the relationship between being a husband and being married. Some modal statements interpreted *de dicto* are quite uncontroversial. Thus,

(5) The shortest spy is necessarily a spy

is taken as true, the necessity arising from the tautology that a spy is a spy.

Both (1) and (5) can be interpreted, however, as statements of *de re* necessity. The following paraphrases emphasize these readings:

(6) The object which is in fact Mary's husband is necessarily married.
(7) The object which is in fact the shortest spy is necessarily a spy.

These statements will be false on any plausible essentialism: the properties of being married and of being a spy are not essential ones of any object.

Some statements turn out true on either reading:

(8) The heaviest fish is necessarily a fish

might be a statement of *de dicto* necessity true in virtue of the tautology that a fish is a fish, or it might be a statement of *de re* necessity true because being a fish is an essential property of any fish.

Distinctions of scope are important in understanding statements of the form,

(9) The F might not have been the G.

The following partial paraphrases bring out three possible interpretations of this ["partial" because (9) implies that the F is the G, whereas none of the paraphrases does]:

(10) It is not necessary that whatever is the one and only F is whatever is the one and only G;
(11) Whatever is the one and only F, it is not necessary that it is the one and only G;
(12) Whatever is the one and only F and whatever is the one and only G, it is not necessary that the former is the latter.

(10) is most naturally understood as denying a *de dicto* necessity. (11), on the other hand, suggests the denial of a *de re* necessity:

that being the one and only *G* is an essential property of a certain object. (12) seems to deny another *de re* necessity: given what (9) implies, that the *F* is the *G*, (12) seems to deny the essential self-identity of an object.

In sum, statements of *de dicto* and *de re* modality are distinguished by the scope of the modal operator. And the law of substitutivity of identity does not hold for any singular term inside that scope but does hold for one outside it (unless there is some other reason for the law not holding).

8.3 Rigid Designation

The ground so far has been familiar enough. I have not called on the theory of designation or on the discussion of singular terms that it prompted. Nevertheless, we shall see that they do have a bearing.

I have earlier claimed (5.5) that if '*a*' and '*b*' are designational names, then if *a* is *b*, *a* is necessarily *b*. So the statement

(13) *a* might not have been *b*

is false. It is false for the same reason that (12) is: it denies the essential self-identity of an object. What is striking about (13) is that distinctions of scope are irrelevant to understanding the statement. Unlike (9), it has only one interpretation.

Similarly, no question of scope arises for

(2) Joe is necessarily married:

ignoring the possibility that (2) deals with an epistemic possibility, it can only mean that Joe has the essential property of being married. (It was for this reason that the statement seemed obviously false.) In this respect (2) is strikingly different from (1), which has, we have just seen, both a *de dicto* and a *de re* interpretation.

It would seem then that whenever a name appears in a modal

statement, it must be taken as outside the scope of the modal operator. In contrast descriptions seem to lead to ambiguities of scope. What is the explanation for this?

At first sight it may seem that a popular distinction introduced by Kripke explains the difference. According to Kripke a name is a "rigid designator": it refers to the same object in each possible world (in which it refers at all). On the other hand, a description is a "nonrigid designator": it refers in each possible world to whatever fits the description (1972, esp. pp. 269-79). The explanation might seem to run as follows. Because descriptions are nonrigid, whenever one appears in a modal statement, the question arises whether the modality stems from the way the object picked out by the description in the actual world is in each possible world (*de re*), or from the way the description picks out an object in each possible world (*de dicto*). A similar question does not arise for a statement containing a name, however, because the name, being rigid, picks out the same object in each possible world. The statement can be concerned only with the modality stemming from that object, the object picked out in the actual world (*de re*).

We can use the theory of names to strengthen this explanation. In virtue of what is a name a rigid designator? Suppose we take 'name' here to refer to designational names only. Such a name designates whatever is causally linked to it in the appropriate way. It can only be causally linked to an object in the *actual* world. So it designates an object in another possible world simply in virtue of that object being *the same as* the object to which it is causally linked in the actual world. It is this that makes the name rigid.

In my view the above explanation in terms of rigid designation of the differing roles of singular terms is either spurious or false. The problem with it is that the notion of rigid designation is explained by the metaphor of "possible worlds." This metaphor typically gives an illusion of explanatory power and understanding where none exists (*pace* David Lewis). We must remove the metaphor. When we do, interest in rigid designation disappears.

If we look to Kripke for guidance here, we get the following account of rigidity: a term is rigid if it does not give rise to ambiguities of scope in modal contexts and nonrigid if it does. That is why names are rigid and descriptions are not.[4] But, of course, this makes the above explanation completely spurious: the distinction between rigid and nonrigid designators simply *labels* the differing roles of names and descriptions in modal contexts.

A more promising way of removing the metaphor is suggested by the attempt three paragraphs back to use the causal theory to explain rigid designation. Without the metaphor all we are left with is: a term is rigid if it is causally linked to an object in such a way as to designate it and nonrigid if it is not. Ignore empty terms (it is not clear how Kripke's distinction was intended to apply to them). The rigid/nonrigid distinction becomes the designational/attributive distinction. And the explanation for differing roles runs as follows: names do not give rise to ambiguities of scope because they are designational; descriptions do give rise to them because they are attributive.

We need not concern ourselves with the power of this explanation because it is simply false; at least it is simply false if I am correct in the earlier across-the-board distinction between designational and attributive singular term tokens (2.5-2.7). It is false because some designational terms are not names, and some of these, notably descriptions, *do* give rise to ambiguities of scope in modal contexts.

The designational/attributive distinction, hence the rigid/nonrigid distinction, has nothing to do with explaining the differing roles of singular terms in modal contexts.[5] The real reason that (designational) names do not give rise to ambiguities of scope here is that *they do not have any descriptive element logically associated with them* (5.8).[6] Descriptions, on the other hand, do have a descriptive element associated with them and so do give rise to ambiguities of scope. It is the descriptive element that generates *de dicto* necessities. Understood in my way the rigid/nonrigid distinction can seem to be explanatory here if we focus on the paradigm designational terms, names, and the paradigm attributive terms, descriptions. For, such names are rigid (in my sense)[7] and have no descriptive element, whereas such descriptions are nonrigid and have descriptive elements. However, if we focus on "imperfect" descriptions like 'the bachelor' (2.7), this illusion of explanation disappears. Such descriptions are typically designational and hence rigid, but they have a descriptive element: though typically no question of denotation arises for them, a question of application does. As a result they can generate *de dicto* necessities. The following might be truly said of a certain person in a corner:

(14) The bachelor is necessarily unmarried.

The necessity arises from the relationship between being a bachelor and being unmarried, just as the necessity in (1) arose from that between being a husband and being married.

Rigid designation does not help to explain the differences between singular terms in modal contexts, but the discussion of it has provided the broad outline of an explanation. I shall now fill out some details. At the same time, I shall consider the truth conditions of modal statements.

8.4 Truth Conditions

My explanation of the observed difference between names and descriptions in modal contexts is as follows: Most names are designational and so are not associated with descriptions in a way that *could* yield *de dicto* modalities. Any description is, of course, associated with a description (itself) in a way that can yield *de dicto* modalities. Therefore, questions of scope do not in general come up for names in modal contexts but always do for descriptions, whether attributive or designational.

In 5.8 (and 3.1) I gave a truth characterization for a simple language containing no opaque contexts. I shall not attempt to give a formal truth characterization for a language including 'necessarily'. However, there is interest in relating the present discussion informally to the earlier characterization.

Ignoring problems of partial designation, the basic idea was as follows. A predication containing a designational term was true if and only if there was an object which the term both designated and applied to and which had the specified property. (To get this conveniently general statement of truth conditions, I deemed a designational name to apply to everything.) On the other hand, a predication containing an attributive term was true if and only if there was an object which the term denoted and which had the specified property. These will work as well for statements of *de re* modality: it will make no difference that the specified property is one of *being necessarily F*. (Of course, there is a problem saying what such a property is and when an object has one, but that is the problem of essentialism not that of the role of singular terms.)

De dicto modalities do require special treatment, however. Consider (1) (construed *de dicto*), for example. It is true if and only if *both* 'Mary's husband is married' is true *and* it is necessarily the case that if 'Mary's husband' applies to anything, then 'married' applies to it. This requires, as it should, that the necessity arises out of a certain semantic relationship between the singular term and the predicate.

(1) contains an attributive description and is a paradigm *de dicto* truth. Assuming that 'Joe' is a designational name, (2) is a paradigm of a sentence that cannot yield a *de dicto* truth. It cannot yield that truth because 'Joe' applies to everything and so cannot yield the required semantic relationship with the predicate.

The approach to truth conditions for *de dicto* statements works well enough, therefore, for the paradigm cases. The more difficult cases concern on the one hand attributive names and on the other designational descriptions.

The approach has the consequence that *any* attributive term can yield *de dicto* truths. Thus, the following (understood *de dicto*) should seem true

(15) Necessarily, Jack the Ripper was a murderer:

'Jack the Ripper' is an attributive name that applies to any person who committed those infamous London murders (2.5), and thus yields the required relationship with the predicate 'murderer'. This result seems intuitively acceptable.[8]

We have observed that names differ from descriptions in modal contexts in not giving rise to scope ambiguities. However, some names—the attributive ones—do give rise to them. The reason that the question of scope hardly ever arises for names in practice is that we (rightly) nearly always construe names as designational.

Consider (14) next. It contains a designational description, 'the bachelor'. With our approach it would be true if both 'The bachelor is unmarried' is true and it is necessarily the case that if 'the bachelor' applies to anything, then 'unmarried' applies to it. The second conjunct raises no special problem but the first conjunct may. For 'The bachelor is unmarried' to be true, 'the bachelor' must both designate and apply to an object. Now suppose that the person we had in mind in the corner were not in fact a bachelor. The condition would not be met. So with our approach (14) would not be true. The truth of (14) depends not only on there being the required connection between 'the bachelor' and 'unmarried', but also on 'the bachelor' correctly making an identifying reference. The latter requirement seems to me appropriate, just as it was for the truth of the nonmodal 'The bachelor is unmarried'. However, intuitions in such cases depend very much on one's theory.

In conclusion, differences of scope distinguish *de dicto* statements from *de re* statements and settle which singular terms are subject to substitutivity. Many names do not lead to ambiguities of scope in modal contexts because they are not associated logically with a descriptive element: they designate but do not apply (except in the trivial sense; see 5.8).

Chapter Nine
CONTEXTS OF PROPOSITIONAL ATTITUDES (1)

A singular term in the context of a propositional attitude is also troublesome. Often it is not in purely referential position; the context is referentially opaque and cannot be quantified into.

In this chapter I shall offer a theory of the ways in which the truth conditions of statements attributing propositional attitudes ("attitude statements") depend on the referential properties of the designational terms they contain. The theory will draw on the earlier theory of designation. I shall take *belief* as my example of an attitude. In the next chapter I shall apply the theory to further problems and discuss some difficulties.

9.1 Background

Quine has noted that not all belief contexts are referentially opaque.

(1) a believes that b is F

can be so understood that it remains true on the substitution of 'c' for 'b' where $b = c$, even though a (being ignorant of the identity) would deny that 'c is F'. In this case the context passes the substitutivity test and so is referentially transparent. Once again we are faced with a syntactically ambiguous form of statement. To read (1) opaquely is to take 'b' as within the scope of the attitude verb; to read it transparently is to take it as not within that scope (cf. 8.2).

We have available to us various paraphrases of the transparently interpreted (1) which emphasize the purely referential role of '*b*'. I shall adopt one of these,

(2) *b* is such that *a* believes it (him, her) to be *F*.

So initially (until 9.6), I shall always use a sentence of this form to attribute transparent belief.

(1) can be used to attribute either transparent or opaque belief. Initially I shall follow Quine in adopting the convention of interpreting sentences of this ambiguous form opaquely.

The need for the distinction between transparent and opaque belief was brought home strongly to Quine by his observation that the following two statements are very different:

(3) Ralph believes that someone is a spy,
(4) Someone is such that Ralph believes him to be a spy.

For (3) to be true, Ralph has only to believe, as we all do, that there are spies. For (4) to be true, he must have picked out someone as a spy (Quine 1966:184).

This has been shown to conflict with another observation of Quine's. He remarked that "the kind of exportation" which leads from (1) (now construed opaquely) to (2) "should doubtless be viewed in general as implicative" (1966:188).

Suppose that Ralph is like most of us and so (3) is true. Believing that spies differ in height, he is likely to believe that one of them will be shorter than any other. If he does,

(5) Ralph believes that the shortest spy is a spy.

Supposing that there is in fact one shortest spy, by exportation (5) yields

(6) The shortest spy is such that Ralph believes him to be a spy,

which, under the same supposition, by existential generalization yields (4). So, from (3), with the help of very weak assumptions of a type commonly true, we have inferred the strikingly different and, if Ralph is like most of us, false (4). It would seem that some restriction must be placed on the rule of exportation.[1]

The problem is that exportation seems to be in order in most cases but cannot be allowed in all. Montgomery Furth suggested to David Kaplan

that a solution might lie in somehow picking out certain kinds of names as being required for exportation. (Kaplan 1968:193)

Kaplan resorts to "standard names" for abstract objects like numbers. These names enjoy "a certain intimacy" with their objects. For other objects he seeks

some other form of special intimacy between name and object which allows the former to go proxy for the latter in Ralph's cognitive state. (Kaplan 1968:197)

This search leads him to a theory which is one of the kinds to be considered in the next section.

Progress in stating the truth conditions of belief statements clearly involves coming to some view of exportation. It had seemed that the opaque (1) was true if *a* were in a condition disposing him to assert '*b* is *F*', and that in such circumstances the transparent (2) would be true because it simply required that *a* be in a condition disposing him to predicate '*F*' of *b* using *any one* of the many methods of referring to *b*. The case of the shortest spy has thrown all this into doubt.

9.2 Vividness and Knowing-Who

Kaplan restricts exportation to "vivid names" ('names' here covers descriptions). Rather than consider Kaplan's theory in particular, let us consider any theory of that type; that is, let us consider any theory that makes the legitimacy of exportation depend on the alleged believer *having a vivid and largely accurate picture of the object in question.* The picture will consist of the conglomeration of images, names and partial descriptions which [he] employs to bring [the object] before his mind. (Kaplan 1968:201)

I shall say that theories such as these have a *"vividness"* criterion for exportation.

Another solution that suggests itself is to allow exportation of '*b*' only if the alleged believer *knows who* (*what*) *b is*. In effect this is Jaakko Hintikka's solution, though his theory of belief contexts was offered before the discovery of the problem.[2] It has been adopted by many others.[3] I shall say that such a solution has a *"knowing-who"* criterion for exportation.

Both of these criteria are too restrictive. Their fault is similar to that of description theories of names. Just as a name may designate *b* even though the speaker knows little of *b*, so the exportation of '*b*' may be in order even though the alleged believer knows little of *b*: he may have almost no picture of *b* nor know who *b* is. The social custom that makes this possible is that of reference borrowing.

The exportation allows us to move from

(1) *a* believes that *b* is *F*

to

(2) *b* is such that *a* believes it to be *F*.

From (2) we can obtain by existential generalization:

(7) Something is such that *a* believes it to be *F*.

Existential generalization is not in question. So the exportation is in order for all and only those cases where (1) implies (7).

Consider some cases. Ralph, a detective, has arrested Jones for the murder of Smith. Alternatively, an arrest is imminent: Ralph has the name, address, and various details about Jones. Ralph believes that Jones is a murderer. And clearly someone is such that Ralph believes him to be a murderer; the exportation is in order. *Vividness* works well here: Ralph has a vivid enough picture of Jones. At first sight, *knowing-who* may also seem satisfactory: it seems that Ralph knows who Jones is. However, suppose that, unbeknown to Ralph, Jones is in fact the Prince of Wales or the famous double agent "5 Fingers." Ralph does not know who Jones is after all, yet the exportation is unaffected.

Knowing-who is an inadequate criterion for exportation right from the start. Both criteria fail when we take account of reference borrowing. Suppose Ralph tells Tom of the arrest of Jones. Or suppose that Tom reads of the imminent arrest of Jones in the newspaper. Tom has faith in Ralph and thus believes that Jones is a murderer. Clearly, someone is such that Tom believes him to be a murderer: once again the exportation is in order. Yet Tom has scarcely any picture of Jones and certainly doesn't know who Jones is: in order to protect his case, Ralph has released very little information.

I believe that Cicero denounced Catiline. So there is someone whom I believe to have been denounced by Cicero. Yet I have no picture of Catiline and don't know who he is. I turn on the radio in the middle of a talk. I express a belief by saying "That man's a good speaker." Someone is such that I believe him to be a good speaker, but again the two criteria are not met. Over the years Tom has heard Ortcutt mentioned by name on several occasions in circumstances which have led him to believe that Ortcutt is a spy. He remembers little else of Ortcutt. The criteria are not met, but the exportation is in order.

One or both of the criteria may not be met in cases built around the following where the exportations are in order. The only thing Tom believes of Gödel is that he proved the incompleteness of arithmetic. The only thing he believes of Einstein is that he invented the atomic bomb. Tom, a Fundamentalist, believes that Jonah was swallowed by a whale. Indeed, though Jonah may have existed, it is likely that all Tom's nontrivial beliefs about him are *completely mistaken*.

Counterexamples like these do not constitute a "knockdown" argument against the theories in question. What we need as well is a better theory of exportation. I shall offer one. In light of this we can see how exportation can be in order despite gross ignorance or error. *Vividness* and *knowing-who* are largely irrelevant to it.

9.3 Having-in-Mind

Think back to the case of the shortest spy. Why do we think that

(6) The shortest spy is such that Ralph believes him to be a spy

is false? I said that (4) required that Ralph has "picked someone out as a spy" (9.1). Similarly, (6) requires him to have picked the shortest spy out as a spy: *he must have that particular person in mind as a spy*. On the other hand, the opaque

(5) Ralph believes that the shortest spy is a spy

can be true even though Ralph does not have anyone particular in mind. Perhaps, then, the exportation of '*b*' in the move from the opaque (1) to the transparent (2) is in order *if a has b in mind*.

This conjecture is very plausible.[4] It is appropriate enough that we should be able to have beliefs *of* an object only if we have it in mind. However, the conjecture is too simple.

The conjecture immediately reminds us of the distinction between attributive and designational terms drawn intuitively in terms of *having-in-mind* (2.5). And that is the first indication that the conjecture is too simple. If that distinction is a real one, it must apply to the singular terms in attitude contexts just as it does to them in other contexts. So, in tackling the problem of exportation, we must consider not only what the alleged believer has in mind but also what *the speaker* has in mind, for whether or not the speaker has a particular object in mind determines whether '*b*' is designational or attributive. And the very plausi-

Contexts of Propositional Attitudes (1) 225

bility of the conjecture gives weight to the distinction and thus shows the conjecture to be too simple. According to the conjecture, we need to distinguish two cases where 'a believes that b is F' is true—one where a has b in mind and one where a does not. Similarly, then, we need to distinguish two cases where a's expression of belief, 'b is F', is true—one where a has b in mind and one where a does not; that is, we need to distinguish 'b' as a designational term from 'b' as an attributive term.

. My suggestion is that the notion of *having-in-mind*, including the distinction that it suggests, supplies the key to explaining the unusual behavior of singular terms in attitude contexts. This is an important argument for the semantic significance of the distinction (2.7).

Of course, in the absence of an explanation of *having-in-mind*, the plausible solution to our present problem in terms of it would seem theoretically unpromising. However, I have offered an explanation for it, at least insofar as it is associated with the use of singular terms. I shall make use of the explanation later.

What we need is a theory of the truth conditions of belief statements, including a theory of exportation, which combines application of the distinction between attributive and designational terms to the terms in those statements with our earlier two intuitions:

(i) That a transparent belief statement can be true only if the alleged believer has an appropriate object in mind.
(ii) That an opaque belief statement may have no such requirement.

I shall first state the central theses of the theory in an informal way, staying close to the ordinary way of expressing these intuitions. Later I shall offer a detailed and more formal treatment in which the talk of having-in-mind is removed: roughly, an alleged believer can have an appropriate object in mind if he has access to an appropriate d-chain.

The theory includes the following four theses:

T1. If '*b*' in (1) is designational and nonempty, then *a* must have *b* in mind for (1) to be true.
T2. If '*b*' in (1) is attributive, then *a* need not have *b* in mind for (1) to be true.
T3. *a* must have *b* in mind for (2) to be true (whether '*b*' is attributive or designational).
T4. The exportation of '*b*' involved in the inference from (1) to (2) is in order if and only if '*b*' in (1) is designational and nonempty.

T3 embodies intuition (i). T2 embodies (ii). T1 is the most dubious, but some such thesis seems necessary if the exportation is ever to be valid. T4 is largely a consequence of T1–T3. *It is my theory of exportation.* Whether '*b*' is attributive or designational determines the sort of truth conditions (1) and (2) have; in particular, it determines whether it is necessary for *a* to have *b* in mind for (1) to be true.

The proof of the pudding lies in the eating. I shall consider some examples. By starting with this informal version of the theory, I hope to bring out the theory's plausibility. As details and precision are added, it becomes harder to see the woods for the trees.

9.4 Paradigm Cases

Consider first the case which made apparent the need for some restriction on exportation—that of the shortest spy.

(5) Ralph believes that the shortest spy is a spy

is true. The description of the case makes it clear that Ralph may have nobody in mind as the shortest spy. Let us suppose that Kaplan is the speaker of (5). Then it is also clear enough that Kaplan has nobody in mind as the shortest spy either: 'the shortest spy' in (5) is attributive (T2).

(6) The shortest spy is such that Ralph believes him to be a spy

may well be false and is certainly not true simply on the strength of (5). (6) is a transparent belief statement and so requires for its truth that Ralph have someone in mind (T3). And it was precisely the absence of any reason for supposing he did that led to our doubts about exportation. The exportation does not hold in this case because 'the shortest spy' in (5) is attributive (T4). T2–T4 are confirmed.

Suppose that Ralph's remarks on examining Smith's body lead Tom, a bystander, to say

(8) Ralph believes that Smith's murderer is insane.

Tom does not have anyone picked out as the murderer and so 'Smith's murderer' is attributive. And Ralph is no better off than Tom. Although (8) is true,

(9) Smith's murderer is such that Ralph believes him to be insane

is not. So the exportation does not hold. Again T2–T4 are confirmed.

The theory prevents exportation in the paradigm cases of its failure, cases where neither speaker nor believer are so related to an object that they can have it in mind. The theory must allow exportation in the paradigm cases of its success. These commonly feature names.

Consider some earlier examples. Ralph has arrested Jones, believing that he is a murderer. Someone is such that Ralph believes him to be a murderer. Tom, who has faith in Ralph, hears of this and believes that Jones is a murderer. Someone is such that Tom believes him to be a murderer. I believe that Cicero denounced Catiline. So there is someone whom I believe to have been denounced by Cicero. And there are examples that can be built around beliefs associated with 'Ortcutt', 'Gödel', 'Einstein' and 'Jonah'. The names in those cases are all designational and nonempty. So the theory would allow the exportation as it should (T4). For the opaque belief statement to be true in each case, the believer should be in a position to express his belief *using the name in question*. If he did, he would have the object in question in mind. This provides evidence for T1.

Both T1 and T4 talk of the nonemptiness of '*b*'. The need for this stems from the fact, pointed out in 6.6, that 'Tom believes that . . . flies' is a predicate that "neither entails existence nor entails nonexistence." Whereas

(10) Pegasus flies,

taken as a literal statement about reality, is not true because 'Pegasus' is empty,

(11) Tom believes that Pegasus flies

may be as true as any belief statement: however wise the speaker is about Pegasus, *Tom* may believe that Pegasus exists. We shall consider how the theory handles this fact. (There is a tendency for writers on opacity to overlook the special problem posed by the appearance of empty terms in opaque contexts.)

If we are construing having-in-mind transparently, as we have said we should (2.4), Tom cannot have Pegasus in mind, for there is no such object as Pegasus. So, having Pegasus in mind cannot be necessary for the truth of (11). Yet 'Pegasus' is designational (6.5). Hence the need to talk of nonemptiness in T1: only if '*b*' is designational *and* nonempty is it necessary for *a* to have *b* in mind for (1) to be true. The need carries over to T4. For,

(12) Pegasus is such that Tom believes him to fly

taken literally can be no more true than (10); and according to T3 it won't be true because Tom cannot have Pegasus in mind. We must not be able to infer the untrue (12) from the possibly true (11). According to T4 we cannot: only a nonempty designational term can be exported.

So far as it goes, then, our theory handles empty singular terms satisfactorily: it prevents a paradigm case of exportation failure. Of course, we should like to know more about the role of empty terms in opaque contexts. How can (11) be true? That discussion must wait until we have dropped the informal talk of having-in-mind (9.8).

9.5 Other Cases

We have tested the theory against the paradigm cases of both successful and unsuccessful exportation. The former cases are those where both speaker and believer have an object in mind, and the latter cases are those where neither has one. Other cases where speaker and believer differ are not so intuitively clear.

Return to the case of Smith's murderer. Tom (the bystander) remarks, on the same evidence as before,

(8) Ralph believes that Smith's murderer is insane.

However, suppose that this remark is made some time after Ralph (the detective) has inspected the body and that by that time Ralph has, unbeknown to Tom, someone in mind as the murderer. Does

(9) Smith's murderer is such that Ralph believes him to be insane

follow from (8)? We would need to include the premise that 'Smith's murderer' was not empty, of course, but, according to the theory, even with that help we could not infer (9) from (8) because 'Smith's murderer' is attributive (T4). This is right. We might paraphrase (8) by

(13) Ralph believes that whoever murdered Smith is insane.

To infer (9) we need to know also at least what the description of the case told us—that Ralph has someone in mind as the murderer. In fact, we need something stronger—he must have the *right* person in mind (T3):

(14) Smith's murderer is such that Ralph has him in mind as Smith's murderer.

The discussion of this case so far confirms the claim made by T4 that exportation is only valid for designational terms. However, it may suggest that some addition to the theory is called for. Does (9) follow from (8) *and* (14)? According to the conjecture that began 9.3, a conjecture that I argued was too simple, it should. If it does, then we would need to add that, given the admittedly strong extra premise,

(15) *b* is such that *a* has it (him, her) in mind as *b*,

the exportation would be in order even where 'b' is attributive.

I suggest that (9) does not follow from (8) and (14) and so no addition to our theory is called for. It is at this point that our intuitions are not so clear (and mine are doubtless laden with the present theory). There is no doubt that if Ralph is *ordinarily rational* and if (8) and (14) are true, then (9) will be true. He has only to apply his general belief about the insanity of whoever murdered Smith to the particular person he has picked out as the murderer. The inference is so childishly simple that we can be certain he has made it, *but there is nothing in (8) and (14) that logically implies that he has made it*. People should accept all the logical consequences of their beliefs, but we have no guarantee that they have always done so and good reason to suppose that they sometimes haven't.

If this suggestion is correct, then the earlier simple conjecture must be mistaken. However, it cannot be said that the case above *shows* it to be mistaken. The case is not that clear. And we might add that the paradigm cases considered in 9.4 confirm the conjecture as much as the theory. This is no surprise, of course, for the theory is just a development of the conjecture (9.3).

In the above case, the speaker has nobody in mind but the believer has. Next, consider a case where the speaker has someone in mind but the believer has not; or so it seems on the surface, at least. We vary the situation following Smith's murder. The ghastly circumstances lead Tom to the view that whoever murdered Smith is insane. He has nobody in mind as the murderer. Ralph, however, has. On the basis of some muttered remarks by Tom, Ralph says,

(16) Tom believes that Smith's murderer is insane.

Is (16) true? Tom's readiness to affirm 'Smith's murderer is insane' gives a reason for thinking it is. 'Smith's murderer' here would be attributive, for Tom has nobody in mind. However, Ralph's use of the term in (16) seems to be designational.

If the term in (16) is indeed designational, then, according to T1, the answer to our question must be "no": (16) could be true only if Tom had Smith's murderer in mind. The importance of this answer can easily be seen. If it is wrong and (16) is true, then T4 must also be wrong, for it allows the inference from (16) to

(17) Smith's murderer is such that Tom believes him to be insane,

which is certainly false. The exportation of a designational term would not be a valid inference.

In the discussion of the previous case, we saw that if my treatment of it were rejected, we would have to add to T4: given the extra premise,

(15) *b* is such that *a* has it (him, her) in mind as *b*,

the inference from (1) to (2) would be in order even if '*b*' were attributive. Now we see that if the present case were to lead us to reject T1, we would need (15) to infer (2) from (1) *even if '*b*' were designational.*

I suggest that the case should not lead us to reject T1. I suggest that if Ralph, in asserting (16), has a particular person in mind as the object of Tom's belief, his assertion is *not* confirmed if all Tom can offer on the subject is a statement that we might paraphrase, 'Whoever murdered Smith is insane'. I further suggest that any discomfort we might feel about this arises from the fact that, even in the circumstances described, 'Smith's murderer' in (16) *may not be designational*. The circumstances are such that Ralph *can* use the term designationally, but this does not *compel* him to do so (2.7). He might still assert (16) so that it could be correctly paraphrased as

(18) Tom believes that whoever murdered Smith is insane,

which *is* true. In the circumstances in which (16) is true, exportation does not hold; where it does hold, (16) is false.

The plausibility of this claim can be increased by complicating the case. The weakness of the case as it stands is that it makes either interpretation of (16) likely enough. Suppose, on the one hand, we add the information that Ralph is aware of the basis of Tom's muttered remarks. In particular, he is aware that they arose simply from an observation of the scene of the crime and with nobody in mind as the murderer. In saying (16), Ralph might just as well have said (18); he is not attributing to Tom a belief of the person he (Ralph) has picked out as the murderer. 'Smith's murderer' is attributive; (16) is true.

Suppose, in contrast, that we add the following information: Ralph has arrested a man for the murder but has not yet identified him. As a result he uses the term 'Smith's murderer' to refer to him. Tom, knowing that Ralph is on the case but not that an arrest has been made, says to Ralph in passing, "Smith's murderer is insane." He has studied the scene independently of Ralph and thinks that this observation may help with an arrest. Ralph assumes, however, that Tom's view is based on a study of the arrested man. (Let us say that Tom is now a colleague of Ralph's.)

Later Ralph describes the unusual personality of Smith's murderer. He includes sentence (16). 'Smith's murderer' is then certainly designational. My claim is that (16) is false in these circumstances: Ralph is wrong about Tom's beliefs.

This is the best I can do to justify T1. I confess to being less than completely persuaded, and in 10.6 I shall consider a case that throws doubt on T1, indeed, on the whole theory. If T1 is correct, then we can allow the exportation of (nonempty) designational terms without restriction. If it is not, then nothing like a simple rule of exportation is ever valid. Indeed, the truth conditions of attitude statements may be left as obscure as ever. I shall assume that T1 is correct. A justification for this is that intuitions about the complicated phenomena of attitude statements are diverse, and there are few theories that even pretend to cover them all. In these circumstances the present theory is worth developing.

9.6 Logic

Before giving more detailed and formal statements of truth conditions, I shall briefly summarize the consequences of the theory for logic.

A logic that applies to attitude statements would have to distinguish in its notation between designational and attributive terms. From now on I shall use 'a', 'b', and 'c' as variables taking designational terms as their values; 'k' as a variable taking attributive terms; and 'F' as a variable taking predicates. The logic will need a special notation for attitude contexts which distinguishes the transparent from the opaque. I shall use a slash ('/') for this purpose as follows:

(19) a believes/b is F †

---

† The sentence token appearing in this line refers to ⌜a believes/b is F⌝. Similarly, all other displayed sentences contain expression variables.

illustrates the opaque form; so b is not in purely referential position.

(20) a believes b/it is F

illustrates the transparent form; so b is in purely referential position (We would need further notational devices to cope with the attribution of "multiplace beliefs," but I shall ignore such complications.)

The most significant feature of the logic would be that it must include a rule allowing the inference of (20) from (19) and

(21) b exists.

This is the rule that allows the exportation of a designational term (T4). [Of course, if the logic is "standard" in that it allows no empty singular terms, then (21) would not be needed. However, I am assuming the logic would be "free."]

Aside from this the logic must *prevent* all inferences to or from singular terms within the opaque context (following the slash). Thus,

(22) a believes/k is F

and

(23) k exists

do not entail

(24) a believes k/it is F;

attributive terms cannot be exported. And (19) and

(25) $b = c$

do not entail

(26) a believes/c is F;

there is a failure of substitutivity within opaque contexts.

(27) *a* believes/everything is *F*

does not entail (19); universal instantiation does not apply here. Ordinary substitutivity (restricted to what precedes the slash) covers the inference of

(28) *a* believes *c*/it is *F*

from (20) and (25). Similarly, ordinary existential generalization (restricted) covers the inference of

(29) *a* believes something/it is *F*

from (20). This, together with the previously allowed exportation, enables us to quantify into a belief context on the strength of the opaque (19). In contrast, we cannot quantify in on the strength of the opaque (22) because the exportation of '*k*' is not licensed.

This brief discussion suggests that a system of quantified logic for attitude contexts based on the theory may not be hard to construct. It would be interesting to compare such a system with recent systems of quantified epistemic logic. The form that these systems take has been greatly influenced by their attempt to give the notion of *knowing-who* a dominant role. The need for this comes, of course, from its supposed role in licensing exportation (9.2). This has led to some implausible features.[5] If the theory presented here is correct, we have no need for this notion in capturing the logic of "*knowing-that*" statements. Further, it seems that the notion cannot be simply captured in terms of *knowing-that*.

9.7 Truth Conditions: First Approximations

It is time to give a more detailed theory of the truth conditions of attitude statements, dropping the talk of having-in-mind. The theory in this section will be a first approximation; refinements and additions will be made in the next section.

Theories of these statements always face an ontological problem. What are the objects to which propositional attitudes are taken? What are the objects of belief, hope, desire, and so forth? I have already taken a stand on this question. Initially I claimed that the objects were sentences in the language of thought, usually the public language of the thinker (3.2). As it stands this is a *relational* account of attitudes: attitudes are relations between people and semantic sentence types (cf. "propositions"). Of course, what I already had in mind is that these relations hold in virtue of relations between people and *tokens*. We shall return to this point. Meanwhile it is worth bringing out the similarities between this account and Frege's.

For Frege the objects of belief are *senses*. 'Cicero is an orator' in

(30) Tom believes/Cicero is an orator

does not have its "normal" referent: it refers to its normal sense. Furthermore, each part of it refers to its normal sense, thus preserving Frege's functionality principle (6.3) ("On Sense and Reference," 1952). So 'Cicero' in (30) refers to a sense. A difficulty for this Fregean treatment, as Kaplan points out (1968:185), is to say exactly what that sense is. We need a theory of sense. In effect what I have offered is such a theory. Frege claimed that the sense *contained* a mode of presentation. I say, roughly, that the sense *is* the mode of presentation, which is the type of d-chain we have described (5.1–5.2, 5.5). D-chains are the mechanisms of reference for names. Other terms have other mechanisms (chapter 7). We stay close to Frege, then, in taking the objects of propositional attitudes to be sentence types consisting of types of reference mechanisms.

However, this relational, Fregean account requires the reification of types. This is unnecessary (1.4). Whenever such a relation holds, it will be in virtue of a relation between a person and a token. And talk of tokens promises more understanding.

Suppose (30) is true. Tom will stand in a certain relationship to a token of 'Cicero is an orator' in his language of thought. Part of that token will be a token of 'Cicero', underlying which will be a mechanism consisting of d-chains[6] grounded in a certain ancient Roman (and not a famous spy called 'Cicero'); at least, it will be so grounded if we assume it was that object that *the speaker of (30)* meant by 'Cicero'. Therefore, underlying the token in thought of 'Cicero' will be d-chains that will be *part of the same causal network*, that will be of the same mode of presentation, as those underlying the speaker's token of 'Cicero'. Similarly, the mechanism of reference underlying Tom's token in thought of 'orator' will be appropriately related to the speaker's token of 'orator'. To say what would be appropriate here, we need theories of reference of the sort talked about in chapter 7; we shall say a little more about this in 9.8.

It is because Tom stands in that relationship to a sentence token of that type that we could say, if prepared to reify types, that he stands in a believing relationship to that type of token.

Daniel Dennett forced a qualification in the view that the objects of propositional attitudes were sentences in the language of thought, for most of the attitudes we have we never entertain. So if Tom's belief is not a "core-belief," there will be no token of 'Cicero is an orator' in his mind to which he stands in the appropriate relationship. Rather, he will be *disposed* to be so-related to a token of 'Cicero is an orator' by his core-beliefs (3.2). I must modify the statement of truth conditions of (30). What I have said applies only to core-beliefs.

If (30) is true but Tom does not have the required core-belief, then he will be in the appropriate relationship to *other* sentence tokens, some including 'Cicero' and some including 'orator', which would dispose him to be in that relationship to a token of 'Cicero is an orator' *were he to entertain one*; Cicero's being an orator is an obvious consequence for Tom of his core-beliefs. And the mechanisms for 'Cicero' and 'orator' in the disposing relationships will be related to those underlying the speaker's (30) in the ways already mentioned.

So if (30) is true, Tom will either stand in a certain relationship to a token of 'Cicero is an orator' or be disposed to stand in it. We can cover both alternatives by saying that he will stand in a certain relationship to a pair of token mechanisms of reference. One member of the pair is a mechanism appropriately related to the speaker's 'Cicero', and the other to his 'orator'. I shall adapt ordinary usage by saying that the relationship that Tom stands in to this pair of mechanisms, in virtue of which he *has* his belief, *is* the *believing relationship*. (This is an adaptation because if belief, in its ordinary sense, is a relationship at all, it is one that holds between people and *sentence types*, as we have seen.) I shall make a related adaptation of my semantic usage by saying that 'belief' *applies to* Tom and to that pair (in that order). [This is an adaptation because 'apply' was introduced for the relationship between predicates and the world (1.3). To take 'belief' as a (two-place) predicate would be to take it as expressing a relationship between people and sentence types.] The role of 'Cicero is an orator' in (30) is to refer to pairs of that sort. The role of 'Cicero' or 'orator' is to refer to mechanisms of the appropriate sort. Let us use the term 'specify' for these modes of reference. What 'Cicero is an orator' specifies in (30) is a function of what 'Cicero' and 'orator' specify; we have preserved the functionality principle.

This somewhat Fregean treatment makes some of my Quinean terminology seem inappropriate. For Quine, 'Cicero' is not in "purely referential position" in (30). For me it refers, but in an "abnormal" way. "Normally" it would designate Cicero, but here it specifies mechanisms of reference involving Cicero and 'Cicero'; it has, as Frege would say, indirect or oblique reference. I shall therefore drop the Quinean phrase. Similarly, Quine's metaphor "opaque" loses its point. Nevertheless, the term has

Contexts of Propositional Attitudes (1) 239

largely broken free of its metaphorical beginnings and is useful, so I shall retain it (and its opposite, "transparent").

The role of singular terms in opaque belief contexts has always presented a difficulty. On the one hand, if we take the singular term itself to be under discussion, the object drops out of the picture. Yet it seems relevant, most strikingly so when the term is "ambiguous." The statement seems to be "about" the object in some sense. On the other hand, if we attend only to the object, we lose the distinction between transparent and opaque belief. What is required is that a person have a belief about an object "under a certain name or description." Both singular term and object seem relevant to the truth conditions. The above account makes them both relevant: Tom's belief must involve a d-chain that concerns not only Cicero but also 'Cicero'.

T1 requires that Tom have Cicero in mind for (30) to be true. This he would have, for the relevant mental states would involve d-chains grounded in Cicero: it is in virtue of having access to such a d-chain that a person can have Cicero in mind (2.4).

I talk of d-chains being part of "the same causal network." Is anything more required for this than that they concern the same name and same object? The discussion suggests there is; they must be linked into networks arising from the same groundings (including the same naming ceremony or suitable substitute). And this seems intuitively correct here. Suppose that there are two distinct communities which never communicate with each other, both communities by chance giving the one name to an object. Could an opaque belief statement, including a name token arising from one naming, be confirmed by an expression of belief including a name token arising from the other? The situation is so unusual that we may have no clear pretheoretical intuitions about it. However, it does seem that if we are to preserve the *point* of opaque belief, we must rule that the statement is not confirmed by such an expression.

The case of the two communities raises the matter of the attribution of beliefs to those who speak another language. Names that travel across languages cause no problem. However, some names get distorted on the journey: 'London' becomes 'Londres'. We have, therefore, to be liberal about what to count as the same name. Nevertheless, this liberality cannot stretch to allow tokens which do not stem from networks with the same groundings to be the same. We cannot allow that foreigners who do not have even a distorted version of the name 'Everest' could believe (opaquely) that Everest is hard to climb. For if we allow that they could, how can we deny that (30) is true if Tom assents to 'Tully is an orator' but dissents from 'Cicero is an orator'?

Discomfort at this lack of liberality can be allayed by remembering that there are also transparent attributions of belief.

(31) Tom believes Cicero/he is an orator

can be true even though Tom does not have the name 'Cicero'. What is required is that he have appropriate core-beliefs involving d-chains grounded in Cicero: he must be able to designate Cicero *by some means or other* (T3). He must be in a believing relation to a pair of mechanisms, one of which is such a d-chain. (31) differs from (30) in being less specific about the mental state that Tom must be in.

How shall we go about stating the truth conditions of (31)? There are various alternatives. Given what we have said about (30), it seems appropriate to say that 'Cicero/he is an orator' "specifies" sets of mechanisms of the appropriate sorts. But then what are we to say of 'Cicero'? If we want to preserve the Fregean functionality principle, it seems we shall have to say that 'Cicero' refers to the mechanisms that may feature in the specified sets, that is, d-chains grounded in Cicero. This mode of reference is not the earlier one of specification, for 'Cicero' would specify only a subset of those d-chains, the ones that are in the same causal network as those underlying 'Cicero' itself. Nor is the mode *designation*, for Cicero himself is not a d-chain and does not feature in the specified sets. We would need a new semantic term to express this mode. We might say that 'Cicero' in the transparent context "t-specifies" the appropriate d-chains.

This terminology has the advantage of clearly preserving the Fregean functionality principle. However, another terminology seems to yield a more felicitous treatment. The customary thing to say about 'Cicero' in (31) is that it *refers to Cicero*, for substitutivity holds here. If we follow that custom in stating the truth conditions of (31), then we must go on to say that the d-chain that appears in the set specified by 'Cicero/he is an orator' *is one grounded in what 'Cicero' designates*. This treatment certainly accords with *some* functionality principle. It accords with the one I have stated before: that the truth conditions of a sentence should be a function of *the referential properties* of its parts (6.3). This *appears* less restrictive than the Fregean one: that the truth conditions of a sentence should be a function of *the referents* of its parts. However, the difference here is "merely verbal"; it is a matter of whether you *call* Cicero, or the d-chains grounded in Cicero, the referent of 'Cicero' in (31); both Cicero and the mechanisms exist and play their respective roles in the semantic theory whatever one says about this.[7] I shall follow the custom and take Cicero as the referent.

Let us now give a more formal statement of the truth conditions of (30) and (31). Ideally we would look for a formal truth characterization covering (30) and (31), like those in 3.1 and 5.8. However, I shall not be so ambitious. My aim is rather to prepare the ground for such a characterization. So I seek statements using my semantic terminology to *talk about* (30) and (31) and their parts; they will not contain translations of these parts, the model is

'Nana is a cat' is true if and only if
$(\exists x)($'Nana' $Des\ x\ \cdot$ 'cat' $App\ x)$,

where '*Des*' abbreviates 'designates' and '*App*' abbreviates 'applies to' (4.6).

As a first step we can say,

(30) is true if and only if
($\exists x$)($\exists y$)('Tom' *Des* x · 'Cicero is an orator' *Spec* y · 'believes' *App* x y),

where '*Spec*' abbreviates 'specifies'.

(31) is true if and only if
($\exists x$)($\exists y$)('Tom' *Des* x · 'Cicero/he is an orator' *Spec* y · 'believes' *App* x y).

The values of 'y' that will make (30) and (31) true are, of course, sets of mechanisms of reference.

Given what I have claimed about these sets, I can do better than this. As a second step I say,

(30) is true if and only if
($\exists x$)($\exists y$)($\exists z$)('Tom' *Des* x · 'Cicero' *Spec* y · 'orator' *Spec* z · 'believes' *App* x $\{y,z\}$).

So (30) is true if and only if there are x, y, and z, such that x is designated by 'Tom', y is a d-chain specified by 'Cicero', z is a mechanism of reference specified by 'orator', and 'believes' applies to x and $\{y,z\}$ (in that order).

(31) is true if and only if
($\exists x$)($\exists y$)($\exists z$)($\exists w$)('Tom' *Des* x · 'Cicero' *Des* y · z *Ground* y · 'orator' *Spec* w · 'believes' *App* x $\{z,w\}$),

where '*Ground*' abbreviates 'is grounded in'. So (31) is true if and only if there are x, y, z, and w, such that x is designated by 'Tom', y is designated by 'Cicero', z is a d-chain grounded in y, w is specified by 'orator', and 'believes' applies to x and $\{z,w\}$ (in that order).

Had I chosen the terminology for (31) that more clearly preserves Frege's principle, I would have come up with the following (equivalent) statement of truth conditions:

(31) is true if and only if
($\exists x$)($\exists y$)($\exists z$)('Tom' *Des* x · 'Cicero' *t-Spec* y · 'orator' *Spec* z · 'believes' *App* x {y,z}).

This statement is equivalent to the earlier one because of the way in which *t-Spec* is explained in terms of *Des* and *Ground*.

9.8 Truth Conditions: Refinements and Additions

The theory of truth conditions just given needs refinement and filling out.

(a) Consider first the problem of empty names. The transparent

(32) Tom believes Pegasus/it flies

raises no new problem. If we treat it like (31) it will not be true because 'Pegasus', though designational, does not designate. The opaque

(33) Tom believes/Pegasus flies

can similarly be treated like (30), but only if we have something more to say about specification.

We can sum up our discussion of specification for names as follows: A name in an opaque context specifies the d-chains in the same causal network as those underlying that name. These will be d-chains involving the name and its "normal" referent. Empty names like 'Pegasus' in (33) have no d-chains underlying them, so clearly some revision is needed if it is to be possible, as it should be, for (33) to be true (9.4). What underlies an empty name is a causal chain of a certain sort forming part of a network. The chain is not a d-chain because it is not grounded: it "arises out of" an imaginative act or the naming sentence in a failed ceremony (6.4). So a name in an opaque context specifies chains that may not be d-chains. However, all the chains are part of the one causal network; they arise out of the same source. I shall mostly overlook the possibility of terms being empty, speaking as if the chains specified must be d-chains.

(b) The statements of truth conditions for (30) and (31) treat the predicate 'orator' the same. For the sentences to be true, Tom must be in a believing relation to a set of mechanisms, including one specified by 'orator'. I said nothing about these mechanisms beyond a gesture toward the discussion in chapter 7. We should note now that our talk of specification overlooks a distinction. The situation for predicates in belief statements is analogous to that for singular terms. Just as a singular term can refer to its "normal" referent (if it is in a transparent context) or to certain mechanisms of reference (if it is in an opaque context), so also can a predicate refer to its "normal" referent or to certain mechanisms of reference. In the former case Tom could evidence his belief using a predicate *coextensive* with 'orator'; in the latter he must use one *cointensive* (synonymous) with 'orator'. Only in the latter case must Tom stand in a believing relationship to a set containing a mechanism *specified* by 'orator'. Our interest is in singular terms and so it will be convenient to continue to overlook this distinction, treating all cases like the latter one.

(c) The examples so far have all concerned names. Other designational terms can appear in belief statements.

Suppose that there has been a series of speakers at a meeting, one of them a politician. Someone says,

(34) Tom believes/the politician is an orator.

This would be true if Tom were in a believing relationship to a set of mechanisms of reference one of which would be a d-chain appropriately related to that underlying 'the politician' in (34). What is appropriate here? Clearly the two d-chains must be grounded in the politician. However, that is not sufficient because (34) is opaque. Suppose that the politician were Cicero. (34) would not be true if Tom's belief involved the name 'Cicero'. It must involve 'the politician' or some translation of that description. So 'the politician' in (34) specifies a d-chain grounded in Cicero and involving such a description.

Given this explanation of specification for designational descriptions, we could state the truth conditions for (34) in exactly the same way as we stated them for (30). And the transparent analogue of (34) can be treated like (31).

Suppose next that someone says,

(35) Tom believes that he is an orator.

Taking 'he' to be a deictic designational term, what possible interpretations does (35) have? One possibility is that 'he' plays the role of a reflexive pronoun referring to Tom. Such sentences require special treatment, and I shall set them aside until 10.3. Suppose that (35) is prompted by some observation Tom has made about the politician. It can obviously be construed transparently. Can it be construed opaquely? It seems not: there seems to be no way of construing it so that Tom must have his belief of the object "under a certain demonstrative," or anything of that sort. So (35) must be treated like (31). [If I am wrong about this and there is an opaque reading of (35), then we should have to say what, on that reading, 'he' specifies.]

Finally, the designational term in an opaque belief may be anaphoric. Such a term specifies whatever the term upon which it depends would specify were it in the place of the anaphoric term.

(d) The focus on beliefs that would be expressed by one-place predications has concealed from us the general need for the set of mechanisms in the believing relationship to be *ordered*. The need becomes apparent when we consider beliefs that would be expressed by multiplace predications. Consider, for example, the difference between

(36) Tom believes that Dick loves Harry,
(37) Tom believes that Harry loves Dick.

To catch this difference I state the truth conditions of (36) and (37), construed opaquely, along the following lines:

(36) is true if and only if
($\exists x$)($\exists y$)($\exists z$)($\exists w$)('Tom' *Des x* · 'Dick' *Spec y* · 'loves' *Spec z* · 'Harry' *Spec w* · 'believes' *App x* $\langle y,z,w \rangle$).

(e) In 9.6 I introduced expression variables, including '*a*' and '*b*', which ranged over designational terms. I can make use of these now to give general statements of truth conditions.

⌐*a* believes/*b* is *F*⌐ is true if and only if
($\exists x$)($\exists y$)($\exists z$)(*a Des x* · *b Spec y* · *F Spec z* · 'believes' *App x* $\langle y,z \rangle$).

['$\langle y,z \rangle$' reflects our new awareness of the general importance of order in the set of mechanisms. '*b Spec y*' is to be understood in the light of the discussion in (a) and (c).]

⌐*a* believes *b*/it is *F*⌐ is true if and only if
($\exists x$)($\exists y$)($\exists z$)($\exists w$)(*a Des x* · *b Des y* · *z Ground y* · *F Spec w* · 'believes' *App x* $\langle z,w \rangle$).

(Both these statements of truth conditions have been simplified by ignoring the requirement that a designational term in a transparent context must apply to the object it refers to: see 5.8.) In 10.1 I raise a doubt about these truth conditions for transparent belief statements.

I have explained the truth conditions of belief statements containing designational terms in terms of various referential properties of its parts using the semantic notions *Des*, *Ground*, *Spec*, and *App*. *Des* and *Ground* have been explained earlier in this work. I have used that explanation here to explain *Spec* for designational terms. *Spec* for other terms and *App* remain largely unexplained.

(f) The rule of *exportation* (T4) requires that from

(19) *a* believes/*b* is *F*

and

(21) *b* exists,

we can infer

(20) *a* believes *b*/it is *F*.

It can easily be seen that this does follow, given the above statements of truth conditions and those in 6.8 for (21). Given that *b* in (21) designates *x*, it follows that the mechanisms specified by *b* in (19) are grounded in *x* and hence that (20) is true.

(g) Where (20) is true, so also is

(29) *a* believes something/it is *F*.

We can *quantify in*. I need to state the truth conditions of (29):

⌜*a* believes something/it is *F*⌝ is true if and only if $(\exists x)(\exists y)(\exists z)(\exists w)(a \text{ Des } x \cdot z \text{ Ground } y \cdot F \text{ Spec } w \cdot$ 'believes' App $x \langle z,w \rangle)$.

Given these truth conditions, (29) clearly follows from (20): if *z* is grounded in what *b* designates, then there is something that *z* is grounded in.

(h) I have said nothing about belief statements containing *attributive* terms. In the absence of a theory of reference for these terms, I cannot say much. However, I can say something about their role in *transparent* statements. Consider

(38) Ralph believes Smith's murderer/he is insane

where 'Smith's murderer' is an attributive term. For this to be true, Ralph must have appropriate core-beliefs involving d-chains grounded in whoever murdered Smith (T3). The truth conditions here are analogous to those for (31) which contains a designational term. The only difference between the two cases is that in (31) the object that the believer must be able to designate is *designated* by the speaker, whereas in (38) it is *denoted* by the speaker.

Making use of the variable 'k' introduced in 9.6 for attributive terms, I can give a general statement of truth conditions for sentences of this sort.

⌜a believes k/it is F⌝ is true if and only if
$(\exists x)(\exists y)(\exists z)(\exists w)(a$ Des $x \cdot k$ Den $y \cdot z$ Ground $y \cdot F$ Spec w
$\cdot$ 'believes' App $x \langle z,w \rangle$),

where '*Den*' abbreviates 'denotes'.

The great difference in the role of attributive and designational terms in belief contexts comes with opaque belief (as the case of the shortest spy showed). Consider

(39) Ralph believes/Smith's murderer is insane.

For this to be true, Ralph would have to be in a believing relationship to what 'Smith's murderer is insane' specifies. What it specifies will depend on what mechanisms 'Smith's murderer' and 'insane' specify. I can say nothing about that beyond noting that the mechanism for 'Smith's murderer' will not be of the sort appropriate for having someone in mind as the murderer (T2); it will not be a d-chain.

(i) For two people to "share a belief" on the account offered here is for each of them to be in a believing relation to a set and for the two sets to be appropriately related to each other. This relationship will involve relationships between mechanisms in one set and the corresponding ones in the other.

Suppose that Tom were to express a belief, 'Cicero is an orator'. What would be required, so far as the singular term is concerned, for Ralph to share that belief? Would Ralph have to be in a believing relation to a d-chain in the same network as that underlying 'Cicero', or would it be sufficient for the d-chain to be simply grounded in Cicero? Must their beliefs concern not only the same object but also the same term? Must they share beliefs in the opaque sense, or is it sufficient to share them in the transparent sense? I suspect that there is no determinate answer to this question.

(j) At the beginning of this section, I discussed the role of empty designational terms in belief statements. Now consider this situation. A person, as wise as can be about Pegasus, wishes to attribute to Tom a belief about Pegasus, where Tom could show evidence of his belief using *any* designational term underlying which could be found a mechanism arising from the mythical character Pegasus: Tom could use 'Pegasus', 'the horse that sprang from the blood of Medusa', or whatever. It seems that the person might attribute this belief by

(11) Tom believes that Pegasus flies.

If so, *there is a third type of belief statement*—a type "between" transparent and opaque. Call it a "semi-opaque" belief statement.

(What goes for belief must go also for having-in-mind. So if Tom can believe opaquely and semi-opaquely that Pegasus flies, he can also have Pegasus in mind opaquely and semi-opaquely: cf. 6.5.)

A transparent attitude statement differs from an opaque one in two respects. First, the designational term in the attitude context cannot be empty if the transparent statement is to be true, but it can be if the opaque statement is to be true. Second, it does not matter to the truth of the transparent statement *which* designational term the person would use to show evidence of his attitude, but it does matter to the truth of the opaque statement. A semi-opaque attitude statement is like an opaque one in the first respect and a transparent one in the second.

For (11) to be true (read semi-opaquely), Tom must be in a believing relation to a set involving a mechanism that arises out of the same part of fiction as the mechanisms underlying the speaker's 'Pegasus'. Tom's belief need not be associated with the name 'Pegasus', but it must have the same "focus" as the speaker's use of that name. So if there is a semi-opaque reading of (11), we would need a new semantic term to state its truth conditions. We might say that 'Pegasus' in (11) on that reading "so-specifies" all mechanisms arising out of that part of fiction.

(k) I have taken the line that animals can have propositional attitudes to tokens in a language of thought, though that language is not of course a public language (3.2).

(40) Fido believes his master/he has come through the gate

may be true. (40) is a transparent statement, for it seems we can make no sense of attributing *opaque* belief, etc., to animals: the particular singular term used to refer to an object can make no difference where the believer uses no singular terms. The general statement of truth conditions works here. For (40) to be true, Fido must be in a believing relation to a set containing a mechanism grounded in his master. Fido must have a "mental representation" of his master.

Chapter Ten
CONTEXTS OF PROPOSITIONAL ATTITUDES (2)

In this chapter I shall develop the theory set out in the last chapter by applying it to some further problems: negative attitude statements (10.1), multiple attitude contexts (10.2), attributions of self-knowledge to others (10.3), opacity in certain verbs (10.4), and "intentional identity" (10.5). I conclude by considering some difficult cases for the theory (10.6).

10.1 Negative Attitude Statements

Quine noted an apparent paradox arising from the rule of exportation (1966:188-89). Consider his familiar story about Bernard J. Ortcutt (1966:185). We can express the situation described as follows:

(1) Ralph believes/the man in the brown hat is a spy;
(2) Ralph believes/the man seen at the beach is not a spy;
(3) The man in the brown hat = the man seen at the beach = Ortcutt.

From (1) we can infer by exportation:

(4) Ralph believes the man in the brown hat/he is a spy.

Hence, using (3),

(5) Ralph believes Ortcutt/he is a spy.

On the other hand, from (2) and (3) we obtain

(6) Ralph believes Ortcutt/he is not a spy.

Quine is not perturbed by this, for to hold (5) and (6) is not to hold

(7) Ralph believes Ortcutt/he is a spy and is not a spy.

My versions of the truth conditions of (5), (6), and (7) conform to Quine's intuitions. For (7) to be true, Ralph must be in a believing relation to a set containing mechanisms for a *contradictory* predicate. However, both (5) and (6) could be true without convicting Ralph of inconsistency: (5) might be true in virtue of Ralph's belief involving a d-chain associated with *one designational term for Ortcutt* ('the man seen at the beach'), while (6) might be true in virtue of his belief involving a d-chain associated with *another* ('the man in the brown hat'). Ralph might have these two beliefs because he does not realize that the man seen at the beach is the man in the brown hat.

This argument is plausible but not entirely convincing. I return to it at the end of the section.

There are clearly two interpretations of the scope of the 'not' in the ordinary opaque belief statement,

(8) Ralph does not believe that the man seen at the beach is a spy.

The more likely interpretation takes it as equivalent to (2). So understood it is an example of what the linguists call "negative raising." However, it can also be understood as denying that Ralph has a certain belief:

(9) Ralph does not believe/the man seen at the beach is a spy.

(9) is true if and only if
$(\exists x)\sim(\exists y)(\exists z)($'Ralph' $Des\ x \cdot$ 'the man seen at the beach' $Spec\ y \cdot$ 'spy' $Spec\ z \cdot$ 'believes' $App\ x\ \langle y,z\rangle)$.

Contexts of Propositional Attitudes (2) 253

So (9) would be true if Ralph had no notion of spyhood; or if he had never heard of the man seen at the beach or had never thought of him *as* the man seen at the beach; or if he had thought of him that way but not as a spy. [I have taken (9) to entail the existence of Ralph, but perhaps it is open to an interpretation that does not entail this; if so, the statement of truth conditions for that interpretation would begin with the '∼'; cf. 6.6.]

The transparent analogue of (9) is

(10) Ralph does not believe the man seen at the beach/he is a spy.

Given (3), we can infer from (10):

(11) Ralph does not believe Ortcutt/he is a spy.

David Kaplan has argued that

in the same sense in which [(6)] and [(5)] do not express an inconsistency on Ralph's part, neither should [(5)] and [(11)] express an inconsistency on ours. Indeed it seems natural to claim that [(11)] is a consequence of [(6)]. (1968:206)

This leads Kaplan to distinguish two "readings" of (11). On my treatment, the statement of truth conditions for one reading, $(11)_1$, is as follows:

$(11)_1$ is true if and only if
$(\exists x){\sim}(\exists y)(\exists z)(\exists w)($'Ralph' *Des* x · 'Ortcutt' *Des* y · z *Ground* y · 'spy' *Spec* w · 'believes' *App* $x \langle z,w \rangle)$.

The scope of the '∼' here is wide; compare the opaque (9) above. For the second reading, $(11)_2$, its scope is narrow. For reasons that will soon become apparent, we need to include in our statement for $(11)_2$ talk of Ralph *having access* ("*Acc*") to certain mechanisms of reference.

$(11)_2$ is true if and only if
$(\exists x)(\exists y)(\exists z)(\exists w)($'Ralph' *Des* x · 'Ortcutt' *Des* y · z *Ground* y · 'spy' *Spec* w · x *Acc* z w · ∼'believes' *App* $x \langle z,w \rangle)$.[1]

$(11)_1$ denies that Ralph believes spyhood of Ortcutt *under any designational term he has for him*; so it is inconsistent with (5), which is true on the strength of one such term, 'the man in the brown hat'. $(11)_2$, on the other hand, denies that Ralph believes spyhood of Ortcutt *under some designational term he has for him*; this is true on the strength of 'the man seen at the beach' and is not inconsistent with (5).

Talk of access to mechanisms is redundant with positive belief statements and negative ones like $(11)_1$; a person cannot have a belief involving a certain mechanism without having access to it; and if he does not have a belief involving any mechanism of a certain sort, he does not have a belief involving any mechanism of that sort to which he has access. However, talk of access is necessary for negative belief statements like $(11)_2$: if we dropped it, $(11)_2$ would be trivially true because it would be true if *anyone* had access to a d-chain grounded in Ortcutt and he, or someone else again, had the notion of spyhood.

Kaplan attempts to establish the need for the second reading by continuing Quine's story

to a later time at which Ralph's suspicions regarding even the man at the beach have begun to grow. Not that Ralph now proclaims that respected citizen to be a spy, but Ralph now suspends judgment as to the man's spyhood. (1968:207)

At this time (6) is false and $(11)_2$ is true. Kaplan suggests that something like $(11)_2$ is needed to express such suspensions of judgment.

This suggestion is a little strong, for $(11)_2$ does not come close to *expressing* such a suspension. However, the fact that there are these suspensions does show the need for the second reading: a suspension *implies* a second reading negative belief statement.[2]

An obvious defect of $(11)_2$ as an expression of suspension of judgment is that it does not imply any lack of belief that Ortcutt is *not* a spy. Indeed, assuming Ralph to be ordinarily rational,

$(11)_2$ will be true if under one designational term Ralph has for him he believes him not to be a spy; for example, if (2) is true.[3] This is to make a judgment, not suspend one.

A more serious defect is that $(11)_2$ does not imply that Ralph has ever considered the question of Ortcutt's spyhood. It simply requires that Ralph have a d-chain grounded in Ortcutt and a mechanism for 'spy', and not have a belief involving them. Yet, clearly, *to suspend judgment on a question, one must have considered it.*

We have, of course, an ordinary attitude verb available to express what Kaplan has shown we need here:

(12) Ortcutt is such that Ralph has suspended judgment on whether he is a spy.

The only question is whether what is needed can be adequately expressed using only the verb 'believes'. The above discussion suggests that it cannot. The best we can do is:

(13) Ortcutt is such that Ralph has considered whether he is a spy and neither believes he is nor believes he is not.

There seems to be no hope of analyzing consideration in terms of belief.[4]

Now (13) clearly implies that Ralph does not have certain beliefs. If we go along with the view that (11) has two readings, part of what is implied is $(11)_2$; there is no question of $(11)_1$ being implied. So I think Kaplan is right in claiming that his story shows the need for $(11)_2$. Kaplan does not consider how we might match up these "readings" with ordinary English sentences. Tentatively I would suggest that whereas

(14) It is not the case that Ortcutt is such that Ralph believes him to be a spy

expresses $(11)_1$,

(15) Ortcutt is such that Ralph does not believe him to be a spy

expresses (11)$_2$; on the other hand,

(16) Ralph does not believe of Ortcutt that he is a spy

is ambiguous between (11)$_1$ and (11)$_2$. However, perhaps there are no simple English negative belief statements that are unambiguous with respect to the scope of negation.

The discussion in this section raises a doubt about Quine's original intuition on exportation and the truth conditions of transparent belief statements. Quine's intuition was that we should, in general, be able to infer transparent belief from opaque belief (9.1). I have gone along with this, provided the exportation is restricted to designational terms. With this view, transparent belief requires belief *with respect to at least one designational term*. However, we may wonder whether transparent belief really requires uniform belief *with respect to all the designational terms the person has for the object*.[5] Call these "weak" and "strong" beliefs, respectively.

I have, of course, already given the truth conditions for a weak belief statement (9.8). Those for a strong one would be as follows:

⌜a believes b/it is F⌝ would be true if and only if ($\exists x$)($\exists y$)($\exists z$)($\exists w$)(a Des x · b Des y · z Ground y · F Spec w · 'believes' App x ⟨z,w⟩ · (v)(v Ground y · x Acc v ⊃ 'believes' App x ⟨v,w⟩)).

This differs from the earlier statement for weak belief only in having the final clause.

Suppose the Quinean intuition is correct and we wish to attribute strong belief. How could we ordinarily do so? It seems we must resort to something like the following:

(17) Ralph believes of Ortcutt under all the names and descriptions he has for him/he is a spy.

This is strangely clumsy if we have a need to attribute strong belief. And it seems that we do have that need. Let us continue

Quine's story still further: Ralph learns that the man seen at the beach = the man in the brown hat = Ortcutt and decides that *that man* is a spy; (17) is true. Since we have the need, we might wonder if the standard transparent forms meet it. If they do, of course, awkwardness will pervade our attempts to attribute weak belief, for example, to capture the earlier situations where it was only as the man in the brown hat that Ortcutt was under suspicion.

A reason for thinking the standard transparent forms do meet this need is the plausibility of the following claim: if a rational person has a belief of an individual that it has a certain property, then he does not believe of that individual that it does not have that property.[6] This claim can only be true, of course, if the transparent forms are construed strongly. Another reason would be given by any dissatisfaction we feel with Quine's calmness in the face of the apparent paradox of both (5) and (6) being true. The paradox would not arise if the transparent forms are construed strongly, because neither (5) nor (6) would be true. However, Quine's calmness did, and does, seem to have some basis. Furthermore, if the transparent form is construed strongly, it is hard to see how *any* negative belief statement could affirm, as for example, (14) seems to, that Ralph does not believe spyhood of Ortcutt under any designational term he has for him. Intuitions here are unclear. Perhaps the transparent form is ambiguous between weak and strong construals. Or perhaps it is vague so that there is no determinate matter of fact for which construal is appropriate.

I shall continue to interpret the transparent form weakly.

10.2 Multiple Attitude Contexts

Not only can I believe something, but I can believe that you believe something, and I can believe that you know that I suspect something, and so on; there can be multiple attitude contexts.

Consider double attitude contexts first. Let us restrict our attention to statements like

(18) Tom hopes that Ralph believes that Ortcutt is a spy,

in which each singular term is designational (and nonempty). How many interpretations does (18) have? Working the changes on the transparent/opaque (t/o) distinction, there seem to be six, which we might represent as follows:

(19) Tom hopes/Ralph believes/Ortcutt is a spy [oo^2];
(20) Tom hopes/Ralph believes Ortcutt/he is a spy [oo];
(21) Tom hopes Ortcutt/Ralph believes/he is a spy [ot];
(22) Tom hopes Ralph/he believes/Ortcutt is a spy [to^2];
(23) Tom hopes Ralph/he believes Ortcutt/he is a spy [to];
(24) Tom hopes Ralph and Ortcutt/the former believes/the latter is a spy [tt].

Suppose that there are indeed these six interpretations. We can extend our earlier theory to yield the following truth conditions:

(19) is true if and only if
($\exists x$)($\exists y$)($\exists z$)($\exists w$)('Tom' *Des* x · 'Ralph' *Spec* y · 'Ortcutt' *Spec* z · 'believes/ . . . is a spy' *Spec* w · 'hopes' *App* x $\langle y,z,w \rangle$).

So (19) is true if and only if there are x, y, z, and w, such that x is designated by 'Tom', y and z are d-chains specified by 'Ralph' and 'Ortcutt', respectively, w is a mechanism specified by 'believes/ . . . is a spy', and 'hopes' applies to x and $\langle y,z,w \rangle$ (in that order). Note that although it is necessary for *Tom* to have access to a d-chain grounded in Ortcutt for (19) to be true, it is not necessary for *Ralph* to: Tom's hope may be real but quite vain.

(20) is true if and only if
($\exists x$)($\exists y$)($\exists z$)($\exists w$)('Tom' *Des* x · 'Ralph' *Spec* y · 'Ortcutt' *Spec* z · 'believes . . . / . . . is a spy' *Spec* w · 'hopes' *App* x $\langle y,z,w \rangle$).

Contexts of Propositional Attitudes (2) 259

This differs from the statement for (19) only in the expression that specifies the mechanism w.

(21) is true if and only if
$(\exists x)(\exists y)(\exists z)\exists w)(\exists v)($'Tom' Des $x \cdot$ 'Ralph' Spec $y \cdot$ 'Ortcutt' Des $z \cdot w$ Ground $z \cdot$ 'believes/ . . . is a spy' Spec $v \cdot$ 'hopes' App $x \langle y,w,v\rangle)$.

(22) is true if and only if
$(\exists x)(\exists y)(\exists z)(\exists w)(\exists v)($'Tom' Des $x \cdot$ 'Ralph' Des $y \cdot z$ Ground $y \cdot$ 'Ortcutt' Spec $w \cdot$ 'believes/ . . . is a spy' Spec $v \cdot$ 'hopes' App $x \langle z,w,v\rangle)$.

(23) is true if and only if
$(\exists x)(\exists y)(\exists z)(\exists w)(\exists v)($'Tom' Des $x \cdot$ 'Ralph' Des $y \cdot z$ Ground $y \cdot$ 'Ortcutt' Spec $w \cdot$ 'believes . . . / . . . is a spy' Spec $v \cdot$ 'hopes' App $x \langle z,w,v\rangle)$.

This differs from the statement for (22) only in the predicate that specifies the mechanism v.

(24) is true if and only if
$(\exists x)(\exists y)(\exists z)(\exists w)(\exists v)(\exists u)($'Tom' Des $x \cdot$ 'Ralph' Des $y \cdot z$ Ground $y \cdot$ 'Ortcutt' Des $w \cdot v$ Ground $w \cdot$ 'believes/ . . . is a spy' Spec $u \cdot$ 'hopes' App $x \langle z,v,u\rangle)$.

I have drawn attention to the difference between the statements for (19) and (20); also those for (22) and (23). Is this difference a real one? In my semantic terminology this question amounts to the following: Do the mechanisms specified by 'believes . . . / . . . is a spy' differ from those specified by 'believes/ . . . is a spy'? In Quincan terminology it amounts to this: Does the exportation of a term within two attitude contexts to a position within only one make any difference? Is there really such a difference of scope as that between oo and oo^2, or that between to and to^2? So far as I can see the answer to these questions is "no." Consider, for example, how Tom would show evidence of his hope if (19) were true. He would assert

(25) Ralph believes that Ortcutt is a spy.

It would not be good enough if he substituted a codesignational term for either 'Ralph' or 'Ortcutt'. *And the same is true for* (20), because the context after 'hopes' remains opaque. Of course, it is hard to be confident of an answer here in the absence of a clear idea of what mechanisms a complex expression like 'believes/ . . . is a spy' does specify. Such an idea would require theories of reference for 'believes' and 'spy' which I have not begun to offer.

No new question seems to be raised by the possibility of n-tuple attitude contexts with n greater than two. Nor by the possibility of attributive rather than designational terms appearing in those contexts.

10.3 Attributions of Self-Knowledge to Others

In a response to Jaakko Hintikka, Hector-Neri Castañeda drew attention to an interesting construction used to attribute self-knowledge to others. He rightly pointed out that

a man, say, X, can know who a certain person Y is, without knowing that Y is he himself. (1967:11)[7]

For example, X, an amnesiac, might know enough about a certain hero wounded 100 times for it to be true that X knows who the hero is without knowing that he himself is the hero. For the latter to be true, he must put his view into the words, "I am the hero."

This indicates that we need to add to the account of attitude contexts in the last chapter. Where the singular term in such a context is a pronoun (often a reflexive one) which depends for its reference *on the singular term used to refer to the person alleged to have the propositional attitude in question*, the statement can be so understood as to be true only if the person would show evidence of his attitude by using a "self-demonstrative"

('I' in English); any other singular term would not suffice. This applies quite generally to attitude contexts. I shall call pronoun tokens with this particular cross-referential property 'reflexive" even if they are not explicitly reflexive, and will follow Castañeda in always using 'he*' as such a pronoun.

These new attitude contexts are curious. We can quantify into them and so they must be transparent; if a knows that he* is F, then someone knows that he* is F. Yet the person in question can show evidence of his attitude by using only one of the many ways of referring to himself, a self-demonstrative. Clearly, then, the attitude statements attributing such attitudes have quite different truth conditions from the standard transparent attitude statements. Let us call them "*transparent."

Some new devices are called for. First, we need a conventional way of expressing these attitude statements. I illustrate my conventions using an example of Castañeda's:

(26) Jones knows/ he* is a millionaire.

For (26) to be true Jones must be in a knowing relation to a set of mechanisms including a d-chain for a self-demonstrative (the "act of perception" that establishes this causal link to the object is, of course, an act of introspection; see 2.6). So,

(26) is true if and only if
$(\exists x)(\exists y)(\exists z)($'Jones' $Des\ x\ \cdot\ Self\text{-}dem\ y\ \cdot$ 'millionaire' $Spec\ z\ \cdot$ 'knows' $App\ x\ \langle y,z\rangle)$.

'Self-dem y' says that y is a d-chain for a self-demonstrative. Alternatively, we could have used "he*' $Spec\ y$' explained as follows: 'he*' specifies d-chains for self-demonstratives.

Ernest Sosa discusses

(27) The spy knows that he* killed the guard,

offering as a paraphrase:

(28) There is a person such that the spy knows he (the per-

son) killed the guard, and that person is none other than the spy himself. (Sosa 1970:886)

As an attempt to explain *transparency in terms of transparency, this clearly fails. (28) would be true if the spy were in a position to assert knowledgeably ⌜a killed the guard⌝ where a is *any* designational term designating himself. However, as Castañeda has made clear, (27) can be understood so as to be true only if the spy were in a position to assert knowledgeably, "*I* killed the guard."

Nevertheless, Sosa later argues persuasively that there *is* a standard transparent interpretation of a statement like (27).

> Suppose several people are disguised blindfold and are filmed dancing. They later grade their own performances without knowing who is who. When they are identified S complains that the others have given him unjustly low marks, until it is pointed out that he has given *himself* the lowest marks. . . . (1970:893)

It seems true to say,

(29) S believed that he himself was the worst dancer,

even though at the time he would not have asserted "I am the worst" but rather, assuming he had the clown disguise, "The man with the clown costume is the worst." He could show evidence of his belief, it seems, by using *any* designational term that referred to himself.

No new devices are needed to treat this interpretation of an attitude statement containing a reflexive pronoun, if indeed there is such an interpretation; it is simply a special case of standard transparency:

(29) is true if and only if
$(\exists x)(\exists y)(\exists z)($'$S$' Des $x \cdot y$ Ground $x \cdot$ 'worst dancer' Spec $z \cdot$ 'believes' App $x \langle y,z \rangle)$.

*Transparency is a species of transparency and so the fact that 'Jones' in (26) might be replaced by an attributive term poses no interesting new problem. Nor does quantifying into *transparent contexts. Consider

(30) Everyone believes/he* is mortal.

(30) is true if and only if
$(x)(\exists y)(\exists z)(Self\text{-}dem\ y\ \cdot\ $ 'mortal' $Spec\ z\ \cdot\ $ 'believes' $App\ x\ \langle y,z \rangle)$.

Each person, if prompted, would be disposed to assert, "I am mortal."

An attitude logic designed to cover *transparency would need one new rule: *transparency implies transparency.

10.4 Opacity in Certain Verbs

Quine has noted an opacity in certain verbs (1960:§32).

(31) The commissioner is looking for the chairman of the hospital board

may not remain true if we substitute 'the dean' for 'the chairman of the hospital board' even though the dean is the chairman of the hospital board: it can be construed opaquely. However, it can also be construed transparently so that it is paraphrased by

(32) The chairman of the hospital board is such that the commissioner is looking for him.

The question of exportation arises here again in the inference from (31) (if opaque) to (32).

We can use the semantic predicates already introduced for attitude contexts to bring out the role of singular terms in such contexts. Construe (31) opaquely and assume the singular terms are designational. Then,

(31) is true if and only if
$(\exists x)(\exists y)($ 'the commissioner' $Des\ x\ \cdot\ $ 'the chairman of the hospital board' $Spec\ y\ \cdot\ $ 'looking for' $App\ x\ \langle y \rangle)$.

On the other hand,

(32) is true if and only if
($\exists x$)($\exists y$)($\exists z$)('the commissioner' *Des* x · 'the chairman of the hospital board' *Des* y · z *Ground* y · 'looking for' *App* x $\langle z \rangle$).

For (31) to be true the commissioner must have a "looking-for-attitude" involving a d-chain specified by 'the chairman of the hospital board': it must be grounded in the chairman (assuming it is nonempty) and involve a translation of that description (9.8). For (32) to be true his attitude may involve *any* d-chain grounded in the chairman.

A propositional attitude logic could be simply adapted for statements containing opaque verbs by including a suitable symbolism for capturing them. The rule that only designational terms can be exported could be generalized to cover these statements.

The last clauses of the above statements of truth conditions say that 'looking for' applies to the person x and an ordered set having one member, a d-chain. Clearly, *order* is of no consequence here. I have persisted with the talk of ordered sets simply in the interests of consistency. And I can feel free here because no attempt is being made to explain this sort of application anyway. Finally, it is worth noting that the sorts of d-chains specified by the likes of 'the chairman of the hospital board', the d-chain *types*, are Elizabeth Anscombe's "intentional objects" (cf. 9.7 on Frege and sentence types). She calls these opaque verbs "intentional verbs" and speaks of them "taking intentional objects" (1965).

Quine mentions other verbs that behave in a similar way: 'hunt' and 'want'. Another is 'worship'. The latter brings out an important feature of these verbs:

(33) Plato worships Zeus

may be true even though Zeus does not exist. In this respect it does not differ from

(34) Plato believes that Zeus is powerful.

Some ordinary semantic verbs seem to behave in a similar way to 'worship'. This has led some philosophers to group them with the above opaque verbs.[8] Thus, we count

(35) 'Zeus' refers to a Greek god

as true even if we are atheists. However, this fact of ordinary language, if it is a fact, seems better explained by taking (35) to involve the fiction operator ("F") so that it is (roughly) paraphrasable by

(36) It is pretended that 'Zeus' refers to a Greek god.

This treats *the application of ordinary semantical terms to empty names* analogously to the way I earlier (chapter 6) treated the *use of empty names*.

(Should this suggestion be false and the ordinary semantic verbs such as 'refer' indeed be "intentional," then these verbs in their ordinary senses are ill-suited to scientific semantics; cf. 1.3, 4.1. However, we could still warp their meanings to suit our purposes.)

'Want' gives rise to opacity in another way:

(37) John wants to catch the dean.

Many other verbs are similar in this respect; for example, 'try' and 'hope'. The following inelegant paraphrase brings out the obvious similarity between such statements as (37) and propositional attitude statements:

(38) John wants he* to catch the dean.

In the light of this, and construing (37) opaquely, I give its truth conditions as follows:

(37) is true if and only if
$(\exists x)(\exists y)(\exists z)(\exists w)($'John' *Des* x · *Self-dem* y · 'catch' *Spec* z · 'the dean' *Spec* w · 'wants' *App* x $\langle y,z,w \rangle)$.

John must stand in a wanting relation to the set of mechanisms for 'I catch the dean'.

Distinctions between opaque and transparent contexts are important in handling ambiguities arising from the use of *indefinite* singular terms.

(39) John wants to catch a fish

is generally understood as indicating only that John wants to catch some fish or other. So understood,

(39) is true if and only if
($\exists x$)($\exists y$)($\exists z$)('John' *Des* x · *Self-dem* y · 'catch a fish' *Spec* z · 'wants' *App* x $\langle y,z \rangle$).

However, suppose that John is after a particular man-eating shark so that (39) is aptly paraphrased by

(40) There is a fish which John wants to catch.

We have moved from an opaque to a transparent construal of (39). Understood transparently,

(39) is true if and only if
($\exists x$)($\exists y$)($\exists z$)($\exists w$)($\exists v$)('fish' *App* x · 'John' *Des* y · *Self-dem* z · 'catch' *Spec* w · v *Ground* x · 'wants' *App* y $\langle z,w,v \rangle$).

Construed transparently, (39) requires that John's wanting attitude involve a d-chain grounded in some fish (so he has it in mind). This is not so when it is construed opaquely; indeed, so construed it can be true even if there are no fish (cf. wanting to catch a unicorn).

In my view, therefore, ambiguities like the above are to be handled in a familiar way by making distinctions of scope. This view has been criticized by Barbara Hall Partee (1972). She argues that such ambiguities as these arise from the use of indefinite singular terms in *other* sorts of contexts. In fact, she claims that a distinction like mine between attributive and designational terms is also necessary for *indefinite* singular terms. I do not find the argument persuasive. It is true that we can distinguish two circumstances in which a person might say, "Tom met a man," one in which the person had someone particular in mind and another where he had not. *However, it does not seem that this distinction has any significance for the semantics of the sentence.* The sentence has just one set of truth conditions. It will be true if *there is some man* whom Tom met, whether the speaker had him in mind, someone else in mind, or nobody in mind.

10.5 Intentional Identity

Peter Geach has pointed to the problem of understanding a sentence like

(41) Hob thinks a witch has blighted Bob's mare, and Nob wonders whether she (the same witch) killed Cob's sow. (1967)[9]

Construing the sentence opaquely seems to have the unacceptable consequence that the pronoun 'she' within one opaque context is bound by 'a witch' within another. On the other hand, there seem to be objections to construing the sentence transparently:

(42) Some witch is such that Hob thinks she blighted Bob's mare, and Nob wonders whether she killed Cob's sow

is an unsatisfactory paraphrase because the reporter who uttered (38) may believe there are no witches. Geach objects also to

(43) Someone is such that Hob thinks she is a witch and has blighted Bob's mare, and Nob wonders whether she killed Cob's sow

because it implies that Hob and Nob have some one person in mind. Geach claims that the attitudes of Hob and Nob may have a common focus even though there is nothing at that focus. There may be "intentional identity" even though there is not actual identity.

(42) and (43) present no interesting new problems for my theory. Thus,

(43) is true if and only if
$(\exists x)[(\exists y)(\exists z)(\exists w)($'Hob' *Des y* $\cdot$ *z Ground x* $\cdot$ 'is a witch

and has blighted Bob's mare' *Spec w* · 'thinks' *App y* ⟨z,w⟩) · (∃y)(∃z)(∃w)('Nob' *Des y* · *z Ground x* · 'killed Cob's sow' *Spec w* · 'wonders' *App y* ⟨z,w⟩)].

The intentional identity is captured by the requirement that the d-chains involved in both people's attitude be grounded in the one object *x*.

Geach's argument that both (42) and (43) may miss the meaning of (41) is very convincing. Furthermore, his intuition that in cases like this there may be a common focus seems to be a good one. We must try to make sense of it.

First, suppose that the situation were simply that the reporter had overheard Hob saying, "A witch has blighted Bob's mare," and Nob saying, "Maybe a witch killed Cob's sow." Neither Hob nor Nob is committed to the view that there is only one witch in Gotham. There would be no ground for attributing a common focus to their attitudes: (41) would not be true.

Next, suppose that both Hob and Nob think there is only one witch in Gotham. They use the definite instead of the indefinite article, yielding an empty description (assuming there are no witches). Then the following is true:

> (44) Hob thinks that the witch in Gotham blighted Bob's mare and Nob wonders whether the witch in Gotham killed Cob's sow.

On the strength of this the reporter would seem to be entitled to assert (41). It seems sufficient for the assumption of intentional identity. And (44), like (42) and (43), poses no interesting new problems. However, its defect as a possible paraphrase of (41) is that it, unlike (41), attributes to Hob and Nob the view that there is only one witch in Gotham.

It is tempting to offer

> (45) Hob thinks a witch has blighted Bob's mare, and Nob

wonders whether the witch who has blighted Bob's mare killed Cob's sow

as a paraphrase of (41). This again gives a common focus with an unproblematic sentence. It avoids the previous difficulty about uniqueness but has another one. It requires that Nob have thoughts about Bob's mare, yet, as Geach points out, he may not. He *might* show evidence of the wonder that goes into making (41) true by using 'the witch who has blighted Bob's mare', but he *might not*.

How can we make any further sense of the intuition that there is a common focus to the attitudes of Hob and Nob? A full answer would require a general account of *indefinite* singular terms and their role in attitude contexts. This I have not given. Nevertheless, I can give a partial answer suggested by the earlier discussions.

I said that

(46) Tom believes that Pegasus flies

(construed opaquely or semi-opaquely) requires for its truth that Tom have a belief involving a mechanism arising out of the myth underlying the speaker's 'Pegasus' (9.8). Now consider

(47) Tom believes that Pegasus flies and Ralph believes that he eats grass.

Clearly, for this to be true, Ralph's belief must involve a mechanism arising out of that same myth. Suppose that Tom expresses his belief, ⌜*a* flies⌝, and Ralph his belief, ⌜*b* eats grass⌝. For (47) to be true, *the mechanisms underlying a and b must be causally related in a certain sort of way*. This causal relationship is the explanation of the common focus. Now, under the same supposition, precisely the same remark applies to

(48) Tom believes a horse flies and Ralph believes he eats grass.

What still needs to be done is to specify the ways in which the mechanisms must be causally related. My earlier discussions of empty names and their roles in belief statements (6.4, 9.8) supply most of the answer for (47). Guided by those discussions, can we now do something similar to solve the problem for (48), because that is also the problem for (41)?

Suppose that the basis for the reporter's (41) was that he heard Hob say, "A witch has blighted Bob's mare," and then Nob say, "Maybe she killed Cob's sow," where 'she' was bound by 'a witch'. Clearly, (41) would be true. So would it be if Hob had said instead, "She has blighted Bob's mare," and both pronouns were bound by someone else's use of 'a witch', even though Hob and Nob did not know of each other's sayings. These bindings involve a causal dependency. Underlying the singular terms Hob and Nob use to express their beliefs—or *would* use, for it is not essential that they say anything—is a causal network similar to that underlying a name. Indeed, if we suppose that the singular terms they would use are both dependent on a *name*—for example, those of Tom and Ralph might both be dependent on 'Pegasus'—the similarity has already been remarked upon (2.6); cross-reference here differs only trivially from "reference borrowing."

In sum, the intentional identity of the objects of Hob's and Nob's attitudes requires that underlying these attitudes there be a common causal network of the sort we have begun to describe. Either that or there is *actual identity* of objects because (42) or (43) is true; or perhaps (44), which requires no common causal basis, is true. Without recourse to causal theories of reference, a sentence like (41) seems quite intractable.

10.6 Difficult Cases

In this section I shall consider three cases which present difficulties for the theory of the semantics of attitude statements presented in chapter 9. The first is a case where the believer seems to have access to an appropriate d-chain, and yet we do not think that he has the object in mind nor that exportation is in order. The second is a case where the believer does not seem to have access to an appropriate d-chain, and yet we may think that he has the object in mind and that the exportation is in order. The difficulty in these cases is not with the intuitions that link the validity of exportation to *having in mind* (9.3), but with the theoretical explanation of those intuitions that makes use of the causal theory of designation. The third case has more widespread implications. The believer does not have the object in mind nor access to an appropriate d-chain, and yet he seems to have a belief "about" that object. This threatens my whole approach to attitude statements

(i) Return to the murder of Smith. Suppose that Ralph finds the words 'Jum Eli' scrawled in blood by Smith's body. Ralph assumes that Smith wrote these words with his finger to indicate the murderer. Alternatively, Ralph finds a piece of an envelope on which is written only the name of the addressee, 'Jum Eli'. As a result of Ralph's comments, Tom says truly,

(49) Ralph believes/Jum Eli murdered Smith.

(Or, if this seems too hasty of Ralph, perhaps Tom should say only that Ralph *suspects* that Jum Eli murdered Smith.) Now, assuming that there was a d-chain grounded in Jum Eli underlying the earlier use of the name by Smith or the author of the envelope, the name in (49) is designational and can be exported. Then, by existential generalization, we can conclude,

(50) Ralph believes someone/he murdered Smith.

Yet (50) seems false. It does not seem that in these circumstances we would feel that Ralph has anyone in mind as the murderer.

In this case the causal link to the object, though of the appropriate sort, is minimal and is not accompanied by any "picture" of the object. If we accept the intuition about (50), the case is therefore a severe test of the theory of exportation, a test which it fails. Perhaps we should reject the intuition. Certainly intuitions about exportation are often not firm. However, this one seems as firm as most. The best we can hope for, it seems, is that the theory will prove strong enough to modify intuitions about cases like this one.

(ii) Suppose next that Dick detects unexplained irregularities in the movement of planets. His examination of these irregularities leads him to conclude that there is a planet of a certain mass in a certain orbit outside the range of our telescopes. He calls it 'Vulcan'. We say truly

(51) Dick believes/Vulcan causes the irregularities.

Assume Dick is right. Then the following may also seem true:

(52) Dick believes something/it causes the irregularities;

we may feel that Dick has something in mind. Yet Dick does not seem to have access to an appropriate d-chain for this to be so. Further, 'Vulcan' seems to be attributive and hence not, according to my theory, open to exportation.

The import of this case for my theory is not perfectly clear because 'Vulcan' is unusual in being a "theoretical" name. The planet in question cannot be perceived and so the use of the name could not arise out of perception of the object. The discussion of theoretical terms (7.4) suggests that this alone is not sufficient to make the name attributive. In that discussion I sought a less demanding causal relation between speakers and object that I called "quasi perception." I hardly began to characterize that relation. Should such a relationship exist between Dick and the planet, then the name would be designational and would pose no problem for the theory of exportation.

However, it seems to me unlikely that, if we knew more about quasi perception and more about this case, we would discover that the relationship between Dick and the planet was one of quasi perception. I suspect that 'Vulcan' is attributive and that Dick does not really have any beliefs "about" that planet. I am inclined to explain away any tendency to see (52) as true as arising out of uncertain intuitions about the semantics of theoretical terms.

(iii) In 9.5 I argued that if Ralph says,

(53) Tom believes/Smith's murderer is insane,

having someone in mind as the murderer, then what he says is false if the following expresses the whole truth about Tom's beliefs on the subject:

(54) Tom believes/whoever murdered Smith is insane.

'Smith's murderer' in (53) is designational, and so Tom must have the murderer in mind for (53) to be true (T1). Tom does not have a belief "about" that particular person.[10] Furthermore, it was central to my whole theory of belief statements (9.3–9.5) that a transparent statement could not be true unless the believer had a particular object in mind; that was T3. Therefore,

(55) Tom believes Smith's murderer/he is insane

is false in these circumstances.

The following case, adapted from one of Stephen Schiffer's (1977:34), throws doubt on all this. Suppose that the newspapers publish (54). On the strength of this, Big Felix who happens, unbeknown to Tom, to be Smith's murderer, says:

(56) Tom believes that I am insane.

On the same ground, his moll says to one of the mob:

(57) Tom believes that Big Felix is insane.

The problem is that (56) and (57) may seem to be true. How *could* they be true? It seems we must construe them transparently for them to be true since the only singular term Tom has for the murderer is 'Smith's murderer'. According to T3, then, Tom must have Big Felix in mind for these sentences to be true. Yet all Big Felix and his moll had to go on was (54), which does not require that Tom have anyone in mind. If (56) and (57) are true, then (55) is too. And it is hard to see how we can resist the conclusion that (53) is too. If we accept the truth of (56) and (57), the whole having-in-mind approach to attitude statements is threatened.

Are (56) and (57) true? I was initially inclined to think that they were. However, I have tested these sentences on various philosophers and have been impressed by the number who think the sentences false. And we should not ignore the arguments and intuitions stimulated by examples in chapter 9 that suggest these sentences cannot be true.

In conclusion, in these last two chapters we have seen that the causal theory of designation developed earlier in the book can be used to offer plausible solutions to many of the problems of referential opacity. It is against this background of apparent success that the difficulties raised in this last section must be judged.

10.7 Conclusion

In this part of the book our concern has been with some semantically difficult sentences, expressing modalities, and attributing propositional attitudes. With such a sentence the main problem is to show how the semantics of the sentence depends on the semantics of its parts. I have argued that, where the sentence attributes a propositional attitude, the theory of designation helps to solve that problem. Earlier, in Parts I and III, I developed that theory. The concern then was with semantically simple sentences, for example, predications. With such a sentence it is fairly clear how the semantics of the sentence depends on the semantics of its parts. So the main problem is the semantics of its parts. The focus in this book was on some of those parts, proper names, and other singular terms that, I argued, are semantically similar to names; all these terms depend for identifying reference on designation. Drawing on ideas from Kripke and Donnellan, I developed a causal theory of designation. The aim was to show that the theory could handle a range of traditional problems of singular reference and avoid criticisms that have been aimed at earlier causal theories of names.

At the end of Part III I discussed briefly the task of extending causal theories of reference to other terms. The hope was to use such theories to show how, ultimately, all language is "hooked onto" the world. Fulfilling this hope would, of course, be a very large enterprise. Certainly it is not fulfilled here. Indeed, even the theory of designation offered is far from a complete one. A complete theory would require much more knowledge of language in general and the mind than I, at least, have. Throughout the book it was necessary to take positions on some of those broad issues. In Part II I confronted some of them in more detail, attempting to show how the theory of designation fitted into an overall semantic program. My stance was a realist one—realist about the external world, about the mind, and about truth and reference. Further, I favored a functionalist theory of the mind and I hankered after physicalism. These various doctrines are often unclear; all of them are controversial. In some quarters it is claimed that the doctrines cannot be consistently combined. For this reason and others, there has been a move away from "full-blooded" realism of the sort adopted here. Sophisticated and—I think it is fair to say—obscure forms of "weak" realism and antirealism have become common. Despite this trend, "full-blooded" realism strikes me as a more promising doctrine in the long run. Furthermore, I think that such realism is supported by the possibility of causal theories of reference.

GLOSSARY OF SPECIAL SEMANTIC TERMINOLOGY

(Consult the sections referred to for more details)

Ability to Designate. A person gains an ability to designate x when he gains access to a d-chain grounded (only) in x (2.2–2.3, 5.1).

Access. The relationship that a person has to a d-chain in virtue of which he has the ability to (partially) designate an object (2.2).

Application. A species or mode of reference.
(1) The relationship between a predicate and the objects it refers to (1.3).
(2) [Derived from (1).] A relationship between a singular term and objects holding in virtue of the term's "descriptive" content; thus, 'the book' applies to all books (2.5–2.7, 5.8).
(3) The relationship between a propositional attitude verb and the ordered pairs it refers to; each such pair consists of a person (or similar object) and an ordered set of mechanisms of reference (9.7–9.8).

Attributive. The use of a singular term, or a token of that use, to refer (without any particular object in mind) to whatever is alone in having a certain property; depends for identifying reference on denotation; cf. designational (2.5–2.7).

D-Chain. Short for "designating chain." A causal chain between object and person consisting of groundings, reference borrowings, and abilities to designate. Enables (partial) designation (2.2–2.3, 5.1–5.3).

Denotation. A species or mode of reference. The relationship between an attributive term and the one and only object it applies to (2.5–2.7).

278 Glossary

Designation. A species or mode of reference.
 (1) (Initial, intuitive.) The referential relationship between a proper name and its bearer (1.3).
 (2) (Final, theoretical.) A referential relationship between a designational term and the object in which the d-chains underlying it are grounded (2.5–2.7).
Designational. The use of a singular term, or a token of that use, to refer to a particular object in mind; depends for identifying reference on designation; cf. attributive (2.5–2.7).
Empty Term. A singular term that does not make identifying reference; for example, 'Pegasus', 'the golden mountain' (6.1).
Grounding. A perception of an object that begins a d-chain and makes it possible for the object to be (partially) designated (2.2, 5.2).
Identifying Reference. A singular reference that picks out one object. The relationship between an attributive term and the object it denotes, and between a designational term and the object it both designates and applies to (2.7, 5.8).
Partial Designation. A referential relationship between a designational term and an object in which a d-chain underlying it is grounded (5.4). (If a term partially designates only one object, then it designates that object.)
Physical Type. A type of entity identified by overt physical characteristics and used as a medium of language; for example, a certain type of sound; cf. semantic type (1.4).
Reference. The genus of which all referential relationships (for example, application, designation, denotation, specification) are species (1.3).
Reference Borrowing. A person's acquisition or reinforcement of an ability to (partially) designate as a result of the exercise of such an ability by another person in an act of communication (2.3, 5.3).
Semantic Type. A type of entity identified by semantic characteristics; thus, a sound token and an inscription token can be of the same semantic type; cf. physical type (1.4).
Specification. A species or mode of reference. The relationship between an expression in a propositional attitude context and

the mechanisms of reference or sets of such mechanisms, it refers to (9.7).

Underlie. A d-chain underlies the token it causes. It is in virtue of being underlain by a d-chain grounded in x that the token (partially) designates x (2.2–2.3).

NOTES

Chapter 1. Description Theories of Proper Names

1. It has, as Searle allows, "enormous plausibility" (1969:163).
2. I use 'name(s)' as short for 'proper name(s)'. I regard nicknames as names. I shall not be discussing the names of abstract objects.
3. In the *Begriffschrift*: see Frege (1952:10). For a more recent expression of such a view, see Geach (1951:474). The early Wittgenstein also held the view that identity was not a relation between objects (1921:5.5301–5.5303). Russell was impressed with the argument for this view (Whitehead and Russell 1910:67; Russell 1956:245) but was able to resist the conclusion with the help of his doctrine of logically proper names. For later Russellian reactions to the difficulty, see Smullyan (1947:140), Fitch (1949:138–39).
4. For example, Shwayder (1956), Wiggins (1965), Linsky (1963).
5. Dummett claims that although Frege held that the sense of a proper name could be that of a definite description, it is unlikely that he held that it always was (1973:App. to ch. 5, esp. 110). However, if 'description' is construed widely to include demonstrative elements, then, even if Dummett were right, it would still be appropriate to see Frege's theory as a description theory of *reference* for names; cf. note 21 and related text. The argument offered in sec. 1.5 is aimed at such theories among others.
6. "Knowledge by Acquaintance and Knowledge by Description" in Russell (1917); Russell (1912:ch. 5); "On Denoting" and "The Philosophy of Logical Atomism" in Russell (1956); Russell (1919:ch. 16); Whitehead and Russell (1910:Introduction). On the theory of logically proper names, cf. Wittgenstein (1921:3.203, 3.22, 3.221).
7. Strawson (1959:181–83); Searle (1958:167–68, 1969:77–88). Geach (1962:43). Almost every article on proper names in the 1960s seemed to mention an identification requirement.

282   1. Description Theories of Proper Names

8. Wittgenstein (1953:§79); Strawson (1959:186–94); Searle (1958:170–73; 1969:166–74); Wilson (1959:532–33). The term 'presupposition-set' is Strawson's. The views of Strawson and Searle have been adopted by many.

9. Field (1972) has pointed out that Tarski's "definition" of 'denotes' (= my 'designates'), consisting mostly of a list of name-object pairings, is a trivial addition to his theory of truth: it lacks explanatory power. What such "definitions" are good for is teaching the use of a semantic term.

10. Cf. Davidson (1977b:251–52).

11. On these last two paragraphs, see Strawson (1959:181–83); Searle (1969:77–96).

12. I know of no description theorist who has explicitly taken this line, but then they do not generally push their inquiry as far as I am now pushing it.

13. Some similar criticisms of description theories are to be found in Donnellan (1972).

14. See, for example, Strawson (1959:191–92); Searle (1958:171–72).

15. See, particularly, Kripke 1972:290–303.

16. Donnellan has neatly summarized this argument (1977:13–15), which he takes (as do I) to be Dummett's main one. I consider modal statements in chapter 8.

17. The main ideas and examples in the following argument are Kripke's, and so the argument is Kripkean. However, he might not approve of what I have done with his ideas and examples.

18. This claim stands in contrast to Strawson's that "if we should embark on a journey through successive presuppositions, we can be sure of reaching an end" (Strawson 1959:193). Kripke's failure to spell 'Catiline' correctly gives weight to his claim of ignorance here.

19. See, for example, Strawson (1959:182n).

20. Once again see Strawson (1959:182n).

21. For example, Dummett (1973:110); cf. note 5. I am not here talking of theories that simply require the association of a "sortal" predicate with the name (but see 2.10).

22. This is to take what Dummett sees as a "heroic course" (1973:137).

23. Another example: I believe that research still goes on as to whether King Arthur was a real man about whom a legend has grown or simply a fictional character.

24. Dummett (1973:140) seems merely to deny them.

25. The terminology is Lakatos's (1970).
26. See, for example, Loar (1976b, esp. 371); and Schiffer (1978). I have read and heard similar views from a number of others. Indeed, in my experience, those who are impressed with Kripke's argument but do not want to relinquish description theories in the face of it, almost invariably adopt a view such as that to be considered here. I have criticized Loar's paper more thoroughly in Devitt (1979b).
27. If we are not given this, we *do* seem to have a violation of (C) despite what Kripke says. (C) requires not only that the account not be circular but also that the notion of reference be ultimately eliminable.

Chapter 2. A Causal Theory of Designation (1)

1. Sections 2.1–2.9 are largely a modified version of Devitt 1974:secs. 1–9. The modifications of secs. 5–7 are fairly extensive.
2. Some causal links between name and object will have to be ruled out as Kripke's example of 'George Smith' (1972:302) and Evans's example of 'Louis' (1973:192) indicate.
3. Kripke has never said much about grounding, but his discussion of "fixing the referent" (1972) suggests a "description theory" of grounding. This is confirmed by his criticism of Donnellan's distinction (1977), a distinction which must, in my view, play a key role in a causal theory of grounding for names (2.5).
4. Cf. Turner 1976, where unreasonably high demands are made of a theory of reference. I return to these questions in chapter 3.
5. See, for example, Fodor (1968:ch. 3; 1975: "Introduction: Two Kinds of Reductionism"); Putnam (1975:362–440). In Devitt 1974, I suggested (p. 186) what now seems to me a fairly crude form of physicalism.
6. Cf. Evans (1973:193).
7. Such notions can be construed opaquely, so that one can mean Tully but not mean Cicero. Our concern is with the transparent construal.
8. I emphasize this point because it was not clear to at least one critic of my 1974 article; see Turner (1976).
9. Cf. Erwin, Kleinman, and Zemach (1976:part 3).
10. In Devitt (1976b), from which the rest of this section is drawn.
11. Donnellan implicitly marks it this way himself in many places (for example, 1966:287).
12. Donnellan does not draw a distinction like this for names (nor does he make the related distinction for demonstratives, which is discussed in the next section). In a note to his paper on names, he remarks:

2. Causal Theory of Designation (1)

> My account of proper names . . . seems to me to make what I call 'referential' definite descriptions . . . a close relative of proper names. (1972:378n.)

Since most names are designational, this is largely right. The explanation for this apparent relationship is that designational names and descriptions are both causally grounded in objects. Donnellan himself does not offer an explanation. Indeed, he does not attempt to explain how designational uses of descriptions are possible or how names are ultimately linked to their objects.

13. I made developments along these general lines in Devitt (1972; 1974). They bring my view close to "the radical two-use theory" which Loar sets up as his opponent in his recent defense of description theories (1976b). However, the radical two-use theory seems to be a straw man. It is not to be found in the only items cited by Loar (nn. 5, 6) as sources—Donnellan (1966) and Kripke (1972)—for they do not make the above developments, and it is different from mine in at least one important respect. I do not identify "the semantical content" of a designational term with its designatum (cf. Loar 1976b:355); see, particularly, my 5.5. The difficulties of such an identification have been obvious since "On Sense and Reference" (in Frege 1952); cf. my 1.2. For a more detailed criticism of Loar, see Devitt (1979b).

14. The question has become particularly pressing with Kripke's recent development (1977) of earlier expressed (1972:343n.) doubts that Donnellan's distinction has any semantic significance. I do not disagree with Kripke's "methodological" conclusion that "the considerations in Donnellan's paper, *by themselves*, do *not* refute Russell's theory of [descriptions]" (p. 255). However, I disagree very much with his substantive conclusion that his discussion makes it "overwhelmingly probable" that Donnellan's distinction is not semantically significant (p. 270). I argue against Kripke in Devitt (1980); see also sec. 5.4. The argument I give here for the distinction is not, of course, one that Kripke considers.

The modifications of my view represented by the change from sections 5–7 of my 1974 paper to the present 2.5–2.7 were partly stimulated by Kripke's article.

15. Kripke thinks they can be otherwise explained with the help of a Gricean distinction between "speaker's reference" and "semantic reference" (1977; cf. Devitt 1980).

16. Kripke (1977) has brought home to me that there are a number

2. Causal Theory of Designation (1) 285

of equivocations in Donnellan's view of his distinction (cf. Devitt 1974). So the following claims may not strictly be Donnellan's. However, many people take Donnellan to be making these claims, and they constitute a clear and interesting view that is certainly derived from his discussion. So, for convenience, I shall continue to attribute the claims to Donnellan.

17. Donnellan allows that in some "extreme circumstances" this may not be the case.

18. This is a common presupposition, as some of Donnellan's references to the views of others show. At one point (1968:210) Donnellan himself claims that dispute here is merely verbal. Yet many of his claims about "reference" have the ring of something far more substantial than this would allow.

19. I prefer the term 'imperfect' to Kripke's 'improper' because, although these descriptions do not perfectly describe the objects they refer to, I shall argue that there is nothing in the least improper about their use to refer to those objects. Kripke does not discuss these descriptions, but he suggests that the case for Donnellan's distinction may be strongest with them (1977:255–56, 271).

20. His remarks here are only suggestive: he is not attempting an explanation.

21. Cf. Evans (1973:194). This goes part of the way toward showing that my theory is not open to Evans's criticism of Kripke's theory: "it has no obvious application, for example, to syntactic ambiguity or to ambiguity produced by attempts to refer with non-unique descriptions, or pronouns." Remarks in 2.6 and chapter 3 go the rest of the way.

22. My argument against the contextual view here would be similar to that against it for names in Devitt (1976b). On the claims of this paragraph, cf. Burge (1974:part 4).

23. McKinsey's criticism (1976) using the example of 'Madagascar' does not give sufficient weight to this feature of my view; see Devitt (1974:sec. 8).

24. See, for example, Gale and Thalberg (1965); references are to be found there to earlier writings by Peirce, Ryle, Mayo, and Ayer.

25. For Quine, of course, there is no such difference; this is a consequence of the thesis of the "inscrutability of reference" (see, for example, Quine 1960:ch. 2).

26. The move from a correct view to a mistaken one is nicely illustrated by Searle's move from his "axiom of identification" to his "principle of identification" (1969:77–88).

Chapter 3. A Semantic Program

1. The program is sketched very briefly in Devitt (1976b:sec. 5). In that paper I claim that a consideration of the problem of ambiguity in names supplies an argument *for* this program and *against* a "possible-worlds program." However, my main reason for opposing that program is its commitment to nonactual possible worlds.
2. Cf. Field (1977) and sec. 5.5 below. I see no need for *conceptual role* beyond what is revealed in the explanation of reference.
3. It has recently become clear to me that I was implicitly committed to a language of thought of this sort in my earlier writings on semantics.
4. See also Harman (1968, 1970, 1974, 1975) for other writings on the language of thought. My views on the language of thought have been heavily influenced by Harman's.
5. I am indebted to Chris Mortenson here.
6. As Kim Sterelny aptly remarked to me.
7. Schiffer's example of the learning of 'grrr' on a desert island (1972:119–36) is an interesting model of this process, aside from the fact that it presupposes that the islanders *already have* the capacity to think that a person is angry.
8. This view has some similarities to the one described briefly by Schiffer (1972:15–16). However, it seems to me that the concession he contemplates there to those who urge the importance of convention in explaining speaker meaning cannot be satisfactorily accommodated within a Gricean program like his for the reasons indicated at the end of 4.9.

Chapter 4. Defense of the Program

1. I am indebted to Kim Sterelny here.
2. Cf. Loar (1976b:360).
3. Perhaps Foster's analogy with explaining the nature of natural laws by setting out the constraints on scientific theories might be considered an argument (1976). Yet the case is quite disanalogous: scientific theories largely *consist of* laws, and so it is reasonable to suppose that we can explain the nature of laws by setting out those constraints; theories of meaning for given languages *do not consist of* meanings.
4. This may well have been Davidson's view all along, of course. See also Wright (1976:217–18), McDowell (1977).

4. *Defense of the Program* 287

5. A similar response applies to Foster's rationale for the interest in competence (1976:2–3).
6. For a good recent criticism, see Levin (1977).
7. Dummett tends to interpret Davidson in this way; see Dummett (1975:113).
8. This interpretation is supported by Davies (1976) and McDowell (1977), two recent works in the Davidsonian tradition. Both are fairly cautious about psychological reality; McDowell, for example, denies that the normal user of the language knows any theory of meaning, either implicitly or explicitly (1977:166–68). However, Davies sees "absolutely no harm in maintaining" that the normal user has knowledge of T-sentences (1976:12). McDowell is also committed to some such view, for he thinks that knowledge of the theory would enable a person "to arrive by inference at the knowledge about particular speech-acts which a fluent hearer acquires by unreflective perception" (1977:170). Davies sees the theory of meaning as "describing" linguistic competence (1976:18–21); McDowell sees it as "a theory of understanding" (1977:165–66). (I am indebted to Barry Taylor for drawing my attention to these works and for some guidance on Davidsonia.)
9. The evidence in a study cited by Tarski (1949:70) suggests that 90 percent of us manage this.
10. See 7.3 and Devitt (1979a:sec. 3) for more on the dependence of our judgments about reference on various theories.
11. I can see no justification for Lewis's constraint (1974:334–35), which treats our lay theory of people (folk psychology) as sacrosanct. And is there only *one* such theory?
12. I hope I shall not be accused of question-begging in using the term "religious." Any such appearance could be removed by a tiresome description of certain parts of the alien's verbal and nonverbal behavior.
13. So I agree with Lewis's "Rationalization Principle" (1974:337).
14. In my experience it is far from obvious to many readers of Davidson (1967) that this is Davidson's view. It is clear to all, of course, that the article *does not offer* any suggestions pertaining to a theory of reference. However, there is a tendency to overlook the fact that the article is *denying any place* for such a theory in a complete theory of meaning. Anyone who doubts my interpretation is invited to read the article again carefully, particularly pp. 305, 308, 310–12. Better, he can read Davidson (1977b), which is quite explicit on the matter.
15. See also McDowell (1977:183–85). McDowell rejects "the quest

4. Defense of the Program

for a causal analysis of denotation" while allowing "the relevance of causal relations in determining what a name denotes" (1977:184). It is not clear to me how much what he allows is worth, given what he rejects.

16. Cf. Field (1975), which is in part a response to Wallace (published, 1977).
17. Note that the Principle of Charity was introduced by Wilson (1959:532) as part of a description theory of names.
18. Cf. Canfield (1977:106) who finds descriptions, unlike names, "seemingly, or presumably, non-mysterious."
19. Dummett's remarks are aimed at Kripke but would clearly be meant to cover any causal theory.
20. Millar (1977:part 4) develops an argument against Dummett along these lines.
21. Cf. Millar (1977:part 3).
22. Cf. Evans (1976), Dummett (1976:107–11), Field (1977:401–2).

Chapter 5. A Causal Theory of Designation (2)

1. I use the plural form not because it is theoretically important to have more than one thought, but because if there *is* one there will almost certainly be several.
2. This greatly expands and modifies the discussion in Devitt (1974:sec. 10).
3. It is convenient to call these causal chains "designating," even though the token they give rise to does not *fully* designate either cat (this will be discussed later).
4. See, for example, Canfield (1977).
5. This common assumption, among others, is rejected by the "incommensurability thesis" of Kuhn and Feyerabend. I have argued against this thesis in Devitt (1979a).
6. Cf. Kaplan's discussion of a similar case (1968:201): in his view the name will be the name of both objects. Cf. also Donnellan (1972:370–71).
7. So McKinsey (1975:239–41; see also 1978:175–76) has misunderstood the admittedly brief discussion of this in Devitt (1974). The misunderstanding is aided by his confusing of the two cases discussed in the second paragraph of the present section (his quotation on p. 239 from my 1974 paper omits a passage that shows there are two different cases in question). This confuses my view of a token of 'Nana' like that in (4) with my view of one like that in (5).

5. Causal Theory of Designation (2)   289

8. This would be Kripke's view; see his discussion of the case of Smith, who is raking leaves in the distance, being mistaken for Jones (1977:263–264). A large part of Kripke's argument against Donnellan (Kripke 1977) rests solely on his intuitions about this case, which he sees as analogous to one of Donnellan's. He makes no attempt to explain these intuitions. Once they are explained, Kripke's doubts about Donnellan's distinction are undermined; the two cases are importantly disanalogous (cf. Devitt 1980; the disanalogy can be detected by comparing the present discussion with the earlier one in 2.7 of "Our neighbor's cat has disappeared," a case like Donnellan's).

9. Kripke seems to recognize this point (1977:274, n. 26), but if the recognition is taken seriously it undermines his position.

10. A desirable feature of a theory, as Kripke points out (1977:269).

11. A similar point can be made more persuasively about Kripke's case of Smith, in the distance, being taken for Jones. The supposed identity of a person in the distance is likely to affect what one thinks he is up to: "I can't imagine *Smith* ever raking leaves."

12. Cf. Kripke 1977:263–64.

13. The development was suggested by Field at the time of his paper but does not appear in it. It will be discussed further in 5.8.

14. Cf. Evans (1973), who has some nice examples of designation change. Evans has intuitions that are similar to the ones here but offers a different explanation. He claims (p. 195) that the phenomenon of designation change is "decisive against" Kripke's theory. Cf. also Dummett (1973:149–50).

15. This greatly expands the discussion of identity statements in Devitt (1974:sec. 11).

16. I have already indicated (at the beginning of 1.5) that the argument against description theories based on the claim that names are rigid designators—the modal argument—is rather theory-laden. However, we have more powerful reasons for rejecting such theories.

17. Bill Lycan has suggested (in conversation) a moratorium on the term 'meaning' in semantics on the ground that all it seems to mean at present is: "whatever about linguistic phenomena most interests *me now*."

18. So my view is of the sort that Schiffer calls "Modes of Presentation as Causal Chains" (1978:186). Schiffer requires that "sameness in modes of presentation" entail "sameness in functional roles" (p. 180). He rejects my sort of view because "sameness of causal chains" does not

have this entailment (p. 188). In my theory it *does*, as can be seen from 5.1–5.3: what goes on in the head has a lot to do with the relevant identity conditions for causal networks.

19. This notion would be like Lewis's *having-the-same-meaning$_2$* (1972).

20. A classical Millian theory of names suggests some such notion of synonymy, as pointed out in section 1.2(i). And in recent times Lewis's *having-the-same-meaning$_1$* (1972) is such a notion if we ignore the consequences of his theory of counterparts.

21. Brian Loar needs no encouragement, it seems. He makes his task of refuting causal theories of names easy by interpreting them in this way *without having any cited basis for that interpretation at all* (Loar 1976b; see also note 13 to chapter 2 above, and Devitt 1979b). Schiffer (1977) contains a similar misinterpretation: 33–34.

22. Field's view of the importance of conceptual role semantics combines badly with his commitment to causal theories of reference. For example, he finds the following requirement "plausible":

> If two names have the same conceptual role (for a speaker at a time) then they must be coreferential. (1977:396)

But such a requirement is not plausible if a central principle of causal theories of names is correct:

> The reference of a name is not determined by what is in the mind of its user.

There is no reason why a name that is differently grounded from another *must* differ from it in conceptual role.

23. Cf. Kripke (1972:348n).

24. Cf. Dummett (1973:136).

Chapter 6. Empty Terms

1. Implicitly, the remark concerns "atomic" sentences with the empty name in "purely referential position."

The tough view was dominant among the founders and developers of modern logic (for example, Frege, Russell, Church).

2. See Cartwright (1960), Caton (1959), Crittenden (1966), and Garner (1969) for examples of such views.

3. Signs of the tender view can be found in many other recent writings.

4. The view that 'exists' is not a predicate goes back to Kant. It has been the orthodox view in recent years.

5. This view is exemplified in Cartwright (1960), Crittenden (1966), and Candlish (1968). There are signs of it also in some of the work of the "free logicians": see, particularly, Leonard (1956) and Hintikka (1966).

6. The behavior of the ordinary semantic verb 'refer' in contexts like these has led some to group it with opaque verbs like 'worship'; cf. 10.4.

7. By 'fiction' and 'fictional work' here, I am referring to myths, fairy tales, (fictional) plays and films, and so forth, as well as novels.

8. To say this is not to say that nothing in the work is intended to have any relevance to the actual world. The "imagined world" may well be so characterized that it has many lessons for our world, and this may be the main point of the exercise. However, what is *explicitly* done is the "characterization of a fictional realm." It is *by means of* this "fictional realm" that "things are said about" the real world: there are parallels, resemblances, and so forth.

9. Note, however, that it is generally *not* true that he *pretends to describe the actual world*. He would be doing this only if he were trying to give the impression of not telling a story.

10. This possibility was pointed out to me by Kendall Walton. I am indebted to him for this and also for drawing my attention to his writings on the subject, in particular to Walton (1973). These led to some improvements in this chapter. They also point out some of the distinctions among types of fiction which would have to be brought out in a fuller treatment of truth conditions than the one here.

11. Erwin, Kleinman, and Zemach (1976, part 2, criticize Donnellan (1974) on the ground that he cannot handle Kripke's suggestion about 'Santa Claus'.

12. Cf. Loar (1976b:356); Loar sees a serious problem for "the radical two-use theory" here; that theory has certain similarities to mine (chapter 2, note 13).

13. Some comments made by Bill Lycan prompted much of this paragraph.

14. See, for example, Erwin, Kleinman, and Zemach (1976:part 1).

Chapter 7. Other Terms

1. Putnam never talks of multiple grounding, but always emphasizes the baptism (1975:200–204, 274). However, his theory so far as it goes,

does not make reference change *impossible*: he could always add multiple groundings to the theory.

2. See Lewis (1970) for some ideas along these lines.

3. Putnam sometimes writes as if the Principle were in some way constitutive, but it seems he means it to be methodological (see esp. 1975:283). An example of such a writing is his claim that the Principle is "a procedure for *preserving reference across theory change*" (1975:281; original emphasis).

4. This is discussed in Devitt (1979a).

Chapter 8. Modal Contexts

1. This terminology is explained in many places in Quine's writings; see, for example, Quine (1960:§§30, 31, 35).

2. See "Three Grades of Modal Involvement" in Quine (1966) on this distinction and other matters bearing on this chapter.

3. See Plantinga (1969) for a discussion of the distinction between *de re* and *de dicto* modalities.

4. Dummett disagrees about names (cf. 1.5 above, particularly note 16 and related text).

5. So I agree with Kripke that Donnellan's distinction cannot be identified with the *de dicto/de re* distinction (Kripke 1977:258-59).

6. Strictly speaking, even names have a descriptive element associated with them in that they are tied to criteria of identity, to general categorial predicates (2.10). However, since such a predicate will always specify an *essential* property of an object, there seems to be no theoretical point in allowing that *this* sort of association with a descriptive element can generate a *de dicto* necessity. Modal statements involving the name and the categorial predicate are best seen as simply true *de re*.

7. Cf. "names are always rigid designators" (Kripke 1972:277).

8. I suggest that the plausibility of Dummett's discussion of 'St. Anne' (1973:112ff.) comes from taking that name as attributive.

Chapter 9. Contexts of Propositional Attitudes (1)

1. This argument is due to Sleigh (1967:28) and Kaplan (1968:192).

2. See Hintikka (1962) and many subsequent writings. Hintikka's approach is not Quinean: he does not accept the distinction between opaque and transparent contexts.

3. See, for example, Stine (1974).
4. Note that it is fairly much in accord with Kaplan's intuitions (1968:204). However, where Kaplan explains *having-in-mind* largely in terms of *vividness*, I explain it in terms of causal links to the object.
5. Stine (1974) contains a useful discussion of these features. Her own system has the implausible consequence that the following is a valid argument (1974:132):
The Morning Star = the Evening Star,
($\exists x$)(a knows x/x is the Morning Star),
($\exists x$)(a knows x/x is the Evening Star),
Therefore, a knows/the Morning Star = the Evening Star.
6. There might be only one d-chain, but that is unlikely (2.3).
7. Kaplan's treatment also seems to accord better with my functionality principle than with Frege's. His "version" or "analysis" of (31) would be:

($\exists \alpha$)[R(α, Cicero, Tom) · Tom B ⌜α is an orator⌝]. (1968:203–4).

I take this "version" to be a step on the way toward a completely metalinguistic statement of truth conditions, that is, one mentioning each of the terms in (31); see, for example, my treatment below. (It is certainly not a translation of (31), for there is nothing in (31) that the semantic term 'R' translates.) It does not seem that this statement will make the truth conditions of (31) a function simply of the *referents* of 'Tom', 'Cicero', 'believes', and 'orator'.

Chapter 10. Contexts of Propositional Attitudes (2)

1. This differs from Kaplan's (46) in requiring for truth under the second reading that Ralph have the notion of spyhood.
2. The rest of this section is largely drawn from Devitt 1976a, a response to a criticism of Kaplan, by Heidelberger (1974). A consideration of Schiffer (1977:33) has led me to some modifications.
3. The last sentence in the passage quoted from Kaplan (1968:206) says very much the same thing.
4. My notational convention is not perspicuous for the concerns of this paragraph and so has not been used in it.
5. This is in effect the "ad hoc restriction on exportation" that Kaplan mentions in note 33 (1968:214).
6. The claim was suggested by the assumption on which Heidelberger based his criticisms of Kaplan:

If a man suspends judgment with respect to an individual's having a certain property then he does not believe with respect to that individual that it has that property. (1974:442)

7. See also Castañeda (1968), Hintikka (1967, 1970).
8. See, for example, Campbell (1968).
9. See also Dennett (1968), Cohen (1968), and Barense (1969).
10. My intuitions about this and about case (ii) above are similar to Donnellan's (1977:20–22).

BIBLIOGRAPHY

Anscombe, G.E.M. 1959. *An Introduction to Wittgenstein's Tractatus.* London: Hutchinson.
———. 1965. "The Intentionality of Sensation: A Grammatical Feature." In Butler 1965:158-80.
Ayer, A.J. 1963. *The Concept of a Person and Other Essays.* London: Macmillan.
Barense, J.G. 1969. "Identity in Indirect Discourse." *Journal of Philosophy* 66:381-82.
Burge, Tyler. 1974. "Demonstrative Constructions, Reference, and Truth." *Journal of Philosophy* 71:205-23.
Butler, R.J., ed. 1965. *Analytical Philosophy.* Second series. Oxford: Blackwell.
Campbell, R. 1968. "Proper Names." *Mind* 77:326-50.
Candlish, S. 1968. "Existence and the Use of Proper Names." *Analysis* 28:152-58.
Canfield, John V. 1977. "Donnellan's Theory of Names." *Dialogue* 16:104-27.
Cartwright, R.L. 1960. "Negative Existentials." *Journal of Philosophy* 57:629-39. Reprinted in Caton 1963.
Castañeda, Hector-Neri. 1967. "On the Logic of Self-Knowledge." *Noûs* 1:9-21.
———. 1968. "On the Logic of Attributions of Self-Knowledge to Others." *Journal of Philosophy* 65:439-56.
Caton, C.E. 1959. "Strawson on Referring." *Mind* 68:539-44.
Caton, C.E., ed. 1963. *Philosophy and Ordinary Language.* Urbana: University of Illinois Press.
Chomsky, Noam. 1965. *Aspects of the Theory of Syntax.* Cambridge, Mass.: MIT Press.

Cohen, L. Jonathan. 1968. "Geach's Problem about Intentional Identity." *Journal of Philosophy* 65:329–35.
Crittenden, C. 1966. "Fictional Existence." *American Philosophical Quarterly* 3:317–21.
Davidson, Donald. 1965. "Theories of Meaning and Learnable Languages." In Y. Bar-Hillel, ed., *Logic, Methodology and Philosophy of Science*, pp. 383–94. Amsterdam: North-Holland.
———. 1967. "Truth and Meaning." *Synthese* 17:304–23.
———. 1970a. "Semantics for Natural Languages." *Linguaggi Nella Società e Nella Tecnica*, pp. 177–88. Milano: Edizioni di Communità.
———. 1970b. "Mental Events." In L. Foster and J.M. Swanson, eds., *Experience and Theory*, pp. 79–101. Amherst, Mass.: University of Massachusetts Press.
———. 1973a. "In Defence of Convention T." In H. Leblanc, ed., *Truth, Syntax, and Modality*, pp. 76–86. Amsterdam: North-Holland.
———. 1973b. "Radical Interpretation." *Dialectica* 27:313–28.
———. 1974. "Belief and the Basis of Meaning." *Synthese* 27:309–23.
———. 1975. "Thought and Talk." In Guttenplan 1975:7–23.
———. 1976. "Reply to Foster." In Evans and McDowell 1976:33–41.
———. 1977a. "The Method of Truth in Metaphysics." In French, Uehling, and Wettstein 1977:244–54.
———. 1977b. "Reality without Reference." *Dialectica* 31:247–58.
Davidson, Donald and Gilbert Harman, eds. 1972. *Semantics of Natural Language*. Dordrecht, Holland: Reidel.
Davies, Martin K. 1976. "Truth, Quantification, and Modality." Ph.D. dissertation, Oxford University.
Dennett, D.C. 1968. "Geach on Intentional Identity." *Journal of Philosophy* 65:335–41.
———. 1975. "Brain Writing and Mind Reading." In Gunderson 1975:403–15.
Devitt, Michael. 1972. "The Semantics of Proper Names: A Causal Theory." Ph.D. dissertation, Harvard University.
———. 1974. "Singular Terms." *Journal of Philosophy* 71:183–205.
———. 1976a. "Suspension of Judgment: A Response to Heidelberger on Kaplan." *Journal of Philosophical Logic* 5:17–24.

———. 1976b. "Semantics and the Ambiguity of Proper Names." *Monist* 59:404–23.
———. 1979a. "Against Incommensurability." *Australasian Journal of Philosophy* 57:29–50.
———. 1979b. "Brian Loar on Singular Terms." *Philosophical Studies*, vol. 37, in press.
———. 1980. "Donnellan's Distinction." In French, Uehling, and Wettstein, in press.
Donnellan, K.S. 1966. "Reference and Definite Descriptions." *Philosophical Review* 75:281–304.
———. 1968. "Putting Humpty Dumpty Together Again." *Philosophical Review* 77:203–15.
———. 1972. "Proper Names and Identifying Descriptions." In Davidson and Harman 1972:356–79.
———. 1974. "Speaking of Nothing." *Philosophical Review* 83:3–31.
———. 1977. "The Contingent *A Priori* and Rigid Designators." In French, Uehling, and Wettstein 1977:12–27.
Dummett, Michael. 1973. *Frege: Philosophy of Language*. London: Duckworth.
———. 1975. "What Is a Theory of Meaning?" In Guttenplan 1975:97–138.
———. 1976. "What Is a Theory of Meaning? (II)" In Evans and McDowell 1976:67–137.
Erwin, Edward, Lowell Kleinman, and Eddy Zemach. 1976. "The Historical Theory of Reference." *Australasian Journal of Philosophy* 54:50–57.
Evans, Gareth. 1973. "The Causal Theory of Names." *Proceedings of the Aristotelian Society*, Suppl. vol. 47:187–208.
———. 1976. "Semantic Structure and Logical Form." In Evans and McDowell 1976:199–222.
Evans, Gareth and John McDowell, eds. 1976. *Truth and Meaning*. Oxford: Oxford University Press.
Field, Hartry. 1972. "Tarski's Theory of Truth." *Journal of Philosophy* 69:347–75.
———. 1973. "Theory Change and the Indeterminacy of Reference." *Journal of Philosophy* 70:462–81.
———. 1975. "Conventionalism and Instrumentalism in Semantics." *Noûs* 9:375–405.

———. 1977. "Logic, Meaning, and Conceptual Role." *Journal of Philosophy* 74:379–409.
———. 1978. "Mental Representation." *Erkenntnis* 13:9–61.
Fine, Arthur. 1975. "How to Compare Theories: Reference and Change." *Noûs* 9:17–32.
Fitch, F. B. 1949. "The Problem of the Morning Star and the Evening Star." *Philosophy of Science* 16:137–41.
Fodor, Jerry A. 1968. *Psychological Explanation: An Introduction to the Philosophy of Psychology.* New York: Random House.
———. 1975. *The Language of Thought.* New York: Thomas Y. Crowell.
Foster, J.A. 1976. "Meaning and Truth Theory." In Evans and McDowell 1976:1–32.
Frege, Gottlob. 1918. "The Thought: A Logical Inquiry." Transl. by A. M. Quinton and Marcelle Quinton. *Mind* 65(1956):289–311. German version, 1918–1919, in *Beiträge zur Philosophie des Deutschen Idealismus.*
———. 1952. *Translations from the Philosophical Writings of Gottlob Frege.* Edited by Peter Geach and Max Black. Oxford: Blackwell. 2d ed., corr., 1960.
French, Peter A., Theodore E. Uehling, Jr., and Howard K. Wettstein, eds. 1977. *Studies in the Philosophy of Language.* Midwest Studies in Philosophy, vol. 2. Minneapolis: University of Minnesota Press. Rev. enl. ed., *Contemporary Perspectives in the Philosophy of Language,* Minneapolis: University of Minnesota Press, 1979.
———. In press. *Foundations of Analytic Philosophy.* Midwest Studies in Philosophy, vol. 6. Minneapolis: University of Minnesota Press.
Gale, R. M. and I. Thalberg. 1965. "The Generality of Predictions." *Journal of Philosophy* 62:195–210.
Garner, R. T. 1969. "On the Use of Proper Names and Definite Descriptions." *Philosophical Quarterly* 19:231–38.
Geach, Peter. 1951. "Frege's *Grundlagen.*" *Philosophical Review* 60:535–44. Reprinted in E. D. Klemke, ed., *Essays on Frege,* pp. 467–78. Urbana: University of Illinois Press, 1968.

———. 1962. *Reference and Generality*. Ithaca, N.Y.: Cornell University Press.
———. 1967. "Intentional Identity." *Journal of Philosophy* 64:627–32.
Grice, H.P. 1957. "Meaning." *Philosophical Review* 66:377–88.
———. 1969. "Utterer's Meaning and Intentions." *Philosophical Review* 78:147–77.
Gunderson, Keith, ed. 1975. *Language, Mind, and Knowledge*. Minnesota Studies in the Philosophy of Science, Vol. 7. Minneapolis: University of Minnesota Press.
Guttenplan, S. D., ed. 1975. *Mind and Language*. Oxford: Oxford University Press.
Harman, Gilbert. 1968. "Three Levels of Meaning." *Journal of Philosophy* 65:590–602.
———. 1970. "Language Learning." *Noûs* 4:33–43.
———. 1973. *Thought*. Princeton, N.J.: Princeton University Press.
———. 1974. "Meaning and Semantics." In M.K. Munitz and P.K. Unger, eds., *Semantics and Philosophy*, pp. 1–16. New York: New York University Press.
———. 1975. "Language, Thought, and Communication." In Gunderson 1975:270–98.
Heidelberger, Herbert. 1974. "Kaplan on Quine and Suspension of Judgment." *Journal of Philosophical Logic* 3:441–43.
Hintikka, Jaakko. 1962. *Knowledge and Belief*. Ithaca, N.Y.: Cornell University Press.
———. 1966. "Studies in the Logic of Existence and Necessity." *Monist* 50:55–76.
———. 1967. "Individuals, Possible Worlds, and Epistemic Logic." *Noûs* 1:33–62.
———. 1970. "Objects of Knowledge and Belief: Acquaintances and Public Figures." *Journal of Philosophy* 67:869–83.
Hume, David. 1739. *A Treatise of Human Nature*. Edited by L.A. Selby-Bigge. Oxford: Oxford University Press, 1888. 1st ed., 1739–1740.
Kaplan, David. 1968. "Quantifying In." *Synthese* 19:178–214. Reprinted in Linsky 1971.

Kripke, Saul A. 1972. "Naming and Necessity." In Davidson and Harman 1972:253–355, 763–69.
———. 1977. "Speaker's Reference and Semantic Reference." In French, Uehling, and Wettstein 1977:255–76.
Lakatos, I. 1970. "Falsification and the Methodology of Scientific Research Programmes." In I. Lakatos and A. Musgrave, eds., *Criticism and the Growth of Knowledge*, pp. 91–195. Cambridge: Cambridge University Press.
Lakoff, George. 1972. "Linguistics and Natural Logic." In Davidson and Harman 1972:545–665.
Leonard, H.S. 1956. "The Logic of Existence." *Philosophical Studies* 7:49–64.
———. 1964. "Essences, Attributes, and Predicates." *Proceedings and Addresses of the Philosophical Association* 37:25–51.
Levin, Michael. 1977. "Explanation and Prediction in Grammar (and Semantics)." In French, Uehling, and Wettstein 1977:128–37.
Lewis, David K. 1969. *Convention: A Philosophical Study*. Cambridge, Mass.: Harvard University Press.
———. 1970. "How to Define Theoretical Terms." *Journal of Philosophy* 67:427–46.
———. 1972. "General Semantics." In Davidson and Harman 1972:169–218.
———. 1974. "Radical Interpretation." *Synthese* 23:331–44.
———. 1975. "Languages and Language." In Gunderson 1975:3–35.
Linsky, Leonard. 1963. "Reference and Referents." In Caton 1963:74–89.
Linsky, Leonard, ed. 1971. *Reference and Modality*. Oxford: Oxford University Press.
Loar, Brian. 1976a. "Two Theories of Meaning." In Evans and McDowell 1976:138–61.
———. 1976b. "The Semantics of Singular Terms." *Philosophical Studies* 30:353–77.
McDowell, John. 1977. "On the Sense and Reference of a Proper Name." *Mind* 86:159–85.
McKinsey, Michael. 1976. "Divided Reference in Causal Theories of Names." *Philosophical Studies* 30:235–42.

———. 1978. "Names and Intentionality." *Philosophical Review* 87:171-200.
Mill, J. S. 1867. *A System of Logic*. London: Longmans, 8th ed., rev., 1961. 1st ed., 1867.
Millar, Alan. 1977. "Truth and Understanding." *Mind* 86:405-16.
Partee, Barbara Hall. 1972. "Opacity, Coreference and Pronouns." In Davidson and Harman 1972:415-41.
Plantinga, A. 1969. "*De Re et De Dicto*." *Noûs* 3:235-58.
Putnam, Hilary. 1975. *Mind, Language and Reality*: Philosophical Papers, vol. 2. Cambridge: Cambridge University Press.
———. 1976. "What is 'Realism'?" *Proceedings of the Aristotelian Society* 76:177-94.
Quine, W.V. 1950. *Methods of Logic*. London: Routledge and Kegan Paul, 2d ed., rev., 1962. 1st Amer. ed., 1950.
———. 1953. *From a Logical Point of View*. Cambridge, Mass.: Harvard University Press, 2d ed., rev., 1961. 1st ed., 1953.
———. 1960. *Word and Object*. Cambridge, Mass.: MIT Press.
———. 1966. *The Ways of Paradox and Other Essays*. New York: Random House.
Russell, Bertrand. 1912. *The Problems of Philosophy*. London: Oxford Paperbacks, 1967. Orig. publ., 1912.
———. 1917. *Mysticism and Logic*. New York: Doubleday Anchor, 1957. Orig. publ., 1917.
———. 1919. *Introduction to Mathematical Philosophy*. London: George Allen and Unwin.
———. 1956. *Logic and Knowledge*. Edited by R. C. Marsh. London: George Allen and Unwin.
Schiffer, Stephen. 1972. *Meaning*. Oxford: Oxford University Press.
———. 1977. "Naming and Knowing." In French, Uehling, and Wettstein 1977:28-41.
———. 1978. "The Basis of Reference." *Erkenntnis* 13:171-206.
Searle, J.R. 1958. "Proper Names." *Mind* 67:166-73. Reprinted in Caton 1963.
———. 1965. "What Is a Speech Act?" In Max Black, ed., *Philosophy in America*, pp. 221-39. Ithaca, N.Y.: Cornell University Press.

———. 1969. *Speech Acts: An Essay in the Philosophy of Language.* Cambridge: Cambridge University Press.

Seuren, Pieter A.M. 1972. "Autonomous versus Semantic Syntax." *Foundations of Language* 8:237–65.

Shwayder, D.S. 1956. "'='." *Mind* 65:16–37.

Sleigh, R. C. 1967. "On Quantifying into Epistemic Contexts." *Noûs* 1:23–31.

Smullyan, Arthur F. 1947. Review of W.V. Quine's "The Problem of Interpreting Modal Logic." *Journal of Symbolic Logic* 12:139–41.

Sosa, Ernest. 1970. "Propositional Attitudes *de Dictu* and *de Re*." *Journal of Philosophy* 67:883–96.

Stich, Stephen P. 1976. "Davidson's Semantic Program." *Canadian Journal of Philosophy* 6:201–27.

Stine, Gail C. 1974. "Quantified Logic for Knowledge Statements." *Journal of Philosophy* 71:127–40.

Strawson, P. F. 1954. "A Reply to Mr. Sellars." *Philosophical Review* 63:216–31.

———. 1959. *Individuals: An Essay in Descriptive Metaphysics.* London: Methuen.

Tarski, Alfred. 1949. "The Semantic Conception of Truth." Reprinted in J. Feigl and W. Sellars, eds., *Readings in Philosophical Analysis*, pp. 52–84. New York: Appleton-Century-Crofts.

———. 1956. *Logic, Semantics, Metamathematics.* Transl. by J. H. Woodger. Oxford: Oxford University Press.

Tuner, Dan. 1976. "Devitt's Causal Theory of Reference." *Australasian Journal of Philosophy* 54:153–57.

Wallace, John. 1977. "Only in the Context of a Sentence Do Words Have Any Meaning." In French, Uehling, and Wettstein 1977:144–64.

Walton, Kendall L. 1973. "Pictures and Make-Believe." *Philosophical Review* 82:283–319.

Whitehead, A.N. and B. Russell. 1910. *Principia Mathematica.* Cambridge: Cambridge University Press. 2d ed., 1927. 1st ed., 1910.

Wiggins, D. 1965. "Identity-Statements." In Butler 1965:40–71.

Wilson, N.L. 1959. "Substances without Substrata." *Review of Metaphysics* 12:521–39.

Wittgenstein, Ludwig. 1921. *Tractatus Logico-Philosophicus.* Transl. by D. F. Pears and B. F. McGuinness. London: Routledge and Kegan Paul, 2d printing, corr., 1963. German ed., 1921.

——. 1953. *Philosophical Investigations.* Transl. by G.E.M. Anscombe. Oxford: Blackwell. 2d ed., rev., 1958. 1st ed., 1953.

Wright, Crispin. 1976. "Truth Conditions and Criteria." *Proceedings of the Aristotelian Society,* Suppl. vol. 50:217–45.

INDEX

Abilities to designate, 27–35, 38–39, 51, 56, 64, 93–94, 129–40, 143, 146–50, 155–56, 277–78; see also Linguistic competence
Abstract objects, 208, 221, 281n
Accessible: usage explained, 29, 277
Ambiguity, 72, 80, 99, 239; in proper names, xi, 9–13, 32–36, 78–79, 132, 136, 140–41, 286n; in scope, 14, 210–16, 266–67, 285n; in demonstratives and pronouns, 43, 132; in thought, 78–79; in indefinite singular terms, 266–67
Anaphoric: usage explained, 43–44
Anscombe, G. E. M., 167, 264, 295
Application: usage explained, 9, 42, 46, 54, 163, 215, 217, 238, 277
Armstrong, D. M., xiii
Attributive terms, 45–47, 54–56, 157, 161–65, 177–79, 202, 213–15, 224–25, 266, 277–78; proper names, ix–x, 40–42, 44–47, 56–60, 157–60, 177–78, 179, 216, 272–73, 292n; definite descriptions, x–xi, 36–57, 157, 160, 178–79, 214–15, 226–27, 229–32, 247–48; demonstratives and pronouns, x, 42–47, 54–56, 178; and emptiness, 42, 170, 177–79; in attitude contexts, 224–27, 229–34, 247–48, 260, 272–73
Ayer, A. J., 16, 285n, 295

Baptism, see Naming ceremony
Barense, J. G., 294n, 295
Benefit of Doubt, Putnam's Principle of, 192, 200, 202, 292n
Bigelow, John, xiii
Burge, Tyler, 285n, 295
Butler, R. J., 295

Campbell, R., 294n, 295
Candlish, S., 291n, 295
Canfield, John V., 288n, 295
Cartwright, R. L., 290–91n, 295
Castañeda, Hector-Neri, 260–62, 294n, 295
Categorial predicates, 63–64, 152, 163, 292n
Caton, C. E., 290n, 295
Causal theories, see Definite descriptions; Demonstratives and pronouns; Designational terms; Grounding; Natural-kind terms; Other terms; Perception, theory of; Proper names; Reference, causal theories of; Reference borrowing
Cause: notion discussed, 161
Charity, Principle of, x, 87, 113, 115–18, 120, 202, 288n
Chomsky, Noam, 70, 295
Church, Alonzo, 290n
Cohen, L. Jonathan, 294n, 296
Conceptual analysis, see Semantics

305

Conceptual analysis (*Cont.*)
  and folk theory, conceptual
  analysis
Conceptual role, 153, 155–57, 195–96,
  286*n*, 290*n*; *see also* Language of
  thought
Confusions, errors, and mistakes in
  referring, xi, 36–37, 47–50, 54, 57,
  71, 79, 82, 135, 139–52, 156,
  191–95, 203; *see also*
  Misunderstandings
Convention, 80–86, 95, 106–7,
  150–51, 155, 178, 181, 286*n*
Conventional meaning, ix, 68–69, 74,
  80–86, 125, 140–41, 165; of a
  proper name, ix, 3–6, 13–14, 20,
  58, 74, 81, 86, 125, 143–46, 150–51,
  154–55; of a definite description,
  37–42, 47–55; of a demonstrative or
  pronoun, 46, 51–52; of a natural-
  kind term, 195–99
Convention T, x, 87, 113–15
Core-thought, 78, 237, 240, 247
Criterion of identity, 5, 16, 60–64,
  151–52, 292*n*; *see also*
  Identification requirement
Crittenden, C., 290–91*n*, 296

Davidson, Donald, x, xii, 67, 86,
  90–96, 98–101, 104–5, 110, 114–25,
  282*n*, 286–87*n*, 296
Davies, Martin K., 287*n*, 296
D-chains (designating-chains), 29–34,
  38–41, 43, 47, 54, 56, 60, 64, 79,
  111, 129, 133, 136–40, 148, 153–58,
  160, 176, 178, 225, 237, 239–45,
  247–48, 252, 254–55, 258, 261, 264,
  266, 268, 271–72, 277–79, 288*n*,
  293*n*; *see also* Abilities to
  designate; Grounding; Reference
  borrowing
De dicto and *de re*, 208–12, 214–17,
  292*n*
Definite descriptions, ix–xi, 5, 25, 27,
  36–59, 133–34, 136, 139, 148–49,
  157, 160, 162, 178–79, 189, 212–15,
  263–64, 268, 284–85*n*, 292*n*,
  imperfect, xi, 50–52, 132, 214,
  285*n*; in modal contexts, 209–16; in
  attitude contexts, 221, 226–27,
  229–33, 239, 244–45, 247–48, 273;
  see also Description theories
Degree of designation, *see* Partial
  designation
Degree of truth, *see* Partial truth
Deictic: usage explained, 42–43
Demonstratives and pronouns, ix–xi,
  16–18, 25, 27, 42–47, 51–52, 54–57,
  132–34, 136, 139, 162–63, 178–79,
  283*n*, 285*n*; in attitude contexts,
  245, 267–70, 273–74; reflexive, 245,
  260–63, 265–66
Dennett, Daniel, 78, 237, 294*n*, 296
Denotation: usage explained, 42, 49,
  53, 277
Descriptions, explanation of the
  application of, 6–7, 124, 126, 200,
  288*n*; *see also* Definite descriptions
Description theories: of grounding, xi,
  283*n*; of proper names, 3–23,
  30–32, 41, 64, 107, 123–26, 132–33,
  136, 152, 160, 168, 187–88, 196,
  199–200, 222, 281–84*n*, 288–89*n*;
  behaviorist interpretation of, 12;
  centralist interpretation of, 12–14,
  32, 132; refutation of, 13–23, 90,
  107, 187–88, 282–83*n*; modal
  argument against, 13–14, 289*n*,
  292*n*; of meaning distinguished
  from of reference, 13–14; of
  reference borrowing, 15–19, 21–23;
  circularity in, 16, 21–23; of natural-
  kind terms, 197, 199–200; of other
  terms, 203
Designation: usage explained, 7–8,
  38, 40–43, 278; change 138, 150–51,
  289*n*; *see also* Abilities to
  designate; D-chains; Designational

terms; Grounding; Partial
designation; Reference; Reference
borrowing
Designational terms, xi, 45–47,
54–55, 111, 129, 135, 137–40, 157,
161–65, 177–79, 207, 213–15,
224–25, 262, 266, 277–78, 284n;
proper names, ix–xi, 40–43, 45–47,
55–60, 111, 129, 152, 154, 157–60,
163, 177, 178–79, 212–16, 227–29,
243, 272–74, 284n; demonstratives
and pronouns, x–xi, 42–47, 51–52,
54–57, 162–63, 178–79, 245,
273–74; definite descriptions, x–xi,
40–59, 160, 162, 178–79, 214–16,
231–33, 244–45, 263–64, 273,
284–85n; and emptiness, 42, 54,
162–63, 170, 177–79; in attitude
contexts, 219, 224–28, 230–34,
243–50, 252, 254–58, 260, 264,
271–74; *see also* Abilities to
designate; D-chains; Grounding;
Reference borrowing; Referential
uses of definite descriptions.
Devitt, Michael, xii, 283–290n,
292–93n, 296–97
Donnellan, Keith, ix–xi, xiii, 25, 32,
36–37, 39–42, 44–50, 52–55, 88,
160, 202, 275, 282–85n, 288–89n,
291–92n, 294n, 297
Dummett, Michael, x, xii, 14, 67,
91–92, 105–6, 118, 124, 281–82n,
287–90n, 292n, 297

Empty terms, 6, 10, 14, 18–19, 40,
42, 44, 62–63, 129, 159, 162–63,
167–88, 201, 213, 265, 268, 270,
290–91n; fictitious, 170–73, 175–77,
179–83; failed, 170, 175–77, 181,
183; in attitude contexts, 183,
228–29, 234, 243–44, 249–50,
267–70
Erwin, Edward, 283n, 291n, 297
Essentialism, 207–11, 215, 292n

Evans, Gareth, 58, 283n, 285n,
288–89n, 297
Exportation, xi, 55, 220–35, 246, 251,
256, 259, 263–64, 271–72, 293n

Failed names, *see* Empty terms,
failed
Feyerabend, Paul, xii, 288n
Fiction operator (F), 172–75, 179–81,
183–84, 265
Fictitious names, *see* Empty terms,
fictitious
Field, Hartry, x, xiii, 71–72, 75, 78,
113, 141–42, 147, 156, 163, 282n,
286n, 288–90n, 297–98
Fine, Arthur, 191–92, 195, 298
Fitch, F. B., 281n, 298
Fodor, Jerry A., 29, 75–76, 99, 283n,
298
Folk semantics, *see* Semantics and
folk theory, conceptual analysis
Foster, J. A., 91, 93, 96, 286–87n,
298
Frege, Gottlob, 4–7, 14, 153–55, 176,
236, 238, 242, 264, 281n, 284n,
290n, 293n, 298
French, Peter A., 298
Functionalism, 29, 275
Functionality, Fregean principle of,
174, 181, 184, 187, 236, 240–42,
293n
Furth, Montgomery, 221
Future objects, reference to, 59–60

Gale, R. M., 285n, 298
Garner, R. T., 290n, 298
Geach, Peter, 60, 267–69, 281n,
298–99
Grammars, *see* Linguists and
grammars
Grice, H. P., x, 67, 82, 88, 118, 299
Grounding, x–xii, 27–34, 38–41, 43,
51, 54, 56–59, 62–64, 79, 81, 111,
129–40, 143–52, 154–55, 157–58,

Grounding (*Continued*)
176–77, 179–80, 184, 190–93, 196, 199, 200, 237, 239–48, 250, 253–56, 258–59, 262, 264, 266–68, 271, 277–79, 283–84n, 290n; multiple, ix, 56–57, 62, 136–37, 139, 147, 149, 151, 158, 190, 192, 291–92n; *see also* Perception, theory of
Gunderson, Keith, 299
Guttenplan, S. D., 299

Harman, Gilbert, 75–77, 79, 91, 96, 103, 106, 156, 286n, 296, 299
Having in mind, 11–12, 32–40, 43, 48, 50, 58, 60–62, 64, 138–40, 157, 178–79, 181, 184, 224–32, 235, 237, 239, 248–49, 266–67, 271–74, 293n
Heidelberger, Herbert, 293n, 299
Hintikka, Jaakko, 222, 260, 291–92n, 294n, 299
Hume, David, 4, 299

Identification requirement, 7, 14, 60, 64, 281n, 285n; *see also* Criterion of identity
Identity statements (and beliefs), 4–6, 132, 134, 143–44, 148–49, 152–56, 163, 182–83, 281n, 289n
Incommensurability thesis, xii, 288n
Indefinite singular terms (variables), 44–45, 266–70
Indeterminacy of translation and inscrutability of reference, 118, 123, 285n
Instrumentalism, 75, 118–21
Intentional identity, 251, 267–70
Intentional objects, 264
Intentions to designate, 138

Kant, Immanuel, 291n
Kaplan, David, xi, 221–22, 226, 236, 253–55, 288n, 292–93n, 299
Katz, Jerrold, 96
Kleinman, Lowell, 283n, 291n, 297

Knowing who, 221–24, 235, 260–62
Kripke, Saul A., x–xiii, 13–14, 19–22, 32, 90, 107, 138, 152, 159–60, 177, 189, 207–9, 212–13, 275, 282–85n, 288–92n, 300
Kuhn, Thomas, xii, 288n

Lakatos, I, 283n, 300
Lakoff, George, 70, 300
Language of thought, 68, 75–80, 83–86, 98, 103–6, 108–9, 130–38, 190, 236–37, 286n, 288n; in animals, 77, 83, 250; *see also* Conceptual role
Leonard, H. S., 183, 291n, 300
Levin, Michael, 287n, 300
Lewis, David K., 80–81, 106, 213, 287n, 290n, 292n, 300
Linguistic competence, 31, 70, 79–80, 87, 93, 96, 100–10, 130, 196–99; and semantics, x, 87, 92–95, 101, 105, 124–25, 197–98, 287n; and semantic propositional knowledge, x, 20, 87, 93–110, 196–99, 287n; *see also* Abilities to designate
Linguists and grammars, 70, 95, 104–5, 252
Linsky, Leonard, 281n, 300
Loar, Brian, xi, 90, 125, 283–84n, 286n, 290–91n, 300
Logic: of attitude sentences, 233–36, 263–64; "free," 234, 291n
Logically proper names, 5, 281n
Lycan, William, xiii, 289n, 291n

McDowell, John, 286–87n, 297, 300
McKinsey, Michael, 285n, 288n, 300–1
Martin, C. B., xiii
Mayo, B., 285n
Meaning, *see* Conventional meaning; Speaker meaning
Meaning, theory of, *see* Semantics
Mechanisms of reference, 69, 74, 154,

156, 174, 180, 187, 189, 198, 203, 236–38, 240, 242, 244–50, 252–55, 258–61, 265, 269, 270, 277, 279; *see also* D-chains
Mental representation, *see* Language of thought
Methodological questions, 7–8, 31, 61, 87–90, 107, 110–21, 196–98, 201–2, 292n
Mill, J. S., 3–6, 301
Millar, Alan, 288n, 301
Mistakes in referring, *see* Confusions, errors, and mistakes in referring
Misunderstandings, 34–36, 57, 137–38, 140, 147; *see also* Confusions, errors, and mistakes in referring
Modal contexts, 207–17, 274, 282n
Mode of presentation, 5, 132–36, 153, 236–37, 289n
Mood, 69–70, 74
Mortenson, Chris, 286n
Multiple grounding, *see* Grounding, multiple

Names, *see* Proper names
Naming ceremony, 26–31, 40–41, 56–59, 61–63, 82, 158, 171, 176–77, 179, 184, 187, 192, 199, 239, 243, 291n
Naming sentence, 26–27, 176, 243
Natural-kind terms, 111–12, 191–99, 202; "observational," 189–91, 203; "theoretical," 199–203, 272–73
Nerlich, Graham, xiii
Nicknames, 58, 183, 281n

Opacity, xi, 6, 55, 161, 179, 207, 219–21, 224–25, 228–29, 233–35, 238–40, 243–46, 248–50, 252, 256, 258, 260, 272, 283n, 292n; in certain verbs, 251, 263–67, 291n; *see also* Modal contexts; Propositional attitude contexts

Other terms, 129, 189–203, 275, 291–92n

Partee, Barbara Hall, 266, 301
Partial: reference, ix, 123, 141–42, 151, 170, 193–95, 201; designation, 142–48, 150, 160, 162–65, 186, 215, 277–79; truth, 142–45, 147–48, 164–65, 195; denotation, 160, 162, 164; application, 162, 164
Peirce, C. S., 285n
Perception, theory of, 27, 30, 39–40, 42–43, 61–64, 133–34, 160, 190, 200–1
Physicalist reduction, 8, 29, 275, 283n
Plantinga, A., 292n, 301
Possible worlds, 152, 212–13, 286n
Pragmatics, 182–83, 197–99
Presupposition-set, 7, 282n
Pronouns, *see* Demonstratives and pronouns
Proper names, ix–xi, 3–36, 40–47, 55–64, 90, 93–94, 106–7, 110–11, 122–26, 129, 132–35, 138–60, 163, 176–87, 190, 193, 195–96, 199–200, 202, 207, 212–17, 222, 274–75, 278, 281–85n, 288–90n, 292n; meaning of, ix, 3–6, 13–14, 20, 58, 74, 81, 86, 124–25, 143–46, 153–57; ambiguous, xi, 9–13, 32–36, 78–79, 132, 136, 140–41, 286n, Mill's view of, 3–6, 290n; in identity statements, 4–5, 132, 143–44, 152–56, 182–83; Frege's view of, 4–7, 153; in singular existence statements, 5–6, 169, 186–88, 291n; Russell's view of, 5–7, 187–88; empty, failed, fictitious, 6, 10, 14, 18–19, 40, 63, 157, 167–88, 228–29, 243–44, 249–50, 265, 269–70, 290–91n; main problem of, 6–8, 11, 26, 64; and partial designation, 142–48, 150, 160, 186; in modal contexts, 152, 211–17; in attitude

Proper names (*Continued*)
contexts, 221-23, 227-29, 236-43, 245, 248-50, 270-74
Propositional attitude contexts, xi, 32, 55, 207, 219-74, 278, 292-94n; and logic, 233-36, 263-64; negative, 251-57; multiple, 251, 257-60
Pseudonyms, 58, 170, 185-86
Psychological reality of language, *see* Linguistic competence
Purely referential position, 207-8, 219-20, 234-35, 238, 290n
Putnam, Hilary, xiii, 29, 88, 190-92, 197-200, 202, 283n, 291-92n, 301

Quantifying in, 207-8, 219, 235, 247, 261, 263
Quine, W. V., xi, 8, 11, 55, 118, 123, 167, 219-20, 238, 251-52, 254, 256-57, 263-64, 285n, 292n, 301
Quotation marks, use of, 11

Rationality, Principle of, 87, 113, 115-18
Realism, xii, 88, 120, 122-24, 275
Reference, causal theories of, ix-x, xii, 8, 57, 67, 73, 83, 115, 126, 140, 189, 270, 275, 290n; partial, ix, 123, 141-42, 151, 170, 193-95, 201; and truth or meaning, xii, 7, 18, 63, 69-74, 87, 92-94, 114, 118-26, 141-43, 161-65, 168, 174, 181, 184-87, 198-99, 282n, 287n; usage discussed, 7-9, 40, 48-49, 71, 88, 153, 169, 186, 265, 278, 285, 291n; identifying, 54, 162, 170, 178, 189, 216, 277-78; change, 57, 151, 191-95, 203, 275, 292n
Reference borrowing, 130, 137-38, 140, 222-23, 270, 277-78; for names, x, 15-19, 25, 28-32, 34-36, 41, 56-57, 58-59, 62-64, 134-35, 146-47, 150, 158, 175, 282n; and circularity, 16, 21-23; for descriptions, 38-39, 44-45; for natural-kind terms, 190-91
Referential opacity, *see* Opacity
Referential uses of definite descriptions, x-xi, 36-40, 202, 284n; *see also* Designational terms
Reflexive pronouns, 245, 260-63, 265-66
Rigid designators, 13, 152, 207, 211-14, 289n, 292n
Russell, Bertrand, 4-7, 14, 50, 167-68, 281n, 290n, 301-2
Ryle, Gilbert, 285n

Schiffer, Stephen, 80, 83, 88, 106, 125, 273, 283n, 286n, 289-90n, 293n, 301
Scope, *see* Ambiguity in scope
Searle, J. R., 82, 281-82n, 285n, 301-2
Self-knowledge, attribution of to others, 251, 260-63
Semantics, ix-x, 8, 25, 28-29, 67-126, 274-75, 282-89n; and linguistic competence, x, 87, 92-95, 101, 105, 124-25, 197-98, 287n; and testability, 7-8, 31, 61, 87-90, 107, 110-21, 196-98, 201-2, 292n; and folk theory, conceptual analysis, 8, 87-90, 99-100, 107, 145, 153, 187, 198, 265, 285n; and truth, 68-69, 108, 124-25, 198-99, 267; and theories of particular languages, 87, 90-92, 286n; and conceptual role, 156-57, 195-96, 286n, 290n; and empty terms, 168-69
Semi-opacity, 249-50
Senses, 4-6, 153, 236, 281n
Seuren, Pieter A. M., 70, 302
Shwayder, D. S., 281n, 302
Singular existence statements, 5-6, 167-70, 183, 186-88, 291n
Sleigh, R. C., 292n, 302
Smart, J. J. C., xiii

Index 311

Smullyan, Arthur F., 281*n*, 302
Sortal predicates, *see* Criterion of identity
Sosa, Ernest, 261–62, 302
Speaker meaning, ix, 11, 33, 69, 74, 80–86, 96, 108–10, 125, 140, 143–46, 154–55, 165, 237, 286*n*; and Donnellan's distinction, 37–42, 289; *see also* Having in mind
Speaker's knowledge, *see* Linguistic competence
Specification: usage explained, 238, 240–41, 243–46, 278–79
Sterelny, Kim, xiii, 286*n*
Stereotypes, 197–99
Stich, Stephen P., 94, 302
Stine, Gail C., 293*n*, 302
Storytelling operator (S), 170–72, 175
Strawson, P. F., 11, 170, 281–82*n*, 302
Substitutivity of identity, 6, 183, 207–9, 211, 217, 219, 234, 241, 260, 263
Suspension of judgment, xi, 254–55, 294*n*

Tarski, Alfred, x, 70–73, 96, 113, 142, 163, 282*n*, 287*n*, 302
Taylor, Barry, xiii, 287*n*
Testability, *see* Methodological questions
Thalberg, I, 285*n*, 298
Thought: notion discussed, 77–78, 131, 160–61; *see also* Ambiguity in thought; Language of thought
Transparency, 55, 161, 178, 182, 207, 219–21, 224–25, 227–28, 233–34, 238, 240, 243–50, 253, 256–58, 261–63, 265–67, 273, 283*n*, 292*n*; *see also* Modal contexts; Propositional attitude contexts
Truth, theory of, x, xii, 69–74, 110–11, 141–43, 147–48, 161–65, 171–74, 179–88, 193–95, 207–74, 282*n*, 291–94*n*; vehicles of, 11, 86; interest in, 63, 68–69, 89–90, 108–9, 150; and semantics, 68–69, 108, 124–25, 198–99, 267; characterizations, statements of conditions for, 71–72, 111–12, 142, 162–65, 168, 179–80, 186–87, 215–16, 237–50, 252–74, 293*n*; partial, 142–45, 147–48, 164–65, 195
Truth-functional connectives, explanation of, 126
T-sentences, x, 87, 95–96, 98–99, 104, 113, 115, 119–21, 287*n*
T-theory, 96, 100, 104–5
Turner, Dan, 283*n*, 302
Types, physical and semantic, 10–11, 31–33, 41, 77–78, 80–81, 85–86, 98, 130–32, 136–37, 141, 150–51, 154–56, 159, 236–38, 264, 278

Uehling, Theodore E., Jr., 298
Underlying: usage explained, 29, 38, 279
Understanding, *see* Linguistic competence.

Verificationism, 118, 122, 124
Vividness, 221–24, 293*n*

Wallace, John, 288*n*, 302
Walton, Kendall L., 291*n*, 302
Wettstein, Howard K., 298
Whitehead, A. N., 281*n*, 302
Wiggins, D., 281*n*, 302
Wilson, N. L., 282*n*, 288*n*, 303
Wittgenstein, Ludwig, 18, 281–82*n*, 303
Wright, Crispin, 91, 286*n*, 303

Zemach, Eddy, 283*n*, 291*n*, 297

DAVIDSON COLLEGE